Retiring Wea[...]
For Dummi[...]

C000259420

Costing Retirement Necessities

Tot up how much you're spending on the following items to get an idea of how much income you're going to need to enjoy a comfortable retirement:

- Household bills
- Loans and mortgages
- Insurance
- Running a car
- Holidays and entertainment
- Rainy day money

And you may want to factor in retirement goals, too:

- Buying a holiday home
- Pursuing a hobby
- Affording life's luxuries
- Helping family

Knowing What You're Worth

Add up the following to find out what you're currently worth:

- Your home
- Your state, private, and workplace pensions
- Any collectables and high-value private possessions
- Your savings accounts and investments

And remember to deduct any debts you have; typical debts include:

- Your mortgage
- Any credit and store cards
- Any personal loans
- Any bank overdrafts

Kickstarting Your Retirement Fund

You may not get rich quick, but these ideas stand you in good stead for a wealthy future:

- Buy a property.
- Have at least three months' salary in rainy day savings.
- Gear up your skills.
- Start a business.
- Don't borrow to pay off debt.
- Don't borrow to buy shares.
- Don't borrow if can use your savings instead.

For Dummies: Bestselling Book Series for Beginners

Retiring Wealthy For Dummies®

Cheat Sheet

Deciding Your Retirement Goals

Fixing a few goals in your mind helps you work out what you need to do between now and retirement:

- ✔ Establish when you would like to stop working (next Monday morning isn't an option!).
- ✔ Decide how much money you'll need.
- ✔ Examine how much money you're on course to receive.
- ✔ Work out if you want any high-value retirement goodies.
- ✔ Calculate how much you're going to need to reach your goals.
- ✔ Think about what you're willing to sacrifice to reach your dreams.
- ✔ Determine what you want to leave behind for loved ones.

Understanding Personal Pension Performance

Personal pension growth depends on these factors:

- ✔ **How much you pay in over the years.** The more you pay in, the more you should get out. From 2006 you can contribute up to 100 per cent of your income (up to a maximum of £215,000) into a personal pension.
- ✔ **When you start making contributions.** The younger the age at which you start a personal pension then the longer the money will have to grow. It's estimated that every £1 you pay into a pension in your twenties is worth £3 that you pay in during your early fifties.
- ✔ **Level of charges.** Your pension provider levies a charge for managing your pension and may levy charges if you stop contributing or want to transfer your pension pot to another provider.
- ✔ **Annuity rate.** Personal pension rules dictate that most people will have to use 75 per cent of their fund to buy an annuity. In recent years annuity rates have fallen, meaning that it costs people more to secure a decent retirement income. If annuity rates fall further, you may have to save more in your pension to enable you to buy an income allowing you to enjoy the finer things in old age.

For Dummies: Bestselling Book Series for Beginners

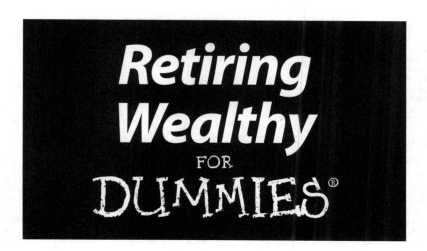

Retiring Wealthy
FOR DUMMIES®

by Julian Knight

JOHN WILEY & SONS, LTD

Retiring Wealthy For Dummies®
Published by
John Wiley & Sons, Ltd
The Atrium
Southern Gate
Chichester
West Sussex
PO19 8SQ
England

E-mail (for orders and customer service enquires): cs-books@wiley.co.uk

Visit our Home Page on www.wileyeurope.com

Copyright © 2006 John Wiley & Sons, Ltd, Chichester, West Sussex, England

Published by John Wiley & Sons, Ltd, Chichester, West Sussex

Wiley also publishes its books in a variety of electronic formats. Some content that appears in print may not be available in electronic books.

British Library Cataloguing in Publication Data: A catalogue record for this book is available from the British Library.

ISBN-10: 0-470-02632-4 (PB)

ISBN-13: 978-0-470-02632-8 (PB)

Printed and bound in Great Britain by TJ International, Padstow, Cornwall

10 9 8 7 6 5 4 3 2 1

WILEY

About the Author

Julian Knight was born in Chester in 1972, educated at the Chester Catholic High School, and later at Hull University. He is the BBC News personal finance reporter and writes for the BBC News Web site; Julian is author of *Wills, Probate & Inheritance Tax For Dummies*, and lives in London with a large mortgage. Before joining the BBC, Julian worked at *Moneywise* magazine and contributed to *The Guardian* as well as many other publications.

11ᵗʰ NOVEMBER '08

TO MY DUDE,

I SEEM TO REMEMBER YOU PASSING COMMENT ABOUT RETIRING RICH! .... WELL THIS BOOK SEEMED LIKE A GOOD PLACE TO START!

AND GIVEN THAT YOU STILL HAVE ONE 24 HOUR FLIGHT TO GO IT MAY PROVIDE YOU WITH SOME READING MATERIAL!

I HOPE YOU FIND THE BOOK USEFUL ... AND THAT YOU PASS ON THE SECRETS TO ROB & I!
ENJOY THE READ.

ALL MY LOVE

XXX.

Dedication

To my grandparents with love.

Publisher's Acknowledgements

We're proud of this book; please send us your comments through our Dummies online registration form located at www.dummies.com/register/.

Some of the people who helped bring this book to market include the following:

Acquisitions, Editorial, and Media Development

Project Editor: Daniel Mersey

Executive Editor: Jason Dunne

Content Editor: Simon Bell

Development Editor: Sally Lansdell

Copy Editor: Martin Key

Proofreader: Andy Finch

Technical Editor: Danny Hackett ACII APFS

Executive Project Editor: Martin Tribe

Cover Photo: © Stockfolio/Alamy

Cartoons: Ed McLachlan

Composition Services

Project Coordinator: Jennifer Theriot

Layout and Graphics: Andrea Dahl, Denny Hager, Stephanie D. Jumper, Heather Ryan

Proofreader: Susan Moritz

Indexer: Techbooks

Publishing and Editorial for Consumer Dummies

Diane Graves Steele, Vice President and Publisher, Consumer Dummies

Joyce Pepple, Acquisitions Director, Consumer Dummies

Kristin A. Cocks, Product Development Director, Consumer Dummies

Michael Spring, Vice President and Publisher, Travel

Kelly Regan, Editorial Director, Travel

Publishing for Technology Dummies

Andy Cummings, Vice President and Publisher, Dummies Technology/General User

Composition Services

Gerry Fahey, Vice President of Production Services

Debbie Stailey, Director of Composition Services

Contents at a Glance

Table of Contents

Introduction

● ●

*R*etirement should be about having fun. In an ideal world you get to kick off your shoes and enjoy some of the finer things in life, travel a bit and do things you never had the chance to do while you were working.

But in truth, what retirement has in store for you depends on the financial decisions you make from now on. Be a wise saver and investor and keep a lid on the amount of money you borrow – then you're doing everything you can to make your retirement dreams reality. On the other hand, become a spendaholic, borrow money right, left, and centre and fail to develop the right skills to boost your earning potential and I'm afraid old age may well involve a grim struggle to make ends meet.

Sadly, lots of people are heading towards the poverty in old age scenario. They are burying their heads in the sand and in some cases hoping the state will ride to the rescue and pay them enough of a pension to live off. As a result, recent estimates suggest that at least one in three adults is headed for old age poverty. But by picking up this book you are already well ahead of the pack.

Taking a conscious decision to plan towards a wealthy retirement is one of the smartest moves you can make. The earlier you set in train your retiring wealthy plan, the greater the chance that it reaches its destination and doesn't hit the buffers. But if you're no spring chicken, no sweat – there are lots of things you can do to secure yourself a great big money pile to see you through your autumn years. Young or older, this book shows you how to draw up your retiring wealthy plan – and follow it through.

About This Book

Retiring Wealthy For Dummies helps you decide on your retirement objectives and plot a route to making them reality.

You can read this book in lots of ways – although I don't advise doing it with a torch under the bedclothes, as it plays havoc with your eyes. Obviously, one way is to start from the front cover and read to the end, as you would a novel. But this is no Harry Potter – you can discover just as much from this book by dipping in and out, zeroing in on the information you require when the need arises.

I'd advise that you start off by reading Part I, which helps you draw up the basics of your big retiring wealthy plan. After then you can go wherever you want – skip to the chapters on pensions or those regarding property if they float your boat.

But do note that this book is supposed to be a work of reference, so you may find a little bit of repetition. That doesn't matter, though – some things about proper saving and investing for retirement can't be said often enough.

Retiring wealthy means playing for big stakes. If you're able to carry away the prize you're in line to enjoy a fabulous retirement.

Conventions Used in This Book

The world of saving and investing is chock-full of jargon, some of it fairly straightforward, the rest seemingly designed to confuse the man or woman in the street (and sometimes the professionals). No worries, one of this book's main aims is to junk the jargon.

I endeavour to explain things in plain English and where I have to use a bit of jargon the phrase appears in *italics* and is followed by a spot-on, easy-to-understand description of what it means.

What You're Not to Read

As you look through this book you see text in grey boxes. The information in these sidebars is interesting (I hope) but not essential to your understanding of the subject matter. So when it comes to these sidebars the choice is yours – you can read them or not. If you don't you're not missing out on vital information.

You may also notice technical stuff icons dotted throughout this book. Technical stuff information is there to give you a bit of in-depth knowledge of an issue raised in the text. But just like sidebars, it's not the end of the world if you ignore technical stuff.

Foolish Assumptions

When writing this book I made some assumptions about you:

- ✔ You're not a money expert.
- ✔ You're willing to make necessary sacrifices.
- ✔ You don't want your retiring wealthy plan to dominate your life.
- ✔ You want to know the downside as well as the up.

You may find other *For Dummies* books published by Wiley useful too – check out *Sorting Out Your Finances For Dummies* by Melanie Bien, *Renting Out Your Property For Dummies* by Melanie Bien and Robert S. Griswold, *Investing For Dummies* by Tony Levene and *Paying Less Tax For Dummies* by Tony Levene.

How This Book Is Organised

This book has six main parts or themes. Each part is divided into chapters relating to the theme, and each chapter is subdivided into individual sections relating to the chapter's topic. What's more, to help you find specific information more easily a table of contents is at the front of this book and a detailed index at the back.

Part I: Plotting Your Way to a Wealthy Retirement

This part equips you with all you need in order to draw up your very own retiring wealthy plan. First, I explain why you need to start saving and investing for your retirement. Later on I look at how to work out what you are worth today and how much you are likely to need to give yourself a prosperous retirement. I show you how to get properly organised and what you can find out from other investors. In addition, I show you how and where to look for unbiased professional advice.

Part II: Laying the Bedrock: Pensions

This part is all about an often misunderstood and underestimated area – pensions. They may be boring but they can also be rather clever and valuable. Pensions are still the main vehicle that most people use to secure a bumper retirement income. I explain all the different types of pension available, including state, workplace, and personal. What's more, I look at stakeholder and self-invested personal pensions – both relatively new kids on the pension block. And to cap it all I explain how you can transfer, top up, and cash in your pensions to get the biggest bang for your buck.

Part III: Building Up a Nest Egg: Saving and Investing

This part is all about putting the basics in place, your money bread and butter if you like. All the standard investments which should form the base of your big plan are covered in this part. Bank savings accounts, National Savings and bonds as well as the ins and outs of savvy stock market investment – you find it all here. Read this part to find out about most of the savings and investment products you ever have to deal with throughout your life.

Part IV: Using Property to Boost Your Retirement Pot

In this part I show you how to maximise the amount of money you make from your own home and other property investments. I also look at the role that property can play in your big retiring wealthy plan. The upside and downside of property investment are examined, as is how to tell a good from a bad mortgage product. And I dedicate a whole chapter to the investment craze of recent years – buy-to-let. For lots of people making money from property has a big appeal and this is the part to check out if you want to know how to do it.

Part V: Alternative Investment Strategies: The Wealth Is Out There

This part contains lots of information you may not easily find in other publications. I concentrate on some investments considered a little off the wall, but if you get them right they can make your fortune. I examine racier stock market investments, derivatives, and even spread betting – but the key is that I do it all in plain English without the use of jargon. What's more, I look at one of the hot investments fields of the moment – collectables, from classic cars through wine and even buying a racehorse. Whatever the collectable I show you how you can make money from it, but I don't forget to point out the potential pitfalls of taking a walk on the investment wild side.

Part VI: The Part of Tens

This part is an essential ingredient in any *For Dummies* book. Each of the four chapters contains ten succinct, must-know facts. I look at how you can boost your income, reduce your tax bill, avoid the money pitfalls, and sort out your personal finances. Taken as a whole, the Part of Tens in this book goes a long way to covering all the financial bases.

Icons Used in This Book

The small graphics in the margins of this book point to bits of text that you should pay special attention to.

The information this icon marks helps you get the best deal possible and highlights some strategies you'd be wise to follow.

Taking to heart the tips and information this icon highlights can make it a lot easier for you to cross the retiring wealthy finish line.

This icon highlights things you really shouldn't do if you want to retire wealthy.

You can gain from this information, but if you do decide to ignore it you aren't putting your retiring wealthy plan ambitions in peril.

Take note whenever you see the little piggy bank icon. The advice that follows explains how you can save money on your savings and investments.

Where to Go from Here

This book aims to help you lay the foundations of your retiring wealthy strategy. It also provides you with a reference, explaining the ins and outs of savings and investing. You can read this book as a whole or zero in on the information you need now and in the future. How you use this book is totally your call.

You may want to make notes as you go along – feel free to jot down comments in the margins. Don't forget to check out the cheat sheet at the front of the book for a good starting point for developing your personal retiring wealthy plan.

You may also feel the need to get some professional help managing your money. This book points you in the right direction to find unbiased, switched-on financial advice.

Part I
Plotting Your Way to a Wealthy Retirement

"Well, we took your high risk investment, put it all on Northern Lass in the 3.30 at Doncaster – it came in last, but that's high risk for you."

In this part . . .

This is where you can start from scratch. Here I tell you why you need to start planning for your retirement. I then talk you through how you can work out your personal worth. By the end of this part you should have a clear set of retiring wealthy goals, and I give you the inside track on the strategies you can adopt to reach them. In addition, I show you how and where to look for unbiased professional advice.

Chapter 1

Building Your Retirement Dream

*Y*ou probably have an image of what life should be like once you retire. Perhaps sun, sea, and sangria appeal or a round the world cruise. Maybe you're looking forward to spending your autumn years pursuing a hobby or enjoying time with the family.

But many people don't start to think seriously about retirement until it's virtually upon them. Up until that age they may have bigger fish to fry. Perhaps they are concentrating 100 per cent on bringing up a family or pursuing their career. If you were to ask a hundred people in their twenties, thirties, and forties what their life goals are, you can bet that planning for a wealthy retirement would come far down the list.

But you've picked up this book – better hurry to that checkout! – which means you're already ahead of the pack. Believe me you're right to take time out to think long and hard about how you're going to pay for your golden years.

In this chapter I explain why it is more important than ever to be the man (or woman) with a plan for your retirement. Fail to plan and you may find that your retirement dreams remain just that – dreams, never making it into reality.

Ticking Away . . . the Demographic Time Bomb

People in Britain – like most people in the western world – are having fewer babies and having them later in life. Boffins have given all sorts of reasons for this phenomenon, from the advent of the contraceptive pill to men wearing tight jeans in the 1970s – don't go there, you don't want to know, believe me! But whatever the reason, the truth is that Britain is an ageing society, where the average age of its citizens is inexorably rising each year. No bad thing you may say – fewer kids means smaller queues at Alton Towers and perhaps the extinction of that most delightful phenomenon, the supermarket aisle tantrum.

However, fewer people being born has a huge impact on your retirement plans and the younger you are the bigger the impact is!

At the same time as fewer people are being born we are all, on average, living longer. A British man can now expect to live into his mid to late seventies while a woman can expect to clock up over eighty years.

These two factors – fewer children and living longer – mean that the ratio of workers to pensioners falls dramatically over the next few decades. In fact by 2050 nearly one in three people living in Britain will be over the age of 60.

The upshot of this change is that the burden of supporting more retired people falls on fewer workers.

This has been dubbed the demographic time bomb, because those in work in 2030 or 2050 – today's children – are not going to want to hand over great big piles of cash to support you in retirement.

Different countries are finding their own way to diffuse the demographic time bomb. The French government is paying couples to have children, while in Britain we have a far more open immigration policy, hoping to attract young people to 'Cool Britannia' with the promise of work.

Don't presume that the state help that is available to retired people today will be available to you when it's time for you leave work. By then the burden on taxpayers of an ageing society may be so great as to mean that a state pension or free NHS healthcare will no longer exist. The key is to be prepared for the worst-case scenario.

Diffusing the demographic time bomb

There may be little you can do about the falling birth rate – no matter how great an effort you put in – but ways do exist for you to copper-bottom your finances to ensure that when the demographic time bomb goes off it doesn't blow your retirement dreams off course.

You need to adopt the know-it-all approach. The saying goes that no one likes a know-it-all, but when it comes to planning for your and your family's future it's best to ignore this and be a bit of a smart Alec. Make sure that you:

- ✔ **Know what you have.** In order to plan for a hopefully wealthy retirement you need to work out what you're worth – in pounds, shillings, and pence – and what you're likely to be worth when it comes to waving goodbye to the working world. See Chapter 3 for how to work out how much you're worth.

- ✔ **Know what you need.** You have to be realistic about the future. What do the state and your employer (through a company pension) provide for you and what do you have to fund for yourself? How much are you going to need to cover the basics such as food, heating, clothing, and a roof over your head? And if you have any debts, such as a mortgage, are they going to be paid off before you get to retirement?

- ✔ **Know what you really want.** This book isn't just about providing for retirement, it's about retiring wealthy. If you have dreams, you need to put a price on them. What, for example, will it cost for you and your loved ones to take the motorhome around Europe, buy that second home in the sun, or take that luxury cruise in the Mediterranean each winter? Once you know what your dreams cost you can more easily gauge if your finances are in shape for you to be able to afford them.

Being a know-it-all helps you answer the burning question that some workers probably ask themselves day in, day out: When can I retire?

Here's some good news: You're probably richer than you think. Spend a little time assessing how much your assets are worth – this gives you an idea of where you're starting out from in your retiring wealthy project. See Chapter 3 for tips on how to assess your financial worth.

One good thing about retirement is that the bills tend to get smaller. Think about it – no longer do you have to pay to commute to work or fork out for overpriced work lunches. What is more, most people have paid off their mortgage by the time they retire, which is a big expense out of the way.

Most people reach the pinnacle of their career and income earning potential in their late forties and fifties. This is also the time when mortgages are paid off and the darling little treasures have flown the family nest. This golden scenario – high income combined with low outgoings – can lead to a sudden injection of wealth, which helps provide for a comfortable retirement.

Avoiding the 'living longer, growing poorer' trap

People are living longer than ever before – I bet you haven't stopped celebrating that one – and this trend is set to continue. Average life expectancy may rise to ninety within a generation.

All this means that you may end up spending nearly as long retired as you do working. And you're going to need to build up enough money while at work to pay for your golden years.

Do the sums: If you live until you're 90 but retire at 65 you need to support yourself for 25 years. If you started work at 21 you have 44 years in which to build up enough cash to see you through at least 25 years. And that's presuming you only have an average life expectancy. Say you keep on going strong until you get the telegram from the Queen – you would have been retired for only nine years less than you would have worked.

Many people, understandably, find the prospect of having to provide for such a long retirement very daunting. But fear not, there are lots of things you're likely to have going for you that help you cross the wealthy retirement finishing line:

   ✔ **Your home.** If you're a homeowner – particularly if you've been one for a good few years – you have a good chance of having a lot of equity in your home. You can free up some of this equity at retirement to provide a healthy retirement income or even borrow money to invest elsewhere – perhaps in a buy-to-let property. See Chapters 13 and 14 for more on using your home to boost your retirement wealth.

✔ **Time is on your side.** To a certain extent, time is your biggest asset. Usually savings and investments grow in value over time by more than prices. Savings benefit from compound interest, where interest piles up year after year. See Chapter 10 for more on how compound interest works and Chapter 12 for stock market investment.

✔ **Getting an early start.** The time factor is crucial to growing your money pot and achieving a wealthy retirement. It therefore follows that a little bit of money saved in early life can grow into a large amount by the time you reach retirement. It has been estimated that every pound you pay into a pension fund in your twenties will, when you retire, be worth double every pound you pay in when you're in your forties.

Interest earned on savings is automatically taxed at a rate of 20 per cent (you have to pay more if you're a higher rate taxpayer at self assessment time). But there are several ways you can reduce the amount of tax you have to pay on your savings.

✔ If you don't earn enough to pay income tax you can claim the tax deducted on your savings back from HM Revenue and Customs.

✔ In addition, every UK citizen over the age of 18 is allowed to pay up to £3,000 a year into a mini cash Individual Savings Account (ISA). Money held in an ISA grows tax-free.

Check out Chapter 10 for more on ISAs and other tax efficient savings.

The golden rule with saving is that you must aim to get a rate of return higher than price inflation. If you fail to beat inflation then you find over time that the amount of goods and services your savings can buy falls. It's best to aim to beat inflation by at least a couple of percentage points – therefore if price inflation is running at around 3 per cent, go for savings accounts which pay at least 5 per cent. Inflation-beating savings accounts don't grow on trees, you have to shop around and study the best buy tables. Check out the moneyfacts Web site at www.moneyfacts.co.uk for a list of the highest paying savings accounts.

Setting Your Retiring Wealthy Target

Try spending some time thinking about what you'd like your later life to be like. Do you want lots of foreign holidays, do you have a hobby you'd really like to pursue and need to fund, or is your idea of bliss merely having enough in the larder, sitting in your garden, and having the grandchildren around?

The richer your tastes the more money you need and the harder you have to save and invest.

Above all, try to be realistic about your goals. If you're on an average salary then, unless you scoop the lottery or win big on the Premium Bonds, you're unlikely to be able to be able to spend winters in Mustique and summers cruising round Monte Carlo in your yacht. See Chapter 2 for more on figuring out your retirement goals.

Financial advisers reckon that in order to have a comfortable retirement, you need an income around two-thirds what you enjoyed during your working life. Therefore, if you earned £30,000 a year on retirement you should aim for an income in later life of around £24,000.

Roping others into your plan

It's likely there is someone special you'd like to take along for the retirement ride. However, you need to talk to this special someone about what you have in mind. And of equal importance, you need to listen to what they have to say on the subject.

It's likely that your ideas won't be identical at first – no worries, you just both have to compromise a little to come up with a joint plan.

Sit down and discuss what you want to achieve, what high value goods you have your hearts set on, and what you are willing to sacrifice to get there. If you have children you probably want to discuss what sort of inheritance you'd like to leave them.

You have a better chance of retiring wealthy if there are two of you with your shoulders to the wheel. Having two incomes coming in means you should have spare cash to save and invest. Couples with two incomes also find that they can afford larger, more expensive, property than singletons; this is because they can borrow a sum based on combined salaries.

A change in the law means that same-sex couples now enjoy the same tax and legal rights as married heterosexual couples. However, to access these rights same-sex couples have to go through a civil partnership ceremony.

Aiming for the retiring wealthy stars

Having said that you should be realistic about your retiring wealthy goals, there is nothing wrong with a little ambition. Okay, you're not going to live the life of Roman Abramovich or the Duke of Westminster, but if you start early, and save and invest hard, with a dash of good investment fortune you can enjoy a bit of the high life.

Think about one big ambition – perhaps you want a home in the sun or you want to extend and improve the family home. Cost this ambition and then go for it.

One of the biggest barriers to retiring wealthy is taking on unnecessary debts. Borrowing big to fund 'here today gone tomorrow' purchases is a mug's game. The rate of interest charged by credit card, store card, and loan providers tends to be very high. Nearly every day I come across people whose lives are blighted by having splashed out cash they didn't have. It may seem very mother henish of me but the simplest advice is, if you can't afford to buy it from your savings or current income, then don't buy it!

The pension image problem

If you played a word association game with someone a few years ago and said 'pension' to them, they probably would have blurted out the following words: boring, complex, solid, and reliable.

Play the same game today and 'boring' and 'complex' would crop up again – but this time so would 'unreliable' and 'crisis'.

Pensions have a major image problem and the reasons for it are not hard to fathom:

- ✔ **Mis-selling:** In the 1980s and 1990s thousands of people were advised by financial advisers to stop paying into their workplace pensions and instead invest in expensive personal pension plans. This advice was terrible and as a result the pensions industry has had to pay out billions in compensation.

- ✔ **Underperformance:** Most pension funds invest heavily in shares and as a result suffered huge losses when world stock markets crashed between 2000 and the spring of 2003. Some of this damage has since been put right as markets have bounced back, but it hasn't stopped pension saving getting a reputation for being unreliable, particularly as providers kept on levying whopping fees even when investment return was falling through the floor. Pension underperformance has been thrown into sharp relief by how well property investment has done, causing many people to ask why they bother with pensions when property can bring home the bacon.

(continued)

(continued)

✔ **Workplace woes:** In the past few years companies have been falling over themselves to cut the amount of money they pay into their workers' pensions. Some company schemes have actually gone to the wall, resulting in tens of thousands of workers losing most of their pensions. Outside the public sector, the old final salary scheme – where workers were guaranteed a pension based on their salary and length of service – has all but disappeared and been replaced by schemes where the workers bear all the investment risk.

✔ **State pension shrink:** Back in 1980 the government abolished the link between the state pension and wages. This wasn't seen as much of a problem at the time, but now the chickens are coming home to roost. The problem is that inflation is generally lower than rises in average wages. This means that the state pension as a proportion of the average wage is shrinking. Today the state pension is worth around only 18 per cent of average salaries; if things go on as they are it's estimated it will be worth just 6–7 per cent by 2050.

✔ **Falling annuity rates:** You now need far more money than you used to need to secure a substantial retirement income. This is partly because interest rates have been falling, but it's also due to the fact that people are living longer and subsequently annuities need to last much longer than in the past. Many people have grown to dislike pensions as they often entail the purchase of an annuity.

Despite all this bad news surrounding pensions, it's worth bearing in mind that they come with absolutely terrific and unique tax breaks. Save in a pension and your government – and sometimes your employer too – gives you free money! Check out Chapters 6 through to 9 for the low-down on pension saving and what role it can and should play in your big plan.

Constructing Your Big Wealth Plan

If you want to enjoy a wealthy retirement you need a plan. Part of this big plan is assessing where you are financially today and where you want to be at retirement. Another key aspect is how you are going to get there.

Rather than invest on a whim, you're best off having an overarching strategy in place. Mostly, it's about deciding your approach to risk. Before you save and invest in anything, ask yourself how it fits in with your strategy.

Your strategy needs to take into account the following:

✔ **Your know-how.** Warren Buffett, the world's most successful stock market investor, has a simple mantra: If you don't know what you're buying, don't buy it. This doesn't mean you have to be able to clone Dolly the sheep before investing in Biotech company shares, but it does mean that you ought to have some grasp over what you're putting your money into. This book should help you get a handle on most things in the world of saving and investment.

✔ **Your age and means.** If you're poor and old then you can afford to take fewer risks than if you're young and well-off. The older you are the less time there is to make up any loss on an investment.

✔ **Your risk comfort zone.** Most financial experts reckon that because you're younger you should take more investment risk, but it doesn't necessarily follow that you must go against what you feel inside. If you don't like risks then don't take them. There is nothing wrong with protecting what you already have. Just be aware that to retire wealthy you're either going to have to take a few risks along the way or rely on earning plenty of cash and saving a high proportion of your income.

Check out Chapter 4 for different strategies you can adopt and how you can tailor your plans to be flexible enough to take advantage of investment opportunities.

One way of guarding yourself and your retiring wealthy plan from the unexpected is to take out insurance. You can insure yourself against virtually anything these days, from illness or injury to whether your wedding day will be spoiled by the rain.

Your money pot is not just for retirement

Charles Dickens' Mr Micawber said 'Annual income twenty pounds, annual expenditure nineteen, nineteen, six, result happiness. Annual income twenty pounds, annual expenditure twenty pounds, nought, and six, result misery.'

Ask anyone with substantial savings and they can tell you it provides a really liberating feeling. Okay you may not be able to tell the boss where he or she can stick your 9–5 job, but having savings gives you options and the chance to invest in your future, or if things go wrong – say you suffer injury, redundancy, or ill health – keeps the wolf from the door.

Most financial experts reckon that before you start ploughing money into property, shares, or exotic investments you should have the equivalent of at least three months' salary in a deposit savings account. Some experts go further and reckon you should have at least six months' 'rainy day' money tucked away.

Obtaining independent financial advice can really help you see your plan through. A good independent financial adviser looks at your present circumstances and recommends what you should be investing in to reach your long-term wealth goal. See Chapter 5 for how to find an adviser.

Keeping a close eye on your plan

One of the keys to bringing off your retiring wealthy plan is to regularly review how well you're doing.

Sit down at least once a year and cast your eye over your savings and investments. Check for the following:

- ✔ **Has the interest rate on your savings account fallen?** If so, perhaps you should look to move to another provider. Regardless, check out the best buy tables again to see if there is a more lucrative home for your money.

- ✔ **Are you making full use of your tax free savings allowances?** You can save up to £7,000 a year in shares tax free or alternatively £3,000 in a mini cash ISA and £4,000 in a mini shares ISA. You should always look to make use of this tax break, particularly the one relating to mini cash ISA.

- ✔ **Is your mortgage rate the best?** People go to huge trouble to get an extra 1 per cent on their savings but leave their mortgage in an uncompetitive deal. Regularly reviewing whether you are with the best and cheapest mortgage provider is one of the smartest financial plays you can make and can save you thousands.

- ✔ **How well are your shares performing?** This isn't simply a case of checking out the share price to see if it's gone up or down. Check to see if any of the company fundamentals have changed, whether it is still making money and crucially paying a good dividend. See Chapter 12 for more on how to read a company share.

- ✔ **Do your investments suit your present circumstances?** Investments that are right for you in your thirties may not be right in your forties or fifties. For example, as you near retirement you should move out of high-risk investments such as shares and look instead to put your money into safer bets such as savings accounts and bonds.

With riskier investments such as shares or derivatives you may be best reviewing your holdings at least once a month. This is because the market can move against your investment in double-quick time and it may be necessary to sell up in a hurry.

Taking note of collective investments

Direct investment in shares isn't for everyone. Unless you know what you're doing you can lose your money, fast. But even though you're not some red-braced City wide-boy it doesn't mean you have to forgo share investing altogether. You can put your money into a collective investment vehicle, such as a unit trust or investment trust.

Collective investments pool investor cash to buy shares in lots of different companies. The idea is that a spread of investment lowers risk for the investor, while the fund manager brings his or her expertise to bear in choosing the right stock.

Unit and investment trusts are hugely popular and most financial experts believe that collective investments can give retiring wealthy goals a real push in the right direction.

There are literally thousands of unit and investment trusts on offer. Some invest in the shares of big companies in large economies like the UK or US, while others specialise in buying up stock in small firms or in emerging economies such as China or India.

Unit and investment trusts are not the only types of collective investment. You can find bond funds which – surprise, surprise – invest in bonds issued by lots of different governments or companies. Alternatively, with-profit bonds invest in both shares and bonds. On the wilder, riskier margins of the investment universe there are venture capital trusts, which invest in lots of different start-up and small companies. This type of collective investment is looked at in Chapter 17.

 Building up a large holding of shares can be expensive and take a very long time. An alternative to going it alone is to pool your money with friends or work colleagues to buy shares. Investment clubs can be both profitable and fun. See Chapter 5 for how to get one up and running.

Understanding the state's role

Each day that you work and make National Insurance contributions you are building up entitlement to the state pension.

The state pension may not seem like much – it is slipping in value relative to average earnings – but it's still likely to play a big role in your retiring wealthy plan.

The state pension gets a bad press, but it actually has a lot going for it:

> ✔ It provides a guaranteed income for life with annual increases linked to prices, known as *index-linking*.

✔ As long as you keep making contributions (over 44 years for men and 39 for women) it doesn't matter if you're a City banker or a bus driver, you're entitled to the same level of basic state pension.

The danger with the state pension is that people pin all their hopes on it.

At present, on average, the state pension makes up just over 40 per cent of the income of people aged between 65 and 74.

Ideally, if you're serious about retiring wealthy, you should aim for the state pension to account for far less than 40 per cent of your retirement income.

Currently, the state pension is worth £82.05 a week for a single pensioner; that's equivalent to just £4,266 over a year (for the 2005–2006 tax year). If you target an income of £25,000 a year – hardly a king's ransom – then the state pension would account for less than one fifth of this sum.

It's up to you to put the pensions, savings, and investments in place to top up what the state pension provides.

You can get a free estimate of how much state pension you have earned to date from the government's pension service. Write to The Retirement Pension Forecasting Team, Room TB001, Tyneview Park, Whitley Road, Newcastle upon Tyne, NE98 1BA.

For more information on the state pension you can check out the government's pension service Web site on www.pension service.gov.uk.

Becoming a Property Tycoon

For many people property ticks a lot of boxes as far as finding a good solid long-term investment is concerned.

Here's what property has going for it:

✔ **It's easy to understand.** You buy at one price, you sell at a higher one (hopefully). If you do buy-to-let your aim is to earn more money in rent than you would have done if you'd invested the money elsewhere.

✔ **It meets a basic need.** Put simply, if you don't own your own home you still have to live somewhere, which means paying rent. In short, a property kills two birds with one stone.

✔ **Its value is transparent.** It's a cinch to tell how much a property is worth – all you need do is check out your local newspaper adverts or estate agency windows.

✔ **It provides equity.** Your home is a major asset and you can use it to secure a higher retirement income – through equity release – or as collateral for funding other property purchases or undertaking home improvements.

You can check out how much property in your neighbourhood is selling for by logging onto the Land Registry Web site at `www.landregistry.gov.uk` and doing a property price search.

Property investment, whether in the form of your own home or, particularly, through buy-to-let, is not all sweetness and light. Drawbacks include the following:

✔ **You can't get your money out quickly.** It takes time to sell property. Unlike shares and savings accounts which can be accessed in no time, even when the market is buoyant it can take months to sell property; when it isn't homes can stay on the market for upwards of a year and in some horror stories even longer.

✔ **You put too many eggs in one basket.** Buying property is the biggest investment most of us ever make. Many people are putting themselves at undue risk by having all their cash tied up in bricks and mortar. It's all very well when the market surges ahead but several times in the past the housing market has crashed leaving homeowners in negative equity.

✔ **Your income fluctuates.** This only applies to buy-to-let property. The reality of life as a landlord is that there are bound to be times when you don't have a tenant paying rent. In landlord speak this is called a *void* period. All the time, though, you still have to fork out for the upkeep of the property, the council tax, and repayments on the mortgage.

Buy-to-let investors have potential additional headaches to cope with such as problem tenants damaging property and not paying rent. See Chapter 15 for how to deal effectively with problem tenants.

Spicing Things Up with Collectables

Investing for your future doesn't all have to be shares, savings accounts, and property. You can mix fun with finances by buying into collectables.

A whole universe of collectables is out there which you can invest in. The main areas include:

- Classic cars.
- Art and antiques.
- Stamps and gold coins.
- Fine wine.

Long-established markets exist in all the above areas, with specialist auction houses buying and selling collectables of all shapes and sizes. And the traditional auction houses have been joined by a new kid on the block – eBay. The online auction site has millions of users around the globe and you can find just about anything you'd ever want advertised there.

With collectable investing it's crucial that you know what you're doing – it's all too easy to pay over the odds. The golden rules are don't invest if you don't know and invest in what you like.

You need to bear some other factors in mind when it comes to investing in collectables:

- **Markets tend to be quite volatile.** In some ways the market in collectables is akin to that in shares – if you get your timing right and buy something which captures the imagination of collectors you can soon see your purchase soar in value. On the other hand, however, buy a collectable which subsequently goes out of fashion and you can be left nursing heavy loses.

- **Markets are susceptible to economic downturn.** Collectables are a bit of luxury and when money is tight, markets tend to suffer. For example, back in the 1980s the classic car market motored away, only to crash when the world economy slowed in the early 1990s.

✔ **Collectables are strictly long-term investments.** Because the market in collectables is quite volatile and dictated by fashion, you have to be prepared to hold on to your investment for a long time. Collectables aren't wise investments for anyone who may need the money they have invested in a hurry.

Generally, you should not have more than 10 per cent of your retiring wealthy pot in collectables. In fact, you may be best off having far less than 10 per cent of your money tied up in collectables, unless it's a real passion and you know exactly what you're doing.

The world of collectables has more than its fair share of con artists. Lots of people operate collectable scams looking to part the unwary with their cash. Scams are particularly prevalent in wine and art – the two most sophisticated collectable markets. See Chapter 16 for how to spot one of these scams.

Understanding the Task Ahead

This book contains no quick retiring wealthy fixes – they don't exist. You have a big task ahead of you, if you want to enjoy the high life in later life.

Even if you enjoy only average life expectancy you're on course to spend over 20 years in retirement. In short, the 40 years or so of your working life are going to have to yield enough cash to pay for your autumn years.

But you do have a lot going for you and you can be successful. Just try to bear the following in mind:

✔ **Have a spread of investments.** Keeping your finger in a lot of investment pies can be a very savvy move. The big idea is that if one of your investments underperforms you may well find another performs well and comes to the rescue.

✔ **Remember patience is a virtue.** You should aim to keep most investments for the long term (more than five years). I say this because the passage of time helps smooth out performance peaks and troughs. Times of underperformance are balanced by periods when the investment does well and over the long term it should all, hopefully, average out. Being a long-term investor means you don't incur fees and charges through chopping and changing investments.

✔ **Get help when it's needed.** Lots of professionals, from stock-brokers to independent financial advisers, really know their onions. As soon as you find yourself reaching the limits of you knowledge, call in the professionals.

✔ **Boost your knowledge bank.** Read newspapers, check out Web sites – read this book! – anything to expand your investment know-how. In the world of getting rich, knowledge really is power. The more knowledge you have the better the chance of making lots of lolly and truly retiring wealthy.

Chapter 2

Figuring Out Your Retirement Goals

*A*t some point, you've probably daydreamed about what retirement may hold for you. In your mind's eye, retirement may give you an opportunity to live it up, splash the cash and follow your dreams, or maybe your ambitions are more modest – quality time spent indulging a favourite hobby perhaps.

In this chapter, I explain how you can turn these daydreams into concrete goals.

Once you have a set of clear, costed goals you can start making the necessary personal and financial moves to guarantee you achieve them.

Assessing How Much Money You Need

How much cash you're going to need at retirement depends on the following two factors:

✔ **When you plan to retire.** The younger the age at which you retire, the greater the length of time over which your money pot has to stretch.

> ✔ **The standard of living you want.** Pretty logical this one. If you want to live the high life then you need plenty of cash. If your ambitions are a little more modest, then you need less money.

Retirement doesn't necessarily mean you stop earning altogether. Even if you're no longer in full-time paid employment you may carry on doing the odd bit of freelance work – after all, why deny the working world the benefit of all your experience?

The older you are the easier it is to gauge how much money you need to live on in retirement. This is because there is less time for things to go awry either with your investments, such as a stock market crash, or with the wider economy, such as a bout of inflation eroding the value of your savings.

Living longer means a bigger retirement pot

Here's some great news. We're all living a lot longer. Life expectancy has shot up in the past couple of decades. If you're a woman born in 1980 you can expect to live until your early nineties. Government boffins reckon that the news on life expectancy is going to get better, with the average woman born today expected to live until they are nearly 100 years old!

This means if you retire in your mid 60s and enjoy just average health you're going to need enough money to live on for at least 20 to 30 years.

And who knows, you may live for much longer than average. Perhaps you're a keep-fit fanatic or you have great genes and come from a family of long livers – rather than enlarged livers.

Best be optimistic: Plan for your money to last 30 or 40 years rather than just 20.

If you want to retire young – particularly since you're going to live longer than ever – then there are no two ways about it, you have to get rich. You can do this through boosting your employed income; saving and investing really hard and really smart; or starting a successful business. See Chapter 21 for ways to boost your income.

Deciding on your standard of living goals

You probably have an idea of the living standards you want to enjoy in retirement.

Your goals will probably be relative. If you spend the later years of your working life as the chief executive of a FTSE 100 company then retirement on £40,000 a year can be considered living on a shoestring! After all as your income increases often so do your outgoings.

The financial experts I've spoken to reckon that most people should aim to secure a retirement income of between 60 and 80 per cent of their working salary. So if you're on £30,000 a year you're going to need a retirement income of between £18,000 and £24,000.

This 60–80 per cent range is just a rough and ready figure. How much you're going to need also depends on your spending ambitions in retirement. You may decide that a life on 60–80 per cent of your earned income isn't enough. After all, you can't fund many trips to Monte Carlo on that sort of money! On the flip side you may think that you can live on a little less.

Generally, life gets less hectic and a little cheaper in retirement. For one thing you don't have the costs of commuting to work or that morning grande latte from Starbucks. What's more, pensioners enjoy cheaper travel on public transport and can earn more cash before having to pay income tax than a younger person can.

Costing retirement necessities

Sit down with a pencil and paper and tot up how much you're spending on the following items. Doing this should give you an idea of how much income you're going to need to enjoy a comfortable – although not spectacular – retirement.

- ✔ **Household bills.** Include council tax, water rates, heating, lighting, telephone bill, TV licence (although if you're over 75, you get a free one), and if you have it satellite or cable television.

- ✔ **Loans and mortgages.** Ideally you should enter retirement with a clean slate. But debt has become a way of life in the UK and many people are likely to find that are still paying off their mortgages and other loans well into their sixties. See later in this chapter for more on how debt can help or hinder your retiring wealthy plan.

✓ **Insurance.** You can insure yourself against just about anything but the basics that most of us have include car insurance and home contents and buildings insurance. How to protect your fortune through insurance is covered later in this chapter.

✓ **Running a car.** After a mortgage, buying, fuelling, and repairing a car usually combine to form your second biggest expense. However, retirement is often a time when people really appreciate their car – it gives them freedom to go where they want, when they want.

✓ **Holidays and entertainment.** These days many people consider a holiday a necessity rather than a luxury. You may also want to eat out, and go to the cinema and theatre perhaps.

✓ **Rainy day money.** You should aim to have between three and six months' income in a savings account to cover emergencies such as urgent household repairs. See Chapter 10 for more on how to build up substantial rainy day savings.

And these are just the basics. If you want to enjoy some of the finer things you need more money. You really can't do retirement on the cheap: You need to be disciplined in your plans and save and invest your way to a wealthy old age.

In recent years, council tax and energy bills have been increasing at a far faster rate than inflation. This is terrible news for people relying on the state pension because that only rises in line with inflation. This is yet another reason for making your own plans rather than relying on the state.

Stretching your retirement goals

You probably want more from your retirement than simply to survive, to make ends meet – otherwise why would you have bought a book called *Retiring Wealthy For Dummies*?

The big thing about retirement is time – time to follow your dreams. But what is the point of having dreams unless you have the financial wherewithal to see them into reality?

The sorts of things that you may want to make happen in your retirement include:

✓ **Holiday home.** How about that dream cottage by the sea or an ivy-clad gîte in France. You're going to need plenty of money to purchase, maintain, and travel to any holiday home you buy. But you can turn a holiday home into a money-spinner by renting it out – see Chapter 15 for more.

✔ **Pursuing a hobby.** Many people look forward to retirement as a time when they get to pursue their hobby. If your hobby is making paper airplanes then you don't need much money, but if it's something a little more exotic and expensive then you need more cash tucked away.

✔ **Life's luxuries.** From fast cars to facelifts, there are a million and one ways to spend your money in retirement. But whatever floats your boat you're going to need the readies.

✔ **Helping family.** Many people see retirement as a chance to spend more time with their family. Often older people are the head of the family and they may feel that they want to give their children or grandchildren a leg up. If you fancy playing the family patriarch or matriarch then needless to say you need the resources.

The above scenarios are just a flavour of what sort of things you may like to do in retirement.

If any of the above applies to you then you're going to need a bigger cash pot than if you were just taking care of the necessities.

If you plan to retire abroad then bear in mind that your UK state pension may be frozen. See Chapter 6 for more on the state pension and living abroad.

Be realistic: If you want some of the finer things in life you may have to carry on working for longer than you'd hoped. The goal is to retire wealthy rather than just early.

Realising Retirement Can Be Sudden

As touched on earlier in this chapter, the age at which you stop work is crucial to assessing how much money you need to live on. The earlier in life you retire the more money you need – simple.

However, predicting when you retire can be far from simple. Some people – particularly those who work in the public sector – have a pretty good idea when they will give up work. Their employer tells them way in advance that they expect them to be gone by a certain age, 60 or 65. These people can plan with certainty.

But for others retirement may come suddenly or can be phased over many years.

Converting your retirement pot into retirement income

When you get to retirement you have the option of buying an annuity. The concept behind an annuity is very simple. You hand over your savings to an insurance company and it pays you an income until you pop your clogs. The amount of income you get depends on how much money you hand over and the annuity rate when you purchase the annuity.

Unfortunately in recent years annuity rates have been falling because people are living longer and interest rates have been historically low. In fact, since the late 1980s annuity rates have halved to around 5% or 6%. This means that £100,000 will buy you an income of around £5,000 to £6,000. This very rough ball-park figure should give you a good idea of what sort of retirement income your savings and investment will buy you. Annuities are looked at in much greater detail in Chapter 9.

The reality in UK industry is that on average workers retire in their early sixties – a few years earlier than the age at which men can claim the state pension – either through their own choice or due to redundancy or ill health.

But even if you think you have job security you should prepare for the possibility that you may stop working earlier than planned.

From April 2006 you can continue to work for your employer and collect your workplace pension. However, the pension scheme has to give the go ahead for you to be paid a pension while staying employed. See Chapter 6 for more on workplace pensions.

In 2006 the government introduces legislation making it illegal for firms to discriminate against job applicants on the grounds of age. However, despite the law change widespread age discrimination is likely to be with us for many years to come. Check out the government's age positive Web site on www.agepositive.gov.uk for more info on the new anti-age discrimination laws, or take a look at Liz Barclay's *Small Business Employment Law For Dummies* (Wiley).

If you're offered early retirement or voluntary redundancy late in your working life you may be best taking independent financial advice as to where to invest any lump sum pay-off you receive from your employer.

Looking at What You've Got Going for You

It may seem that you have a long, long way to go to have enough cash even to cover basic retirement living expenses. But don't lose heart: You probably have lots of things going for you, such as the following.

The younger you start the better the result can be

The simple truth is that the younger you start saving and investing for your retirement the better the chance you have of building up a whopping retirement pot. Here are three ways that starting young and having time on your side can benefit your retiring wealthy strategy:

- ✔ The money you save and invest has a longer time in which to grow.

- ✔ You probably have a long working life ahead of you during which you can save and invest really hard.

- ✔ You can afford to take a few more risks with your investments because you have time to recover financially if they go wrong.

 It has been estimated that every pound you save in your twenties results in the same amount of money being available to you in retirement as three pounds saved in your forties. See Chapter 3 for more on how time can affect the value of your savings, investments, and assets.

 Don't get depressed if you didn't start young: It's never too late to start saving for your retirement. Middle age can present lots of opportunities to save and invest plenty of cash. See below for more details.

Your finances are turbo charged later in life

If you're not a twenty or thirty something no problem; you can still scale the retiring wealthy peak with aplomb. Think about the wealthiest people you know – are they in their twenties or thirties?

(And by wealthy I mean people who have access to real assets not just designer clothes and a sports car.) Er, probably not. The people with real wonga tend to be the middle-aged. Generally, they have the largest houses, fattest savings, and biggest share dealing accounts.

This is all because a bit of money magic is introduced into your finances as you reach your forties and fifties. Here's how it works.

Middle age should mean that you are at the top of your career and from an earnings perspective you've probably never have it so good.

The kids have probably flown the family nest and are striking out on their own. This is great news as it stops the little treasures draining your finances.

You may have repaid your mortgage. All that money you borrowed in your twenties or thirties to buy your home has probably now been repaid – happy days! This takes a big weight off your finances.

Increasingly people are finding that their little treasures are staying at home into their twenties or even thirties. This phenomenon has been given a name – kippers – which stands for kids in parents' pockets eroding retirement savings. Funny? Yes, but from a personal finance perspective, kippers are no laughing matter.

From April 2006 you are able to pay 100 per cent of your income – up to a maximum of £215,000 – into a personal pension. This represents a huge increase in the level of contributions that you're allowed to make into a pension scheme and frees people up to build up a big pot of pension money fast if they've got a lot of disposable income. See Chapter 7 for more on personal pensions.

You're probably richer than you think

It may not feel like it when you open your credit card statement each month but you're probably far wealthier than you imagine. Firstly, the value of your assets, shares, savings, and investments is probably far higher than you think. Ask any home insurer and they can tell you that people regularly underestimate or have no real clue as to how much their personal possessions are worth.

What's more, it's not all about what you're worth today but what your current financial circumstances mean for your future. Even if your savings and investments are dwarfed by a great big mortgage debt then no worries – as long as you can afford repayments of course – because this is a really important investment that can provide a much needed financial boost in later life. See later in this chapter for more on using debt to boost your wealth prospects and Chapters 13 to 15 for how owning property can make your old age more financially secure.

 Why not spend a couple of hours working out your financial worth? Assessing your wealth gives you an idea of how close, or far away, you are from being able to finance a wealthy retirement. See Chapter 3 for the low-down on working out how much money you're worth.

Discovering How to Manage Debt

In William Shakespeare's *Hamlet,* the character Polonius advises 'Neither a borrower nor lender be.' But Polonius was no money guru. If you follow his advice and never borrow then I'm afraid you're unlikely to make enough money to retire wealthy.

Borrowing can be a way to invest for your future, allowing you to earn more cash that can help you to fund your retirement dreams.

Here are some ways in which the right sort of borrowing can give your life and retiring wealthy plans a real kick start:

- ✔ **Buying a property.** For the vast majority of people taking on a mortgage is the only way to buy their own home. And buying a property is one of the best investments for your future you can make. In fact, over the past few decades owning a home has been a star investment. No wonder, therefore, that literally millions of people have been prepared to borrow big to fund a property purchase. See Chapter 14 for clever mortgage tactics.

- ✔ **Gearing up your skills.** Few people can afford to go to university without borrowing money to live on or to pay tuition fees. A university education should make you more employable and help you earn more cash. Likewise, borrowing to re-skill during your working life can really pay dividends. All in all, skilling up can be one of the best investments you can make.

✔ **Starting a business.** Borrowing is often essential to building a successful business. Nearly all successful entrepreneurs need to borrow at some stage to turn their business dreams into money making reality. The financial rewards for building a successful business can be enormous. In short, make it in business and you will be able to retire wealthy. For more on building a successful enterprise check out *Starting a Business For Dummies* by Colin Barrow (Wiley).

Borrowing, of course, has a downside. Borrowing for short term gratification or without thought for repayment can hang like a dead weight around your neck, pulling your finances under and potentially scuppering your retiring wealthy plan.

If you're serious about grabbing the retiring wealthy prize you need to be disciplined and ignore the siren calls of the lenders to borrow more money.

That's not to say you have to be some sort of money hermit, averting your gaze from every snazzy shop window or car showroom just in case you feel tempted to buy something you can't really afford. Hey, we've all splashed the cash from time to time on a nice holiday or the latest iPod. The key is not to let it get out of hand.

Unless taking on debt can help you bring in more income or invest in property then it slows your progress towards retiring wealthy.

Try and bear in mind some simple rules for managing debt:

✔ **Don't borrow to pay off debt.** If you watch daytime TV you've probably seen ads from lenders offering to consolidate your debts into one manageable monthly repayment – isn't that nice of them? No it's not! Consolidation loans work by extending the period of the loan and securing it against your property. In the long run you end up paying far more in interest and if you don't keep up repayments you lose your home.

✔ **Don't borrow to buy shares.** This is far more common than you may think. During the dotcom boom plenty of daytraders – private investors who gave up their day jobs to work for themselves buying and selling shares – borrowed money to invest in shares which were 'sure-fire winners'. These sure-fire winners turned into losers and a number of daytraders were bankrupted. Risky investment and debt don't mix!

✔ **Don't borrow if you have savings.** It may not be as convenient or as flashy as whipping out a gold card in a shop but if you can pay for something from your savings it's much better for your finances. The reason for this is that the interest you pay on a loan is bound to be much higher than what you can earn from savings.

Beware the debt nasties

There are three types of debt – good debt, bad debt, and really bad debt. Lumber yourself with the latter and you can end up counting the cost for years, really setting back your retiring wealthy plans.

Here's a spotter's guide to some really bad debt. Needless to say avoid the following like the plague:

- ✔ **Doorstep lenders**. Some lenders turn up at your door offering no hassle loans normally of a few hundred or thousand pounds. Sign up for one of these doorstep loans and you can end up paying upwards of 100 per cent interest.

- ✔ **Store cards**. If you've bought any high value item in a shop such as a TV, sofa, or washing machine you've probably been asked if you'd like to take out a store card. The salesperson may even have offered you a 'special' discount on the item you were buying if you agreed. These store cards are a really bad deal, charging on average about 10 per cent more than a standard bank credit card.

- ✔ **Overdrafts**. These days banks, as a matter of course, give their customers an automatic pre-approved overdraft of a few hundred or thousand pounds. It may be tempting to dip into this cash reserve but don't. The interest rate charged on overdrafts is often very high – often around 20 per cent or even 30 per cent – and the charges for late payment can be punishing. Banks and building societies make millions each year out of overdrafts – don't let them take you for a ride.

- ✔ **Credit card cheques**. A few years ago some credit card providers started sending their cardholders 'blank cheques' telling them that they could write themselves a loan if they wished. Lots of people took them up on this offer and are now regretting it. This is a marketing gimmick with a sting in the tail as the loan usually attracts a higher rate of interest than standard credit card purchases. What's more, fraudsters try and get their greedy hands on these cheques to swindle you out of your cash. Best advice is: If you receive any of these cheques through the post, shred them!

There are two types of debt you need to get familiar with – unsecured and secured. Credit cards and personal loans are usually unsecured: If you fail to repay an unsecured debt then you end up on a credit blacklist. Secured loans are a very different kettle of fish as any money loaned to you is secured against property, so if you fail to repay then the lender comes along and takes your home. Gulp!

The simplest way to get on top of your debts is to identify the debts that are charging you the highest rate of interest and pay these first. By taking this course, in the long run you fork out less in interest payments. The only exception is mortgage debt, which you should always aim to pay first each month because if you don't make payments you can lose your home.

If you'd like help managing your debts then pay a visit to your local Citizens Advice Bureau (CAB). They will advise you how to get out of the red and back into the black and can even talk to your lenders to ensure they give you some much-needed breathing space. For your nearest CAB office check out the yellow pages or the organisation's Web site at www.nacab.co.uk.

Taking Your Loved Ones Along for the Retirement Ride

If you have a partner or family you are unlikely to be planning a solo retirement – although it's one way of ensuring you always have custody of the remote control. You naturally want to take your partner along with you for the ride (or should that be a post-retirement luxury cruise?). If this applies to you, it's time to get your nearest and dearest in on the act. After all, it's pointless saving and investing really hard if your partner is a secret spend-thrift running up huge debts. Ultimately they're going to drag your finances down to their level.

You need to sit down with your loved ones and talk about what you'd like retirement to hold. Perhaps your ideas about retirement differ. Your partner may want nothing more than to give up work while you want to work until you drop because you just love it. Whatever the scenario, you can only help the matter by talking things through.

Hopefully, you can come to an agreement over where you want to be in your golden years and how you intend to get there.

Of course, if you have a partner on board you have an even better chance of scooping the retiring wealthy prize. Two incomes are better than one as are two savings accounts and even two properties.

Here's an action plan for how to effectively join forces with your partner to drive for that retiring wealthy finishing post:

  ✔ **Establish when you both want to stop work.** One of you may be younger and therefore have longer to go to build up a full state pension entitlement. You should agree the dates at which you can both retire. If there is an age gap, perhaps the older person in the partnership can carry on working for a little while to build up a big enough cash pot to allow the younger person to retire earlier than would otherwise be the case.

✔ **Decide between you how much you need.** You need money to take care of life's basics plus cover emergencies, not forgetting a few of life's luxuries of course. You may have very different ideas of how much money you both need in old age. See earlier in this chapter for more on what sorts of expenses your funds need to cover in later life.

✔ **Examine how much you're on course to receive.** See Chapter 3 for more on how to tot up your personal worth. When you've totted up your joint worth you may find you're a long way short of what you need.

✔ **Discuss if there are any high value retirement goodies you want.** This can be anything from a flashy motor to a home in the sun. If there is something really special you want to aim for, then the sooner you start working as a team the better the chance you have of reaching your combined goal.

✔ **Calculate how much you need to reach your joint goals.** In order to buy retirement income for you both to live on – normally through an annuity – you need a big pot of cash. See earlier in this chapter for more on turning a pot of cash into an income you can both live on.

✔ **Agree on what you're willing to sacrifice to reach your dreams.** It stands to reason that in order to build up a big enough cash pot to enjoy a comfortable retirement you have to save, invest, and work really hard. You can't do any of this without making sacrifices whether that is curbing your spending – perhaps going to Cornwall instead of Cancun this summer – paying a portion of your income into a pension or simply setting time aside to monitor your savings and investments.

✔ **Determine what you want to leave behind for loved ones.** If you have children it's likely you'd like them to benefit financially on your death. If that's the case you want to ensure you've enough money to take care of your combined needs in retirement and leave a tidy legacy for your children, perhaps taking out a life insurance policy to benefit them as well.

An increasing percentage of marriages end in divorce. If you take a trip to splitsville you can find your retiring wealthy plans take a battering.

Good news for same sex couples

A recent law change means that same sex couples who go through a civil ceremony can enjoy the same tax and legal advantages that were once only open to married heterosexual couples. This means that same sex couples can now pass property and money to one another free of Capital Gains or Inheritance Tax. However, unmarried cohabiting different-sex couples do not benefit from the law change because the government argues that they always have the option of getting hitched.

If you divorce the court may well award part of your pension entitlement to your spouse. Such awards are getting more commonplace and are decided upon a case by case basis.

You and your partner may want to both visit an independent financial adviser (IFA). An IFA will be able to look at your two sets of finances and plot a course for both of you to follow to your retiring wealthy goals. However, good independent advice doesn't come cheap. See Chapter 5 for the low-down on seeking professional money advice.

Protecting Your Retiring Wealthy Plan: Buying Insurance

You don't need me to tell you that life doesn't always go to plan. In fact, sometimes things can all go horribly wrong. A bout of ill health or suffering an accident can damage your long-term earnings potential and with it your hopes of ever retiring wealthy.

But help is at hand. Seemingly, for every unfortunate event an insurance product is available to soften the blow. Of course, insurers are in the business of making money and try to set their premiums so that they take in more money than they end up paying out to claimants. However, this doesn't mean that insurance is a bad deal. Some people love the peace of mind that having insurance offers.

The types of insurance that you may want to consider include:

- ✓ **Income protection cover.** This pays you an income if you become unable to work due to ill health or injury.

- ✓ **Critical illness cover.** This pays a lump sum if you suffer a major health event such as cancer or a stroke.

✔ **Private medical insurance.** If you fall ill you should be able to receive prompt private medical attention at no cost. No NHS waiting list for you!

✔ **Redundancy insurance.** This does exactly what it says on the tin: Lose your job, through no fault of your own (so no taking out a policy and telling the boss where to get off!), and you should receive an income for a set period or until you get a new job.

✔ **Legal expenses insurance.** Suing and being sued are getting more common. Have a prang in the car or cause any sort of injury to a member of the public and it may end in court. Luckily, you can insure yourself against someone suing you successfully.

Each of the insurance schemes above has its merits and drawbacks. If you like the look of any of them, you'd be best off taking independent financial advice or talking to an insurance broker.

Mortgage and loan payment protection insurance has been hitting the headlines of late for all the wrong reasons. Consumer groups claim that insurance is overpriced and has lots of get-out clauses for the insurer so that they don't have to pay out. What's more, if you take out payment protection insurance all it does is cover your loan repayments. It doesn't for example pay you an income you can live off.

When it comes to insurance cheapest isn't necessarily best. You need to examine the policy small print for any hidden nasties. For example, some income protection products will only pay out if you're injured and are unable to do any work whatsoever while others will pay if your condition merely stops you from doing your current job. As you can imagine, it's much better to have the latter type of policy than the former.

Understanding the Time–Wealth Trade-off

Unless you're super lucky and win the lottery, have a real head for business, or are a very high wage earner then the road to retiring wealthy can be hard going. However, you can do it – picking up this book qualifies as a start – but you have to be realistic about your plans. Lots of people would love to retire early. But to be a doer rather than just a dreamer, you're going to have to have a lot – and

I mean a lot – of money tucked away. Your savings and investments may have to keep you going for thirty or forty years post retirement.

What's more, by calling it a day early you're potentially missing out on many years' earnings and as mentioned earlier in this chapter your fifties and sixties can be the time when you make the biggest strides towards retiring wealthy.

Be honest, what would you rather do: Retire wealthy or retire young?

I suspect that when you think about it you would go for the latter choice. After all you want to have fun in retirement – how much fun are you going to have if you're living on a pittance?

Retirement is a major life change and it can take some adjusting to. Several organisations run pre-retirement courses explaining how to best meet some of the key challenges that retirement brings such as sensible budgeting and claiming state benefits. As the big day nears you may be best going on one of these courses. Contact the Pre-Retirement Association on 01483 301170 or the Retirement Trust on 0207 378 9708 for course details.

Chapter 3

Knowing How Much You're Worth

I'm going to commit a bit of a social faux pas now and ask a direct question:

How much are you worth?

I know no one likes talking money. We tend to judge how much our friends and family are worth by looking at things like the size of their house, what they do for a living, and even where they like to holiday. What we don't do is ask the 'How much are you worth?' question outright. But when planning for a wealthy retirement, assessing how much you're worth right now is crucial. If you look at making your way to a wealthy retirement as a journey it's important to know where you're starting from. By the end of this chapter, I want you to look yourself in the mirror and answer the 'What am I worth?' question. By knowing the answer to this you're better able to judge how far you have to travel, what you have to do to get there, and what factors can help or hinder you in reaching your retiring wealthy destination.

Understanding What Makes Up Personal Wealth

Here's a piece of good news: You're probably much richer than you think. People frequently underestimate their financial worth. Home contents insurers know this and that's why many of them insist on people insuring their personal property for a minimum of £15,000.

When measuring your wealth, look at lots of different areas of your life. These include:

- **Your home:** If you own a home, this is likely to be your biggest asset.

- **Your state, private, and workplace pensions:** These are meant to give you an income in old age and can be worth a tidy sum.

- **Collectables and high value private possessions:** Items like cars, jewellery, and works of art, which should hopefully grow in value over time.

- **Savings accounts and investments:** You may have money tucked away in a building society or shares and bonds. You can read more on these in Chapters 10, 11, and 12.

You cannot accurately assess your personal worth without taking all your debts into account. You need to subtract your debts, such as mortgage, personal loans, or credit cards, from your assets which include premium bonds, savings, and so on, to reach your final personal worth figure.

Many people – particularly if they have not been a homeowner for long – actually owe more than they are worth. If after doing the sums you find you fall into this category, don't panic! After all, you need a mortgage to buy property, which can turn out to be one of the best investments you can make.

Working out the value of your home

Your home is the granddaddy of all your assets. Due in part to rapidly increasing property prices, homeowners increasingly see their home as providing the key to comfortable old age.

Lots of sources of information are out there to help you work out the true value of your property, and they're all free:

- ✔ Look in local newspapers to see the asking prices of similar properties.

- ✔ Search property Web sites for prices of similar homes in your area, such as www.Rightmove.co.uk, www.property finder.co.uk, and www.assertahomes.com.

- ✔ Ask a couple of local estate agents to put a value on your home or check out their window displays for properties like yours.

Assessing how much your pensions are worth

Your pension is important. For most people, apart from some savings, a pension is all they have to live on in retirement.

Pension income is likely to provide the bedrock of your finances in retirement. So rather than waiting until then to see what pension is coming to you, try to get a heads up now!

Three main types of pension are available in the UK:

- ✔ The state pension.
- ✔ A workplace pension.
- ✔ A personal pension.

Measuring what the state pension will pay you

The UK state pension is based on the contributory principle. This means the size of the state pension you can expect at retirement is based on how many years you make National Insurance contributions.

Many people – women in particular – do not work long enough to make sufficient National Insurance contributions to earn the right to a full basic state pension, because they take time out of the workforce to bring up children or look after elderly or sick relatives. Pension experts call this an *impaired contribution record*.

You can find out whether you're on course for a full state pension by writing to the government's pension service at the following address:

The Retirement Pension Forecasting Team, Room TB001, Tyneview Park, Whitley Road, Newcastle upon Tyne, NE98 1BA.

You can also apply online at www.thepensionservice.gov.uk/ resourcecentre/e-services/home.asp or ring up for a forecast on 0845 3000 168; you'll need your NI number when you ring. And the good news is pension forecasts are free!

The basic state pension in 2005 is worth £82.05 per week (2005–2006). In order to be entitled to a full state pension you need to have made 44 years of National Insurance contributions if you're male or 39 years if you're female. For more on how the state pension works see Chapter 6.

The state pension increases each year in line with inflation. Usually average wages rise faster than inflation, which means that over time people living off the state pension are getting poorer relative to those people earning a wage. At present the basic state pension is worth around less than 20 per cent of the average salary. By 2050 the state pension is predicted to be worth less than 10 per cent of average wages.

The state pension age is likely to rise over the next few decades from 65 to 67 or even 70. For more details on dangers of relying solely on the state pension see Chapter 1.

Working out your workplace pension

Many UK employees save towards their retirement through a workplace pension.

Some employers pay money into their employees' pension scheme and this turbo charges their value. If you have been a member of your workplace pension for a long time it may now be worth a tidy amount of cash. In fact, for many people the workplace pension can end up paying them far more than the state pension. Workplace pensions are important, so see Chapter 6 for more information.

If you want to find out how much your workplace pension is worth, ask the board of trustees who administer your scheme or your own HR department for a statement. If your workplace pension is administered by an insurance company, they should be able to supply you with an up-to-date statement.

Few people stay with one employer for the whole of their working lives. This means that they end up opening up lots of different workplace pensions. Keep a track of all your workplace pensions as this gives you a fuller picture of what income you can expect in retirement.

Gauging the value of your personal pension

If you have a personal pension, it should be very simple to find out what it's worth. Your personal pension provider – usually an insurance company – should send you an annual statement outlining the size of your pension pot.

In future most people will use their pension pot to buy an annuity (the law used to require you to do so). An *annuity* is an income for life and the price of buying an annuity has gone up over the past decade. See Chapter 9 for more on annuities.

The Financial Services Authority (FSA) has a free-to-use pensions calculator on its Web site. The calculator works out how much pension you can expect from the state and personal pensions based on how long you have to go until retirement, how much you are contributing now, and expected investment returns. Check out the FSA's nifty device on www.pensioncalculator.org.uk.

Totting up your savings pot

All that's needed to add up your savings is a little bit of research. The banks and building societies you have savings with send you an annual (or more frequent) account statement. Simply sit down with the most recent batch of statements and a calculator and work out how much you've tucked away. Trying to project this forwards to when you retire is tricky as you don't know what will happen to the interest rate on the account. See 'Projecting Your Wealth Forwards' later in this chapter for more on the positive effects that interest can have on your savings over the long term.

Taking a look at shares

Millions of people own shares, from pinstripe-suited City types to Mrs Miggins running the local pie shop. If you want to find out why share ownership is so popular, flick through to Chapter 12.

The vast majority of investors only own a handful of shares in former publicly-owned companies such as BAE, BP, or British Gas. If you're one of these, working out how much your total shareholding is worth is pretty easy: most national newspapers list the share prices of the UK's biggest companies. Simply multiply the price printed in the paper by the number of shares you hold to calculate the total value of your shareholding. If you're not sure how many shares you own you can contact the company in question and ask them.

If you're what is called a 'serious' investor – which doesn't mean you have to wear a permanent frown, just have lots of cash invested in shares – then plenty of painless ways exist to work out what your total holding is worth:

- ✔ Try one of the free share-tracking services offered by Internet service providers.
- ✔ Check out a financial Web site such as `www.motleyfool.co.uk`.
- ✔ Use a computer program such as *Microsoft Money* to track your gains.

You only need to enter the name of the share and the number you hold and these whizz-bang options track their value.

Many people use a stockbroker to buy their shares. These shares are held in what's known as a *nominee account*. This means that they're in the name of the stockbroking firm rather than your own. No sweat here, as your stockbroker sends you statements detailing your holdings and their value.

How much is my collectable worth?

Checking out how much your collectable is worth today shouldn't be much of a stretch; the following list gives suggestions for finding out the value of some common collectables:

- ✔ If antiques float your boat then check out the latest auctions. Details of your nearest auction room can be found at `www.auctionguide.com`.

- ✔ If you're the proud owner of a classic motor then a quick Internet search should reveal an owners' club. These club Web sites should give you an idea of what your car should fetch on the open market. If this fails, check out magazines such as *Classic Cars* and *Practical Classics*.

- ✔ If you're an art buff or a stamp collector contact a gallery or shop and ask for a valuation.

Placing a price on collectables

Not only is collecting a hobby, it can also be an investment. Collecting classic cars, wine, art, antiques, and stamps can be both a passion and a way of making a profit. Even if your collectable doesn't turn into a goldmine you can still enjoy the possession – driving a classic car or even partaking of a case or two of vintage wine (for purely medicinal purposes of course). But be warned – to turn a profit the collectable has to be widely desired and there has to be a market for it. I'm afraid that much cherished collection of bus tickets or milk bottle tops is not going to support you in old age.

Knowing what your collectable is worth now is the easy part (if you're struggling, check out the sidebar 'How much is my collectable worth?' for inspiration); working out whether it'll grow in value in future is a touch trickier.

Whether a collectable becomes a fashion victim or the next must-have can be just down to pure luck; so banking on collectables to provide you with a comfortable retirement becomes a high-risk business. You may find that your collectable, like bell-bottomed flares or leg warmers, goes out of fashion. For example, in the 1980s the classic car market went through a boom with vintage cars changing hands for silly money. Yet during the 1990s the market collapsed and has only just started to show signs of recovery. See Chapter 16 for more on the ups and downs of collectables as an investment.

For a collectable to be of value, keep it in good condition. Valuable items such as classic cars, wine, or art all have to be stored correctly and this can cost money. For example, wine should be kept in a temperature-controlled warehouse, for which you'll need to pay storage costs.

Coming to a Final Reckoning

So you've worked out what your home, savings, investments, and collectables are worth. Now the miserable bit – you need to subtract your debts.

Typical debts include:

- ✔ Mortgage.
- ✔ Credit and store cards.
- ✔ Any personal loans.
- ✔ Bank overdraft.

Work out the total amount you owe and subtract that from the total you have calculated for your savings and so on.

Once you've factored in your debts you should be at a final reckoning and can answer the question posed at the start of the chapter: 'What are you worth?'

If you look at your debts and decide you want to pay off a loan or mortgage early to maximise your savings in the long run, remember that fees called *early redemption* or *early payment penalties* are often added to your loan.

Projecting Your Wealth Forwards

So now you know the value of your home, savings, shares, and collectables. What do you do with this knowledge?

You can try to project your wealth forwards to see how much all these possessions and investments may be worth to you in retirement.

Trying to see into the future doesn't involve reading Tarot cards or going to see Mystic Meg (no appointment necessary, she should know you're coming!). It's simply a case of doing a bit of maths. Money experts work on the principle that investments should grow in value at between 5 per cent and 7 per cent a year.

Investment growth is never steady. One year your investments may grow in value by say 5 per cent, the next you can have a bumper year and they may grow at 20 per cent. But then due to a property market crash or share price collapse your investments may take a battering and actually fall in value. Nevertheless, over the long term – say 20 or 30 years – it's fairly safe to work on the 5 per cent or 7 per cent investment growth rates.

If you want to see how much your investments will be worth if they grow at 5 per cent, it's time for some number crunching on your calculator:

1. Enter into the calculator how much you're worth today. Multiply it by 1.05 (to represent 5 per cent growth). If, for example, you're worth £100,000 today, multiply this figure by 1.05 and you will get £105,000.

2. Repeat for each year until your planned retirement date. Multiply your figure from step 1 by 1.05 and you will get £110,250, and so on. Eventually over 20 years your £100,000

should balloon to £265,330 presuming a 5 per cent annual growth rate.

If you don't want to number crunch (and I don't blame you!), use the free online compound interest calculator on the Motley Fool Web site at www.fool.co.uk/school/compound.htm.

3. Now follow the same procedure to find out what you'd be worth if your investments grew at 7 per cent a year on average. Enter into the calculator how much you're worth then multiply it by 1.07 (the equivalent to 7 per cent growth) for each year until your planned retirement.

The figures you come up with may pleasantly surprise you, but don't go on a shopping spree! Remember this is a projection; you haven't got this money yet.

These calculations give you an idea of your foundation – where you should be at when it's time to collect that carriage clock and wave goodbye to the world of work

But bear in mind that the final figure doesn't give you the whole picture. You need to bear in mind that prices rise over time eroding the value of your cash. Therefore, if your investment grows at 5 per cent in a year but prices rise by 3 per cent in real terms (after inflation) you're only enjoying 2 per cent growth.

One very important thing needs to be thrown into the mix: What will happen to your income?

Providing that all things go well in your career you should reach the peak of your earnings potential from your late forties or early to mid fifties. In addition, this is a time when you may have paid off your mortgage and the children have flown the family nest. Different ways to maximize your income and help you to improve your situation in retirement are explored in Chapter 21.

Generally the greater number of investments you have – savings, shares, and property for example – the more steady growth is over the long term. Having a spread of investments helps secure a wealthy retirement.

Projecting your wealth forwards is a very inexact science – it gives you some ballpark figures only. Don't rely on calculations you make now to bail you out in several decades time.

Facing Up to Life Changes

Forest Gump famously said life is like a box of chocolates. If that's the case, for every delicious strawberry cream there is a not-so-tasty praline centre lurking beside it. The course of life, like true love, never does run smooth. You may be happy to know that the rest of this section will be a metaphor-free zone!

You have to work into your retirement plan the possibility that life can bowl you a few googlies (I know I promised, but I couldn't resist). Some all-too common problems that can stop you working and earning include:

- ✔ **Getting divorced:** Pay a visit to splitsville and your former spouse may be able to claim a large slice of your property, savings, and even your pension.

- ✔ **Losing your job:** If you can't work due to either ill health or redundancy you are likely to have to dip into your savings to pay the household bills.

- ✔ **Being sued:** Recently the number of cases where one member of the public sues another has increased sharply, as people have used no-win no-fee law firms.

All the above are real 'hide behind the sofa and don't come out until it's all over' scenarios, but nevertheless you would be wise to put plans in place to protect your finances. The great American golfer Jack Nicklaus once said if you haven't lost then you can win! Likewise, if you have a plan in place to cope with worst-case scenarios you're in with a shout of carrying away the retiring wealthy prize.

You have two options to protect yourself and your finances:

- ✔ Build up a cash reserve – rainy day money. How best to do this and what size of reserve you should aim for are explored in the sidebar 'Preparing for a rainy day.' The cash reserve tactic is best suited for problems that go on for months rather than years.

  If you fall ill and are unable to work for a long time, you have to largely exhaust your reserves before the state will step in and pay some benefits such as jobseekers allowance. In fact, savings of over £3,000 can bar you from collecting full job-seekers allowance.

- ✔ Take out insurance against accident, unemployment, or life threatening illness. In short, name something horrible that can happen and you bet there is an insurance you can buy. However, cover can be expensive and not all products on offer are good ones; in fact some are poor and overpriced. If you want to buy insurance you may be best seeking financial advice from an expert, see Chapter 5 for more on this.

Not all life changes have to be bad news! You may find for example that the stork pays an unexpected visit and you or your partner gives birth. While a baby may be a welcome arrival, they are expensive and can throw your financial plans out of kilter.

The best place for your rainy day money is a savings account from a building society or bank. Don't agree to a long notice period on such accounts. Lots of instant access accounts are available, paying high rates of interest. Check out independent Web site www.moneyfacts.co.uk for an up-to-date best buy list. For an explanation of the different types of savings accounts offered, see Chapter 10.

Preparing for a rainy day!

So you want to enjoy the high life in retirement? I thought so. But before you start down the road to a wealthy retirement you need a little cash tucked away in case something untoward happens in your life such as illness, injury, or a period of unemployment. Everyone should aim to put this rainy day money in place first before they start investing in property, shares, or some other scheme designed to secure a wealthy old age.

A good rainy day cash float should:

✔ Be large enough to cover your living expenses for at least six months.

✔ Be easy to get your hands on, which means in a savings account rather than invested in either shares or property.

Chapter 4

Picking a Money Philosophy

● ●

In This Chapter

▶ Taking lessons from an investment 'sage'

▶ Going against the herd – contrary investing

▶ Understanding the core–satellite approach

▶ Helping others while helping yourself

● ●

*A*t some point, you can bet your bottom dollar, all successful investors get asked the same question: 'What is the secret of your success?'

Some reply with some folksy homespun philosophy. Others speak in City-trader talk, more akin to computer binary than everyday English.

Whatever the reply, one thing's for certain: They all have a money mantra. They don't normally start off with this mantra in mind – they arrive at it usually through a combination of trial and costly error.

If you're serious about retiring wealthy you'll tread a similar path, making mistakes but – crucially – learning from them. In this chapter I give you a little bit of a head start, distilling the knowledge of successful private investors and outlining some money strategies you can pick or choose from.

You never know, perhaps, one day someone may ask you to tell them the secret of your investment success.

Listening to the Sage of Omaha

Why spend the time drawing up your own investment philosophy when you can simply use someone else's?

Warren Buffett is acknowledged as the world's most successful investor. Back in the 1960s Buffett bought Berkshire Hathaway, a struggling provincial American textile firm. He used the company as a launch pad to buy shares in other firms he believed were undervalued. Over the years Berkshire Hathaway has grown into one of the largest investment companies on the planet, making people who bought shares in it a fortune.

Warren Buffett is now in his seventies but still heads up the firm, and every year shareholders gather to hear what he has to say on the state of the markets. Buffett's homespun investment philosophies have earned him the nickname the Sage of Omaha and they influence investor thinking around the globe. This is because Buffett's been there, done it, and not only bought the t-shirt but bought the company that made the t-shirt in the first place.

Here are some of the lessons dished out by the sage over the past five decades. They all relate to share investment but, in reality, you can apply them to any class of investment:

- **Have faith in your investments.** If you feel an investment is right then you should aim to invest for the long term, which can mean decades rather than minutes or hours. Being in it for the long term means that you minimise stockbroking and other charges and you benefit fully from the long-term growth in an investment. See later in the chapter for more on the long-term approach to investing.

- **Have proper understanding.** Buffett talks about something he calls the 'circle of competence' being key to sound investing. In short, this means that you should only invest in things that you actually understand. Therefore, if you're not au fait with the Internet or its impact in the wider world perhaps you ought to steer clear of dotcom shares. Likewise, if you understand property then you may be best sticking to that.

- **Pay a 'rational' price.** Not overpaying for an investment seems a bit of a no-brainer but countless investors fall into this trap every day. Think back to the late nineties: Investors were routinely paying top whack for shares in Internet companies that were little more than an idea, a promise of growth in the far flung future. Remember what happened then! Buffett has always crunched the numbers (looking at boring but vital things like a company's profitability) and won't invest unless he has a 'margin of safety'. In short this means he goes for bargains that give him a bit of built in profit just in case the wider market turns against his investment choice.

> ✔ **Be a choosy investor.** When Buffett applies the lessons out-
> lined above to the stock market he finds few shares that actu-
> ally fit the bill. During the course of the 1990s Buffett only
> held shares in 10 companies. This was at a time when stock
> markets were going mad and lesser mortals were buying and
> selling hundreds if not thousands of shares.

Don't invest simply for the sake of it. No investment is better than
a bad one. Remember, you can always earn interest on your cash
through a savings deposit account. It may be boring but it's a lot
more sensible than taking the plunge and buying an investment
you don't understand.

Taking the Long-Term View of Investing

Very few, if any, investment moves you make pay off over the short
term. You have to allow your savings and investments time to work
their magic. When it comes to successful saving and investing,
patience is a virtue.

Generally, financial experts reckon that once you make an investment choice you should stick with it for at least five years and
often much longer, because the passage of time can help smooth
out performance peaks and troughs. Times of underperformance
are balanced by periods when the investment does well and over
the long term it all averages out.

As for savings accounts and fixed return investments like National
Savings bonds, time allows compound interest to weave its spell.
See Chapter 3 for more on how compound interest can boost your
wealth.

But the 'make sure you're in it for the long term' mantra doesn't
always hold true. If you trade alternative investments like options
and futures, spread bet, or buy company shares then you may be
specifically aiming for a quick killing. However, you shouldn't
touch these types of investment with a barge pole unless you're
prepared to lose every penny (and sometimes more) of what you
invest.

If you chop and change your investments regularly you run the risk
of incurring high fees. For example, each time you buy or sell
shares you have to pay stockbroker fees and stamp duty. Likewise,
buy or sell property and you have to pay stamp duty land tax,
estate agency, and legal fees.

The warning not to chop and change investments doesn't apply to savings accounts. Banks and building societies have a nasty habit of launching savings accounts paying a market leading rate of interest, only to lower their rate once they have attracted people to deposit money. Guard against this and review the rate that your savings accounts are paying at least once a year. If you find that your savings account provider has done the dirty and lowered rates then move your money to the current top payer.

Going against the Herd: Being a Contrary Investor

Here's an investment truth: The herd or market sometimes gets it wrong. If you can spot when the herd or market is making an error you can scoop a tidy fortune. This is called contrary investing and it's all about spotting a gap between widespread investor perception and cold reality.

Understanding (and taking advantage) of the herd

If, for a moment, you think of the investment universe as a part of the African game reserve, at any one time you will see herds running in different directions either looking for a safe haven or chasing a prize.

Sometimes it's good to join the herd, other times you should hang back to see what happens or even bolt in the opposite direction. This section shows some classic examples of when you should consider going against the herd.

In essence, contrary investing is all about trying to obtain an investment El Dorado. If it comes off, a contrary investment call means you buy at the bottom and sell at the top.

When an investment bubble is growing

It seems every generation has its very own investment bubble. This is when prices run away from real investment value.

For example, in the late 1980s and early 1990s UK house prices soared and it got to the stage that the price of an average property was five or six time average salaries. First-time buyers were priced out of the market and thus choked off demand. At the same time interest rates rose and literally hundreds of thousands of people couldn't keep up their repayments. A contrary investment strategy would have been to sell property when prices were racing away from salaries and then buy back in once the market crash had taken place.

When an investment has been 'oversold'

Markets (in other words the herd) often react to bad news by over-selling. They pile out of an investment in the hope of collecting their profit and moving on to pastures new (we're back in that African game reserve again!). However, often the market is not discerning in what it sells. For example, a really bad set of UK retail sales figures may prompt a wholesale sell off of retail shares. Yet a good retailer doesn't turn into a dog overnight. A general market sell off can be a great opportunity to pick up a bargain with the hope that ultimately the herd will return and you can turn a tidy profit.

When bad news breaks

Not too long ago oil giant Shell got itself into difficulty for over-stating its oil reserves. The market reacted badly and shares in Shell – a hugely profitable company – were sold off. In fact, shares in the company fell nearly a third in double quick time. A contrary investor who was brave enough to invest on this bad news made a real killing as there was no more bad news from the company and world oil prices doubled pushing Shell's profits into orbit. Guess what happened? The herd piled back into Shell and the shares soared.

Bad company news should give you pause for thought. Bad news should mean one of three things: It's time to sell up and ship out, it's time to sit tight, or it's an opportunity to buy big into a company you believe will come right in the long term.

Working a contrary strategy into your big plan

Of course, it goes without saying that contrary investing is risky. The herd may have abandoned an investment for good reason – it may well be a real dog!

So best exercise some caution. Here are some tips on working contrary investing into your big plan:

- ✔ **Have an investment core in place.** Make sure you have a nice tidy cash pile in place to take care of necessities if things in your life go wrong. You also want money in steady investments such as property or bonds before even considering making a contrary investment play. See later in this chapter for what should make up your investment core.

- ✔ **Don't over commit.** As mentioned above contrary investing is about as high risk as you can get so don't bet your life savings on it. Only invest money you can afford to lose, because there's a good chance of you doing just that.

- ✔ **Make sure you do your homework.** You have a far better chance of being a successful contrary investor if you approach it seriously. If you're not serious about your investments, you're soon parted from your cash. See Chapter 12 for how to assess a company share.

If you win big through contrary investing it should be nothing more than a little extra icing on your investment cake. If you lose cash then it shouldn't matter that much as long as you have core investments in place and don't over commit funds.

Who let the dogs out?

Going to the dogs doesn't involve a betting on Dashing Boy in trap six, it simply means buying the poorest performing shares during the previous year – in stockbroker speak these are called the dogs of the index. You may think once a dog always a dog but surprisingly large numbers of shares bounce back sharply after their year of turmoil.

Buying dog shares is the ultimate in contrary investing. You're betting that the market has oversold the shares and that eventually the City types will realise this and pile back in – boosting your coffers in the process.

Of course, some of your picks are true dogs and can end up going to the wall – or should that be put down? But, hopefully, enough will return to wet-nosed, waggy-tailed health!

Buying dog shares is a popular investment strategy and you can see which shares have performed the worst by checking out the *Financial Times* or the market data section of the BBC News Web site at www.bbc.co.uk/business.

Needless to say dog investing can be very risky. Remember, you may get bitten.

Adopting the Core–Satellite Approach

The core–satellite approach is used by lots of successful long-term private investors. Often they don't realise they are doing it as it seems to come very naturally. The core–satellite approach is beautifully simple and if followed properly can offer the twin benefits of investment growth and security. It's unlikely to get you rich quick but when you're taking a long-term view of investment and reaching for that retiring wealthy prize it's not all about speed – in fact, getting rich slow does most people just fine!

Core–satellite explained

Core investments are those that you shouldn't do without – they may stay with you in one form or another for most of your life. You look to core investments to protect you from the worst life can throw at you, while at the same time growing steadily in value. Ideally, you should look to spend your early working years building up this investment core.

Having an investment core gives you the financial security to add satellite investments. *Satellite investments* are simply everything in the investment universe which aren't core ones. They are investments you don't have to have, which you can take on a case-by-case basis. Satellite investments tend to be riskier than core investments but potentially more rewarding.

These satellite investments, if they go well, should inject some much needed growth into your retiring wealthy project but if they go wrong, no worries, you can still rely on your core investments to keep the wolf from the door.

Core investments tend to be low- to medium-risk, while satellite investments tend to be medium- to high-risk.

Some people put the cart before the horse and invest in higher risk satellite investment such as shares before building an investment core. In truth there isn't much wrong with this, just as long as they can afford to lose the money they have invested and are young enough to be confident in their future earning potential.

What makes up core investment?

A typical investment core is made up of the following:

- **Your main home.** Your home serves the dual purpose of pro-viding a roof over your head – meaning you don't have to pay rent – while hopefully enjoying capital growth. Later down the line, all going well, the idea is that you can sell up, move somewhere cheaper, and pocket the profit. Alternatively, you can remortgage against the increased value of your home to purchase a buy-to-let property.

- **Six months' income on deposit.** This is money held in savings accounts, which can be used if you find that you are short of cash. This so-called rainy day money provides you with the bedrock on top of which you can add more exotic investments in the hope of securing higher returns. See Chapter 3 for details on the best home for your rainy day cash.

- **Government and large company bonds.** Buying government bonds and those issued by large companies can offer a steady stream of income and the chance of capital growth. Even under the worst case scenario the bond issuer buys back the bond at a specified later date for its original value. But you are running the risk that the bond issuer will default. For this reason, money invested in bonds is considered more at risk than in a savings account. Check out Chapter 11 for the inside track on bonds.

- **Some stock market collective investments.** Medium-risk collective investments such as unit trusts, which invest in the shares of large UK companies, can make up part of a core investment portfolio. Collectives should give you a higher rate of return than a savings account but your money is at risk from a general stock market crash or from the fund that you choose to invest in turning out to be a real dud. See Chapter 12 for more on collective investments.

- **Pension saving.** This can take the form of a workplace or pri-vate pension provision. There are many different types of scheme, some riskier than others, and they are explained in full detail in Chapters 6, 7, and 8.

Generally, putting money into collectives is safer than direct investment in company shares. This is because collective funds buy shares in lots of different firms; the idea is that more will pay off than fall flat. However, if you put your cash into the shares of a single company then you stand a greater chance of sustaining heavy losses.

Some stock market collective investments can be high risk, such as funds which invest in technology company shares or emerging markets. As a rule, such high-risk collectives should not form part of your core investments.

Identifying 'satellite' investments

In truth, you can categorise satellite investments as being either medium or high risk. You can also class investments which have a limited resale market as being satellite.

Here are some typical satellite investments:

- Single company shares and bonds issued by medium or small sized companies.

- Alternative investments such as hedge funds, options, spread bets, and venture capital trusts.

- Unit and investment trusts that invest in shares of small companies or companies listed on overseas stock markets.

- Buy-to-let property, particularly if you have to borrow a lot of cash to make the purchase happen.

- Collectables such as classic cars, stamps, and antiques.

 Just because I've lumped several investments together under the 'satellite' banner it doesn't mean they all hold the same risks. For example, a hedging investment like a future may well be a lot riskier than say buying shares in a major oil company. See Chapter 10 for more on what makes up high-, medium-, and low-risk investments.

Paying Less Tax as a Way of Life

Most people are probably paying more tax then they need to. When it comes to paying for retirement people who are not tax aware are already at a disadvantage. After all, every penny extra you pay in tax is money that could have been invested towards providing a prosperous old age.

Ignorance of the tax system is widespread. But you don't need to know every nook and cranny of the tax system – there are accountants who can do that for you – just be aware of some of the basic tax breaks and loopholes you can use to cut the amount of cash you hand over to HM Revenue and Customs. Check out Chapter 18 for ten ways to cut your tax bill or take a look at *Paying Less Tax For Dummies* by Tony Levene (Wiley).

If you have complex tax affairs – for example you're self employed – you'd be best to see an accountant. They can draw up your tax accounts and may well be able to suggest some nifty ways to cut your tax bill. See Chapter 5 for more on finding a good accountant.

Getting the Balance Right: Reducing Risk as You Get Older

When it comes to what you save and invest in, you have to take into account your age. The older you are, the nearer you are to retirement and the fewer risks you should take with your money. This is for a number of reasons including:

- ✓ **Your earnings potential starts to drop.** Most people spend their twenties and thirties in education or training and finding their feet in the world of work or running their own business. All this hard work, hopefully, pays off in their forties and fifties as they ascend the greasy pole, reaching their maximum earnings potential. But as the fifties roll by you often become less attractive to employers. They may see you as not being around for the long term or harder to train than a young thrusting twenty or thirty something. What's more, as you get older there's a greater risk of suffering illness which may stop you working altogether.

- ✓ **You have less time to make up losses.** Investments can go down as well as up. If you're young then you have the time to sit tight during a period of investment underperformance, following say a housing market or stock market crash. But when you're older you may want the money invested to pay for your retirement. At this stage sitting out investment underperformance in the hope that things will eventually come good may not be an option.

Virtually all investment experts reckon that as you get older you should gradually sell high- and medium-risk investments, using the cash to buy into low-risk ones.

 When deciding on your own money philosophy, realise that it has to evolve over time. The gung-ho tactics of your twenties or thirties are not suited to your fifties and sixties.

Remembering That Knowledge Equals Power

The bigger your bank of investment knowledge is, the greater the chance of retiring wealthy. The simple equation is that investment know-how gives you a chance to spot opportunities to grow your wealth. If you'd like one overarching money philosophy it should be: Get familiar with the world of investment.

Here are some ways to arm yourself with investment knowledge:

- **Monitoring the media.** The number of articles published regarding shares, savings accounts, and the property market seems to grow each week. Sometimes it feels like you need to call a taxi just to transport the Sunday newspapers home, so full are they with articles, features, and information. And it's not just the papers, there are huge numbers of Web sites dedicated to all types of investment. With the modern media and the Internet at your fingertips it has never been easier to be in the know.

- **Looking around you.** You can tell an awful lot about which investments are hot and which are not just by keeping your eyes and ears open. For example, next time you're in a supermarket look at the checkout queues. Are they long? Do you think the special offers are really special or not? How about the fixtures and fittings and ease of navigation of the shop – is it top drawer or can there be improvements? These are all good pointers to whether you should invest in the shares of the retailer. As a consumer you're at the sharp end and you may be able to spot a failing or good, undervalued company even before its own management or the City does.

Careless talk costs money

Some people try and expand their knowledge by logging onto investment chat rooms. Generally, people in these chat rooms know nothing about very little – they speculate about this share or that share, spreading idle and often inaccurate gossip. In fact, I have come across anecdotal evidence of downright false information being posted on some of these sites to create interest in a dud share (which the poster is desperate to sell of course). Best not waste your time with investment chat rooms.

Monitoring the media and looking around you are part of doing your investment homework. This applies to all investments, not just shares. For example, if you're looking at buying a buy-to-let property check out what the local schools are like or the property's proximity to transport links – these are factors which can heavily influence its letting potential.

Being your own adviser

If you have the knowledge and the time you can manage your own investment strategy. After all, apart from your nearest and dearest, who other than yourself truly has your best interests at heart?

If you're going to take your big plan in your own hands you need to be properly organised:

- ✔ Set time aside to study potential investments.
- ✔ Regularly monitor the performance of your savings and investments.
- ✔ Keep up to speed with events in the wider economy, as they may impact your investments.
- ✔ Keep your records up-to-date and safe – this way you're better able to monitor investment performance and fill out tax self assessment forms.

Realising sometimes you need to take advice

You may be a well organised saver and investor, in it for the long term, but there are bound to be times when you find yourself in need of a little help. Ideally you should seek independent financial advice when you find yourself at the limits of your knowledge or simply feel that your retiring wealthy plan can do with being given the once over by a fresh pair of expert eyes. See Chapter 5 for how to find good unbiased financial advice.

Taking Economic Factors into Account

Being a savvy investor is not just about weighing up whether a company share is worth buying, nor is it all about buying property in the right location. To be smarter than the average saver or investor you have to keep one eye fixed on what's going on in the UK economy.

Remember the balcony scene from Monty Python's *Life of Brian*? Brian, played by Graham Chapman, tells the crowd that has gathered outside his window in the belief that he is the Messiah that they don't need to follow him or in fact anyone because they are all individuals. The crowd responds in unison 'Yes we are all individuals'.

In the similar way we may think of ourselves as individuals, existing in our own economic bubble, but we're not! In reality, our finances are very sensitive to what's going on in the wider economy.

Using changes in the economy to your advantage

Therefore, keep abreast of economic events and you can position your retiring wealthy plan to take advantage or at the very least not be too damaged by changes in the economy. Here are some key economic factors you should keep an eye out for:

- ✔ **Rising prices.** Inflation can erode your financial position in double quick time. We save and invest not for the sake of it but so that we can exchange our cash pot for goods and services later in life. Rising prices mean that your savings and investments are exchanged for fewer goods and services in future. Unless, of course, the value of your savings and investments grows at the same or a faster rate than prices.

- ✔ **Interest rate moves.** As rates rise then the cost of borrowing goes up but so should the return on savings. If rates fall the opposite occurs. The key is to be on the right side of this equation. When rates are high make sure you're a saver earning top notch interest but when rates are low you have the option to borrow to invest – perhaps in a buy-to-let property using a second mortgage – but *not* to splurge in the shops.

- ✔ **Economic recession.** This can lead to your employer getting into trouble and having to lay off staff (possibly including yourself) or if you're a business owner a recession can mean your customers disappear and you have to fold. You see, all those boring GDP figures they announce towards the end of the news bulletins are important.

✔ **Stock market booms and crashes.** It seems each generation has its own stock market boom followed seemingly inevitably by a crash. Remember the late nineties when everyone ploughed into technology and dotcom shares only for them to come down to earth with an enormous thud? A stock market boom can be a great way to get rich quick but you have to time your exit right or else you're be left holding the baby. Sometimes in the past stock market crashes have affected so many people's finances that they have plunged the wider economy into recession.

Coping with rocky economic times

It's pointless knowing which economic factors to look for if you don't know what to do when you spot them! The question you should ask yourself is how do I protect my big retiring wealthy plan should a major economic shift take place? This is the $64,000 question – or even more with inflation!

Here are some sensible strategies you can adopt when particular events occur:

✔ **Inflation increases.** Check that the rate you're getting on your savings accounts at least keeps place with inflation. You may also want to consider an index-linked investment such as National Savings bonds (see Chapter 10 for more on these). The return on index-linked investments automatically increases when prices rise.

✔ **Interest rates rising.** If you have a mortgage then interest rate rises can be a real killer as your repayments go up. However, interest rate rises aren't all bad news – if you're a saver you should be getting a higher return for your money.

✔ **Interest rates falling.** This is good news for borrowers and it may be time to overpay on your mortgage (if you're allowed) in order to reduce your overall debt level. Falling rates aren't good for savers and it should prompt you to question whether you would be better off investing your spare cash in say shares or property.

✔ **Economic recession.** This is a real batten down the hatches time. If you see a recession looming you should focus on getting your finances in order – ensure that you have enough savings to keep you going should you lose your job or your business fold.

✔ **Stock market booms and crashes.** Many investors adopt a *stop loss* tactic when it comes to share investments. The concept of stop loss is simple: Once your share investments have lost a certain percentage of their value you automatically sell. You can alter your stop loss position to take account of share price rises so that as your shares rise in value so does your stop loss mark. This way the stop loss can help your shares crystalise price gains as well as halt a slide. See Chapter 12 for more on stop loss and share investing generally.

The key is to keep in the know. Set time aside to check out what is happening to interest rates, inflation, stock markets, and the economy as a whole.

Lots of sources of information are out there from news Web sites to newspapers all brimful of the latest data and analysis.

The truth is that most people don't have a clue what the inflation or even interest rate is – more fool them! The first they know that something is awry is when their share portfolios become worthless, the letter from the mortgage company arrives telling them their repayments are about to go up, or the P45 lands on their desk at work.

If you're particularly worried about the effects that higher interest rates may have on your mortgage repayments then you ought to consider opting for a long-term fixed-rate mortgage deal. Under one of these deals no matter what happens to interest rates in the wider economy your mortgage repayments stay the same. However, these deals do come to an end and if rates fall you're stuck on the higher fixed rate. See Chapter 14 for more on mortgages.

Making It on Your Own: Starting Your Own Business

Starting your own business can be one of the best routes to a wealthy retirement. If you manage to build a successful business it's likely to be your life's one really big investment – potentially dwarfing your home – not just in terms of pounds and pence but also time and energy.

But, needless to say, being an entrepreneur isn't easy and isn't right for everyone. If you've ever watched BBC's *Dragon's Den* TV programme you know that for every genius, money-making idea there are dozens if not hundreds of really daft ones. You can't be half-hearted in business and before you start spending valuable time and money you should ask yourself some blunt questions.

- ✔ **Do you really have the time and energy to devote to your enterprise?** The world of small business is a million miles away from the nine-to-five existence most of us pursue.

- ✔ **Are your family and partner onside?** You should give your loved ones a say because if you're going to be serious they may have to cope without you around for long periods of time.

- ✔ **Have you got the business 'X-Factor'?** Is your idea strong enough, do you truly believe in it, and what's more is there someone out there doing it already?

- ✔ **Are you tough enough?** You have to be thick-skinned to be a business type, prepared to talk tough with suppliers and late paying customers, not to mention hiring and firing staff.

These questions are just a starting point. You must draw up a comprehensive business plan in order to secure the finance (which, in turn, may entail remortgaging your home). In addition, once you're up and running you have to advertise, market your business, secure and insure premises, hire staff, and keep proper accounts.

Running your own business is a long but potentially rewarding journey and many helpful books are available. Check out the following books (all published by Wiley):

- ✔ Liz Barclay's *Small Business Employment Law For Dummies*

- ✔ Colin Barrow's *Starting A Business For Dummies*

- ✔ John A. Tracy and Colin Barrow's *Understanding Business Accounting For Dummies*

- ✔ Paul Tiffany, Steven Peterson, and Colin Barrow's *Business Plans For Dummies*

Few business greats make it without borrowing big at the start. However, the sad fact is that the majority of businesses fold in their first year. If this happened to you would your personal finances be able to survive the fallout and what would happen to your retiring wealthy plan?

Helping Yourself While Helping Others

Many people associate making money with exploitation. But it really doesn't have to be this way. It's possible to boost your bank balance without trading in your moral compass. You can go for a socially responsible investment (SRI), also called ethical investment.

The idea is simple – make the investor some money without harming people or planet.

Ethical investment funds

These are unit trusts which pool investor cash to buy shares in companies with a track record of looking after employees and the environment. You can get light green or dark green ethical funds. The greener the shade of the fund, the stricter the rules governing what it can invest in. Light green funds may invest in a variety of firms while dark green stick purely to firms which have spotless ethical practices. Like a standard unit trust you stand to gain from the growth in the underlying investments through a rising unit price.

Credit Union accounts

These are non-profit organisations which pool investor money to lend to people who may be turned down by the mainstream banks. Credit unions do a great job in some inner city areas and surprisingly few borrowers default on their loans. This can be a great way to put something back and many credit unions pay depositors a healthy rate of interest. Check out the Association of Credit Unions Web site at www.abcul.org for more information.

A few years ago the FTSE4Good stock market index was launched. This index contained firms that are noted for their ethical trading policies. Once the index came into being several ethical funds launched promising to track the index. Tracking is simple and has nothing to do with wild animals – a fund which tracks an index buys all the shares in the index according to their value. Therefore, a tracker will buy more shares in a big expensive company and fewer in a little cheap one. The idea is to replicate the performance of the index a whole.

There are an increasing number of financial products being launched tailored to the Muslim faith. Under Muslim Sharia law the paying and receipt of interest is banned but financial firms such as the Muslim bank of Great Britain and Lloyds TSB have designed nifty products that comply with this law but allow people to buy their own homes and operate a current account.

It pains me to write this but ethical investments often underperform non-ethical ones and may not be the most efficient route to retiring wealthy. A recent study of the performance of shares in companies that pride themselves on their ethics found that they lagged behind those of tobacco, drug, and arms manufacturers. The stock market can be a brutal environment and the bottom line is often what a firm's actions mean for profit rather than for the planet!

Chapter 5

Getting Help with Your Retirement Plan

· ·

In This Chapter

▶ Working out if you need to call in a pro

▶ Grappling with financial advice

▶ Working with a stockbroker

▶ Clubbing together with friends and family to boost wealth

· ·

*Y*ou don't have to plan your way to a wealthy retirement single-
handed. Not only do you have this book to help plot your
path to a cash-rich old age, but you'll find a whole array of people
out there who can pull for you, too.

In this chapter, I show you how to harness the power of friends,
family, and professionals in a bid to boost your wealth. I also
explain some of the dangers that lurk out there from high charges
to real sharks looking to take a bite out of your cash pile.

Calling in a Financial Pro

If you're all alone, pick up the phone, and call . . . no, not
Ghostbusters, but a financial expert. You'll discover an army of
financial advisers and stockbrokers, all ready and willing to give
you advice on how to retire wealthy and offering you investment
packages to help you save. However this advice doesn't come
cheap and there are some hefty health warnings to take on board.

 You don't have to take advice – you can plot your own course,
choosing and buying your own financial products. The sidebar
'Buying financial products', later in this chapter, provides a guide
to the different ways of buying a financial product.

Choosing the right type of advice

Before asking for financial advice, you need to work out which sort of expert to consult. Your choices are:

- ✔ **Financial advisers:** In short a financial adviser works for a bank or insurance company and sells only their employer's investment and savings products – plus a limited number from other providers.

  Financial advisers should look after their clients' welfare but are usually paid commission by the providers of investment, insurance, and savings products. Earning commission for these products is controversial and has prompted some to ask whether such advisers are serving their clients' interests or their own? What's more, many financial advisers only have basic industry qualifications, as the number of products they have to get their heads around tends to be quite small.

- ✔ **Independent financial advisers:** Also known as *IFA*s, these experts search the whole marketplace for the best savings and investment products for their clients. They offer a choice of either paying a fee for advice or collecting commission from any product sold.

  Good IFAs thrive on building up a long-term relationship with their clients; they are in it for the long haul and if the client grows wealthy, so do they.

- ✔ **Stockbrokers:** Stockbrokers offer telephone, Internet, and even face-to-face services for dealing on the stock market (see Chapter 12 for more on making money on the stock market). You can use them just the once for a single share purchase or you can entrust them to oversee your share investing for decades.

  Stockbrokers offer a sophisticated advice service – at a cost of course – or they can simply execute your purchase or sale instruction. In short, the service you get from a stockbroker can be as personal or as remote as you want or are prepared to pay for.

- ✔ **Accountants:** The world of tax can be both confusing and intimidating and you may well need some help. Employing an accountant protects your finances from an unexpected tax grab. An accountant is someone who has specialist knowledge of tax and looks out for lots of little loopholes to cut your tax bill. See the sidebar 'Letting an accountant take the strain' for how to choose a good accountant.

Letting an accountant take the strain

Hopefully as you get older you'll get richer – particularly if you follow the advice in this book. I don't want to put the frighteners on you but the wealthier you get the more interest the tax authorities will take in you. Higher rate taxpayers have to fill in devilishly complex self assessment tax forms, with failure to do so resulting in a fine. When the tax authorities start taking a keen interest, you may decide to have someone in your corner – this is when accountants come in.

Accountants immerse themselves in the tax system looking for loopholes to exploit on their clients' behalf. Check out Chapter 18 for more on saving tax but if you have complex financial affairs you may be better off getting professional advice.

Be aware that accountants don't come cheap. Accountants either charge a flat fee for performing a specific task such as completing a self assessment tax form or by the hour. Expect to pay anything up to £100 or even £150 an hour for a good accountant, so only use them if it's absolutely necessary.

You can find an accountant through the Institute of Chartered Accountants, www.icaewfirms.co.uk, or the Association of Certified Chartered Accountants (Acca), www.acca.co.uk.

Working with a financial adviser

Whether to choose an IFA or financial adviser (the difference is explained in the previous section, 'Choosing the right type of advice') seems the ultimate no-brainer – the IFA seems to offer far better prospects. But, hold on a sec, far more people use financial advisers than IFAs, and for three main reasons:

- ✔ **They're thick on the ground:** Financial advisers can be found in nearly every bank branch.

- ✔ **They're cheaper:** Financial advisers are often paid by commission from the products they sell rather than through up-front fees.

- ✔ **They're not commitment freaks:** Financial advisers tend to advise on one particular aspect of your finances – say a mortgage or a pension – and you never see them again. Some clients like to pick and choose when they need a little help.

Good IFAs don't come cheap. They usually charge £80–150 for each hour they spend working on your finances. However, the first consultation is usually free. Be prepared to spend between £750 and £1,000 for an IFA to do a financial makeover for you. In addition, some IFAs charge a retainer fee, normally around £20–30 a month.

In return they will keep your finances under review – and also provide a nice little earner for themselves.

 At your first meeting the adviser should hand over a menu of charges. This outlines how much you can expect to pay for particular services, such as undertaking a full financial review or advising on a new mortgage.

Telling a real pro from an also ran

Financial advisers, independent or not, usually love to show off. You'll often find their business cards plastered with loads of acronyms each denoting that they have passed some financial advice exam. But don't let yourself be blinded by the blizzard of letters after their names – some are relevant to you, others maybe not. It's pointless going to see an IFA who is the UK's number one egghead on mortgages when you need advice purely on pensions!

 IFAs and financial advisers often have framed copies of their exam certificates in their offices – check these out when you go and see them. If they don't have any certificates on display why not ask them to produce them for you to cast your eye over. Table 5-1 gives a list of what all the letters mean.

Table 5-1	Financial Adviser Acronyms	
Basic Qualifications	*Advanced Qualifications*	*Highest Qualifications*
FPC: Financial Planning Certificate (this is the basic must-have industry qualification)	AFPC: Advanced Financial Planning Certificate	FISA: Fellow of the Society of Financial Advisers
CeFA: Certificate for Financial Advisers	MSFA: Member of the Society of Financial Advisers	FIFP: Fellow of the Institute of Financial Planning
IAC: Investment Advice Certificate	MAQ: Mortgage Advice Qualification	FCII: Fellow of the Chartered Insurance Institute
CIP: Certificate for Investment Planning	PIC: Professional Investment certificate Cert IM: Certificate in Investment Management CeMAP: Certificate in Mortgage Advice and Practice	

Basic Qualifications	Advanced Qualifications	Highest Qualifications
	AIFP: Associate of the Institute of Financial Planning	
	ALIA: Associate of the Life Insurance Institute	
	FLIA: Fellow of the Life Insurance Association	

Some financial advice qualifications are graded. For example, all advisers will have an FPC but there are three grades 1, 2 and 3 – 1 being the easiest and 3 being the hardest.

It's very unlikely that you'll find a financial adviser or IFA with every one of the above qualifications – for one thing they'd have to have a business card the size of a snooker table. Just look to see if they are suitably qualified in the area that you need advice in such as mortgages or insurance.

Generally, IFAs are better qualified than financial advisers, which means that they are likely to have more letters after their name. If you only need basic advice relating to one particular area you may be best going to an IFA with basic or advanced qualifications instead of an adviser with the very highest grade exam passes. Usually, the more qualifications an IFA has the more money they are likely to charge for their advice.

Preparing to meet a financial adviser

Your first meeting with an IFA or financial adviser is crucial. The first meeting should be free so make the most of it!

Here is a basic outline of what you should be looking to achieve during your first meeting.

- ✔ Firmly establish that the adviser has the right qualifications to give you the advice you need.

- ✔ Check how the adviser expects to be paid, either by fees or by taking a commission from any product that they sell you.

- ✔ Aim to tell the adviser as much as possible about your circumstances and your financial goals.

The adviser should ask you to bring along details of your financial circumstances. Before the meeting make a list of your investments and their value. See Chapter 3 for how to work out how much you're worth.

The adviser should give you their terms of business at your first meeting. This may look like a very, very boring document – and I'm afraid looks aren't deceptive – but it's worth reading as it sets out how they will treat you and who you can complain to if they make a mistake.

Protecting yourself from mis-selling

Both financial advisers and IFAs have been hit by scandal during recent years. Many financial advisers and IFAs have been found to have mis-sold pensions, mortgages, and some savings products.

Mis-selling – the dreaded M-word – occurs when an adviser recommends a product that isn't suitable for the client – usually the product is far too risky. Reasons for mis-selling range from incompetence to greed. In the past some advisers have put the earning of commission over the interests of the client.

The industry regulator – the Financial Services Authority (FSA) – acts to fine and ban some advisers, and compensation gets paid to some victims. Nevertheless, some people have had their life savings wiped out by being sold the wrong product.

If you feel you have been mis-sold you need to know what to do; the following section 'Making a complaint about an adviser' shows you how to go about this.

Some easy ways to stop yourself falling victim to mis-selling include:

- ✔ **Only taking advice from someone properly qualified to give it:** You can find out whether an adviser is regulated on the FSA Web site by checking out www.fsa.org.uk.

- ✔ **Asking to see the adviser's qualifications:** Lots of industry qualifications exist and the main ones are shown in the section 'Telling a real pro from an also ran', earlier in this chapter.

- ✔ **Asking for references:** You wouldn't employ someone for your company without taking references so don't appoint someone to look after your finances without the same safeguards. A good IFA will be happy to supply references.

- ✔ **Going on personal recommendation:** Often the best way of tracking down a good financial adviser or IFA is to ask your friends who they use and if they were happy with the service. Word of mouth is always better than trusting to pot luck.

- ✔ **Sorting out at the start how much the advice will cost:** Talk to the financial adviser or IFA at the outset about how they are going to get paid – sadly they won't do it out of the goodness of their heart. If you pay by fees ask for a quote – like you would with a builder or any other professional – setting out what is to be done and how much it will cost.

✔ **Walking out if in doubt:** One thing the UK isn't short of is financial advisers and IFAs. If you have any doubts whatsoever on meeting a financial adviser then head for the door.

Making a complaint about an adviser

In a perfect world financial advisers only ever recommend the right products to their clients and everything goes swimmingly. Sadly, though, this isn't a perfect world and mis-selling occurs quite regularly – see the previous section in this chapter for more on mis-selling.

If you buy a financial product on the recommendation of a financial adviser or IFA that turns out to be a complete dud you may be able to claim compensation for your loss. However, if you put in a claim for compensation simply because you are disappointed that an investment recommended to you has performed badly you're unlikely to win compensation. The key to winning compensation is to show that the product recommended either did not meet your financial circumstances or you were lied to about the risks associated with the product recommended.

You have to jump through a few hoops to get your money back – a clear-cut procedure is in place:

1. **Put your complaint in writing to the firm that recommended the financial product to you, asking them to respond to your complaint within a specific period of time, perhaps a month.**

2. **If the firm doesn't hold up its hand and admit its guilt, or offers you too little money in compensation, then write to them again saying that you are unhappy and that they should improve their offer or you will take your case to the Financial Services Ombudsman (FOS).**

   If you accept a compensation offer from the firm you automatically forgo the right to take your complaint to the Ombudsman. Be absolutely sure that the money offered is adequate to cover your losses.

3. **If the firm writes back stating that they will not be making the offer you want then that is the end of the internal complaints procedure and you can now take your case to the FOS.**

The *Financial Services Ombudsman* (FOS) adjudicates on disputes between consumers and financial companies and IFAs. If you want to lodge a complaint against a financial adviser or firm after following the complaint procedure, the FOS is contactable on 0845 080 1800 or through their Web site www.financial-ombudsman.org.uk.

An FOS investigation usually takes between six and twelve months from start to finish, and they do not charge for the service. Roughly half the time the Ombudsman finds in favour of the complainant and can order firms to pay compensation.

If you make a complaint, never send original documents to the firm you're complaining about – they may get 'lost' and scupper your claim. Only ever deal in photocopies and make a record of all telephone conversations and letters between you and the firm you're claiming against.

The FOS only looks at cases once the internal complaints procedures of the firm you have a beef with are exhausted.

Working with a stockbroker

Stockbrokers are your way into the stock market. You can find out more about the stock market by reading Chapter 12, or watching the Eddie Murphy movie, *Trading Places*. Of the two choices, I recommend reading Chapter 12.

The stock market is very complex and investors who don't know what they are doing can lose their shirt. But specialists called stockbrokers are available out there to help you. If you want to buy shares you have to use a stockbroker, as they are the only people allowed to offer access to the stock market; they are a go-between between you and the City.

You give stockbrokers money and tell them what shares you'd like to buy and they buy them for you – simple eh? Erm no, I'm afraid! Stockbrokers offer a variety of services depending on what you ask them to do:

- ✔ **Advisory service:** Your stockbroker offers advice on what shares you should buy and then it's up to you whether to follow their advice. Advisory services are often only made available to people willing to invest tens of thousands of pounds. An ongoing monthly or annual fee is usually levied.

- ✔ **Discretionary service:** Under this type of arrangement you give the stockbroker the discretion to make your share investments for you. The stockbroker constructs a portfolio in line with your financial circumstances and what you are looking to achieve through investing – whether you're investing for the sake of dividend income or you're looking purely for the share price to grow. Again management fees are levied.

✔ **Execution only:** The no-frills airline approach to stockbroking! No advice on what shares to buy is offered, you simply instruct the stockbroker to buy shares for you. A one-off fee is charged for the trade. If you go for execution only you only have yourself to blame if you end up losing your shirt.

Whether you go for advisory, discretionary, or execution only is a matter of how much money you want to invest and how confident you are in your abilities to pick a winning share. Many people invest in the stock market for a bit of fun with the added appeal that they maybe able to turn a bit of a profit – if this applies to you then you may find that execution only is for you. Wealthier investors often go with an advisory or discretionary service while those with less money to spend often go down the execution only route. Bear in mind that execution only is by far the cheapest option. Chapter 12 gives advice on making the most of your dealings on the stock market.

Look for a stockbroker who pays interest on any cash that you have in your share account that is not invested in shares. And try to keep your share dealings to a minimum to save money in stockbroker trading charges.

Stockbrokers tend to be large scale businesses employing highly paid analysts, whose job is to pore over the accounts and study the financial health of companies which have shares listed on the stock exchange.

Some stockbrokers offer low-cost trades but you may be asked to sign up to an expensive advisory service.

Several factors to consider when choosing a stockbroker are:

✔ **Dealing costs:** How much does the broker charge you for buying or selling shares? Compare charges from at least three brokers to ensure that you are not paying over the odds. Remember, every penny you pay in dealing costs eats into your potential profit.

✔ **Ease of administration:** Can you trade online or over the phone, and how easy and quick is it to trade? How regularly does the firm keep you updated as to your holdings? Stockbroking is a very competitive business, so most firms offer hassle-free ways to manage your account.

✔ **Analysis:** If you choose to have an advisory account with a stockbroking firm, you'll probably find that you get regular analyst notes regarding the shares you already own as well as the low-down on how other shares are performing and predictions of their future performance.

The level of interaction with the stockbroker depends on whether you go for an advisory or execution only relationship. If you choose an *advisory* relationship you may end up speaking to a particular broker but she will only be the voice on the phone of the stockbroking firm – what you are paying for is the general package offered by the stockbroking firm such as analysts notes. If you go the *execution only* route then you can judge a broker on price and administration but you won't be getting specialist analyst notes or advice on which shares to buy or sell.

In the past some analysts have been accused of being too cosy with the firms they are analysing. This has led to accusations that analysts sometimes overplay the positives and downplay the negatives. Remember, an analyst may have plenty of expertise but you maybe best doing your own research just to put what they have to say in context. See Chapter 12 for more on how to properly assess a company share.

Bringing Friends or Family On Board

The big advantage that couples or groups of savers have over singletons is that they enjoy two (or more) incomes rather than just one, while at the same time the age-old saying 'two can live as cheaply as one' has a lot of truth to it.

Couples, or groups, therefore usually have more money to save and invest than singletons. Joint-savers have the whip hand over single savers in the following ways:

- ✔ **Taking more risks:** Having more cash to save and invest gives couples the where-with-all to adopt a slightly more risky investment strategy – perhaps ploughing more money into shares or buy-to-let property (see Chapters 12 and 15 for more on these). And as mentioned throughout this book, taking a few risks can help you build up a tidy pile of money for retirement.

- ✔ **Taking on larger mortgages:** Crucially couples with two incomes should be able to borrow more cash to buy property than singletons. Mortgage lenders base how much they are willing to lend on both incomes rather than just one. This means that couples can afford bigger homes and have a greater chance to invest in buy-to-let property. They can also often afford a larger deposit too.

✔ **Taking advantage of two tax allowances:** Each person has a certain amount of money they can save, invest, and earn each year without paying tax. If two of you are striving for a wealthy retirement you can re-jig your finances to make the most of it. Remember, the less tax you pay the more you can save, invest, and even – if the mood takes you – spend! See Chapter 21 for more on tax savings strategies, and Tony Levene's *Paying Less Tax 2005/2006 For Dummies* (Wiley).

If you give money to your partner in order to make the most of your tax allowances but then split up you may find it tricky to get your cash back! The same goes for unreliable friends.

Getting your partner in on the act

Crossing the wealthy retirement finishing line may be easier if two people are saving and investing hard rather than just one. If you are married, or in a long-term relationship, try persuading your partner into your big retiring wealthy plan. After all, you're probably not saving just for your own prosperous old age . . . you will want your loved ones to share in your good fortune too.

Pool your resources with your spouse or long-term partner and team up to use all available tax allowances to the max. Why not sit down together and talk about the sort of life you'd like in retirement and how you think you're both going to pay for it? The sooner you talk about it together the more of a chance you have of achieving a wealthy retirement.

Remember that few couples retire at the exactly the same time – often one person in the relationship carries on working sometimes for years after their other half has put their feet up. When planning your retirement with a partner try to bear this in mind.

You don't have to be married, or even in a relationship, in order to plan a financial future with someone. Take buying a property for example. Buying property with friends is becoming increasingly popular – anything to be able to clamber onto the property ladder.

Making an investment club work for you

Investment clubs allow people with relatively little cash to have a stake in the shares of lots of different companies. No wonder investment clubs are proving so popular with now more than 100,000 up and running throughout the country. If you're not a member of an investment club you probably know someone who is.

Buying financial products

At some point on your route to retiring wealthy you're going to have to buy a financial product, whether it be a mortgage or a savings account. Literally thousands of different financial products are on offer out there – from complex pension products to pet insurance. Nevertheless, there are only three ways of buying financial products – one involves taking advice, the other two are do-it yourself – and they are as follows:

✔ **Direct from supplier:** Many people prefer to make their own choices of financial products and will buy it direct from the bank or insurer. If you buy a financial product direct from a provider you only have yourself to blame if it goes wrong.

✔ **Through a financial adviser or IFA:** Products bought this way come with advice tacked on. The financial adviser or IFA should review your finances and only recommend products that match your circumstances and your needs. See the section 'Choosing the right type of advice' for more on this.

✔ **Through a third party with no advice:** Some investment product providers – usually operating bond or share funds – have struck up deals with large IFA firms to help shift product in bulk. The IFA firms offer these products to the public on a 'no advice' basis – also known as *execution only*. The big plus point for investors is that invariably product charges are discounted or have been dropped all together. These have become known as fund supermarkets. However, like buying direct from the supplier, if it goes wrong you have no one to blame but yourself.

Whichever way you choose to buy financial products should depend on how confident you are in your knowledge and judgement of what to buy.

The idea behind an investment club is simple. Friends pool their resources to invest in shares. Usually club members sign up to a monthly direct debit, which goes into an investment account. Members then vote on what shares they would like to buy using this cash. Members also vote on whether to sell shares that they hold. In short, clubs are run by members for members, with no help from financial advisers or banks.

Share investing can be high risk, so don't plough your entire fortune into an investment club.

The organisation Proshare promotes wider share ownership and in particular the spread of investment clubs. Proshare's Web site has all sorts of useful info for people looking to set up a club. Log on to www.proshare.org.

It's always best to have a cash float saved in a high street bank or building society savings account or National Savings before deciding to sign up to an investment club. Investing in shares is risky and it's possible to lose your entire investment, so savings help cushion the financial blow should your club pick a dud!

When you mix money and friends it's best to do things by the book – be fair and completely open so you all know where you stand. Here are some dos and don'ts of investment clubs:

- **Regular contributions:** Do ensure everyone contributes the same amount of money each month and make sure it's a sum that everyone in the club is comfortable with and can afford to lose if investments turn sour.

- **Harness the knowledge of members:** If someone has worked in a particular industry for many years then they are likely to know about the companies involved in it. The best performing clubs tend to have members from lots of different backgrounds.

- **Keep an eye on all shares bought:** Buying a share is only half the trick, knowing when to sell is equally important. Adopt a policy of members becoming 'share champions'; once a share is bought it's their responsibility to monitor its price and report back to members.

- **Meet regularly:** You should aim to meet at least once a month to review the club's shareholdings. Only in this way can you keep up-to-date with what's going on. If you don't meet regularly your club can wither on the vine.

- **Be prepared to act swiftly:** The stock market waits for no investor! Be fleet of foot and meet when something dramatic happens, such as a share price crash. Be ready to have a members' meeting at short notice.

- **Keep proper accounts:** The oldest investment clubs in the UK have been around for more than 50 years but members come and go, so keeping a tight rein on the books is essential. The club should appoint members to draw up accounts and to make sure that the wishes of the club are acted upon: For example, contacting the club's stockbroker when it comes to the time to buy or sell a share.

- **Draw up a constitution:** Okay, so your club may not be the United States of America but you need a set of rules to run things by. At your first meeting agree a club constitution, setting out conditions of entry and exit into the club, and who does what.

- **Don't play the blame game:** If a share purchase goes wrong (which isn't uncommon), don't apportion blame to whoever championed it or first proposed its purchase.

Part II
Laying the Bedrock: Pensions

"What a beautiful little long term pension policy.....I mean....baby!"

In this part . . .

Pensions – love them or loathe them, they are bound to play a part in your retiring wealthy plan. Despite recent bad press, pensions can be pretty useful things, helping secure a long-term retirement income. Therefore, you need to know all about them, from the state pension through workplace and personal schemes. As far as pensions go, knowledge equals power and the chapters in this part contain all you need to know.

Chapter 6

Making the Most of State and Workplace Pensions

*F*or many the word pension is an instant cure for insomnia. But stifle those yawns and put the coffee pot on. It's worth staying up for this chapter.

Your state and workplace pensions may well prove to be your biggest source of retirement income.

In this chapter I lay bare both state and workplace pensions so that you can make a better decision about the part you want them to play in your retiring wealthy plan.

Realising the Importance of Your Pension

Pensions have had a really bad press of late. It seems that whenever the word pension is used in newspapers or TV news reports it is invariably followed by the word crisis!

This idea of a pensions crisis follows widespread anger at minimal rises in the state pension, mis-selling of personal pensions, and the collapse of some workplace pension schemes.

Reading and listening to some of the doom-laden reports you'd think that the whole pension system was headed for collapse and that you'd be wise to ignore pensions altogether, perhaps investing your cash elsewhere – in property, for example.

But in reality pensions aren't headed for the knacker's yard. Although things aren't quite as rosy as they once were for UK pensions, state, workplace, and personal pensions are still set to be the chief vehicle that most people use to cross the retiring wealthy finishing line.

If you work or have worked in the past you've already built up a state pension. Your state pension won't be enough to pay for living the high life, but it can provide a more than useful backstop.

And workplace and personal pensions – as I explain below – offer unique tax breaks that can help supercharge your retiring wealthy plans.

All in all, pensions – state, workplace, and personal – provide the foundation upon which you can build your retiring wealthy project. Fail to understand pensions and what they offer and you may well be missing a trick.

Understanding the great pensions tax break

The next sentence may be a tad dull, but it's probably the most important in this book.

When you make contributions to workplace and personal pensions something magical happens: The government gives you tax relief on your contributions. In effect this means that for basic rate taxpayers, for every 78p they pay into a pension the government matches this with 22p. Higher rate taxpayers benefit by even more. For every 60p they pay into a pension the government gives them 40p in tax relief.

How does this fact benefit a basic rate and a higher rate taxpayer, both paying into a workplace pension?

Christine is a basic rate taxpayer; her gross annual salary is £20,000. Her workplace pension scheme asks members to pay in 5 per cent of their salary. In Christine's case 5 per cent of her gross salary equals £1000 a year. Hypothetically if the 5 per cent contribution were to come from her net salary then it would only be £780.

Blossom is a higher rate taxpayer; her gross annual salary is £40,000. She is a member of the same workplace pension as Christine and pays 5 per cent of her gross salary into it, equal to £2,000 a year. The true cost to Blossom would be £1,200, although her pension would be swelled to the tune of £2,000.

In effect the government is subsiding Christine and Blossom's pensions to the tune of several hundred pounds a year. Over the long term – say 20 or 30 years – this makes a huge difference to both pension pots.

You earn a state pension when you make National Insurance (NI) contributions. If you're an employee NI is deducted from your gross income in the same way as income tax. The longer you pay National Insurance contributions the more chance you have of earning an entitlement to a full state pension. See later in this chapter for more on this.

One of the key advantages of a workplace pension is that your employer may – and often does – make a contribution to it.

Remembering the pension tax break has strings attached

Allowing pension contributions to be paid from gross rather than net income is a whopping tax break. The government wants to ensure that the money is used for the purpose of providing a retirement income rather than as just a way of dodging tax. Therefore there are strict rules imposed on pension investment such as:

- ✔ Money invested in a workplace or personal pension cannot be accessed by the saver until they have reached the age of 50. This rises to 55 in 2010.

- ✔ Most of the money saved in a pension goes to buying an annuity – an income for life – before age 75 or may be used by the workplace pension fund to buy the scheme member a guaranteed income.

- ✔ From April 2006 the size of a person's pension pot is capped at £1.5m. This is set to rise to £1.8m in 2010.

In short, with pension investment you trade flexibility and control for a tasty tax break.

An exception to the no pension until you're at least 50 rule is made for people who take early retirement from an occupational scheme due to ill health.

Although most of the cash saved in a pension has to go towards providing retirement income, schemes allow members to take up to 25 per cent of their money as a tax-free lump sum. The scheme member is free to do with this money as they please. See Chapter 9 for more on the tax-free lump sum.

Getting to Grips with the State Pension

For a large percentage of the UK population the pension provided by the state is all they have to live on in retirement. Relying on the state pension alone is a one-way ticket to a miserly old age. The current basic state pension for a single person is £82.05 a week. Fancy living off that? No, I thought not!

But saying that you shouldn't pin your retiring wealthy hopes on the state pension does not mean that it is irrelevant and that you should ignore it.

The state pension system can provide you with part of the retiring wealthy answer – a base from which you can plan your assault on the big wealth prize. Get to know the ins and outs of the state pension. The benefits of the state pension are as follows:

✔ **It provides a regular and increasing income.** The income provided by the state pension may not be a king's ransom but it's not to be sniffed at. In order to buy an annuity – an income for life – equivalent to the current state pension you'd have to have a pension pot worth between £60,000 and £70,000. What's more, the state pension is guaranteed to rise each year at least in line with prices.

✔ **It is tax free.** The state pension is so small that it flies under the income tax personal allowance. Of course, if you have other sources of income they may take you above the personal allowance threshold – then you start to pay tax.

✔ **It is free of National Insurance Contributions (NICs).** Once you're sufficiently long in the tooth to receive the state pension then you no longer have to worry about making NICs. In your autumn years the boot is on the other foot and you benefit from what's in the NIC pot rather then paying into it. After a life toiling away you may think you deserve to let others work for you.

Building up entitlement when not working

Home Responsibilities Protection (HRP) has been around since 1978 and is designed to protect the National Insurance contribution records of people caring for a child or sick or disabled person. In short HRP helps you protect your state pension.

You're entitled to HRP if you meet any of the following criteria:

✔ You get child benefit for a child under 16.

✔ You get income support because you're looking after someone.

✔ You're in receipt of Carer's Allowance or are a foster parent.

If any of the above cover you, contact your local benefits office and ask them for details of HRP. You may be automatically enrolled for HRP but double check that you have been. After all, if you don't take advantage of HRP and as result fail to build up enough National Insurance credits then you won't receive a full state pension.

One year of HRP equates to one year of full National Insurance contributions.

The state retirement age for women is set to rise to 65. However, if you're a woman born before 5 April 1950 you will be able to retire at 60. If you were born between 6 April 1950 and 5 March 1955 you come under a transitional arrangement and your retirement age will be set according to your birth date and fall somewhere between 60 and 65. Check out the government's pension service Web site at www.pensionservice.gov.uk for more on how this transitional arrangement works.

If you retire with less than 25 per cent of the qualifying years for a state pension then you won't get anything at all. People aged 80 or over can claim a non-contributory pension worth 60 per cent of the state pension.

Relying on the state alone is not an option

According to a recent survey most people would prefer that the state took care of them in their old age through the basic state pension. However the basic state pension in 2005–06 is £82.05, hardly a king's ransom!

And over time it is widely predicted that the state pension is going to become even less generous, particularly when compared to the incomes of those in work.

The reason for this is that the state pension rises in line with prices and not average earnings. Prices traditionally rise more slowly than wages. As a result those living off a state pension have found their income falling behind that of wage earners. Today the state pension is worth 29 per cent of average earnings – by 2030 it is predicted to fall to 15 per cent.

Relying on the state pension for support is no way to retire wealthy. In fact over the next few decades it may well be a guaranteed ticket to poverty-ville!

The UK has one of the least generous state pensions in Europe. In countries such as France and Sweden the state pension is worth over half average earnings. What is more, on the continent the age at which the state pension is paid is earlier and the level of pension is equal to around half national average income.

The demographic time bomb – described in all its gory detail in Chapter 1 – may mean that the UK state pension age increases at some point during the next decade. Instead of being able to claim your state pension at 65 you may have to wait until 67 or even 70.

A few years back the government introduced the pension credit. The pension credit guarantees a minimum income – £109.45 a week for a single pensioner and £167.05 per week for couples – to Britain's poorest pensioners while at the same time topping up the savings of those with small private or occupational pensions. All very good. However, the government has hinted that this is only a temporary measure and may be abandoned in years to come. For more information on the pension credit or the state pension you can check out the government's pension service Web site on www.pensionservice.gov.uk.

Working out the value of your state pension

Many people assume that because they have worked they are automatically in line for the full state pension at age 65. But you need to make full NI contributions for 44 years if you're a man or 39 if you're a woman to earn the full state pension. Not making contributions for long enough to earn a full state pension is a surprisingly common problem – roughly a third of men and four fifths of women have what is catchily called an *impaired contribution record*.

Repairing a state pension

If you're heading for a state pension shortfall you're allowed to fill in any gaps in your NI contributions dating back up to six years.

For example, during the 2005–06 tax year it is possible to make voluntary contributions dating all the way back to 1999–2000.

Your pension forecast sets out how much state pension you have built up to date and, crucially, how much it is likely to be worth at age 65, assuming you continue to pay full National Insurance contributions.

In addition, the forecast should highlight any shortfall in National Insurance contributions and indicate how much you would need to contribute in order to make it up. The forecast letter should tell you how to actually make up the gap in your contribution record – in short, where to send the cheque.

Of course, you may decide to let sleeping dogs lie and not repair your state pension. It costs you cash to do so and perhaps it's money you feel would be better spent paying off your mortgage or investing in shares. Bear in mind, though, that most financial experts suggest that in nearly all instances when there is a chance to do some repair work and make up missing contributions then it should be seized with both hands and then some!

After all, as mentioned earlier in this chapter, it takes an awfully large pension pot to buy an income equivalent to the state pension.

The HM Revenue and Customs will tell you exactly how much it will cost you to make up the gap.

Many of these people were unaware that they faced a state pension shortfall until they actually reached age 65 – when it was too late to do anything about it.

Don't let the size of your state pension be a surprise. You can get a free estimate of how much state pension you have earned to date from the government's pension service. Write to The Retirement Pension Forecasting Team, Room TB001, Tyneview Park, Whitley Road, Newcastle upon Tyne, NE98 1BA or call the Department of Work and Pensions on 0845 3000168 and ask for form BR19. Alternatively, you can do it online at www.thepensionservice.gov.uk/resourcecentre/e-services/home.asp.

Women are more likely than men to suffer a state pension shortfall because they take time out of the workforce to bring up children and look after elderly relatives.

When UK citizens take up residency abroad, they automatically stop making UK National Insurance contributions. As a result, they can find when returning to the UK that they have not paid enough National Insurance to be in line for a full state pension. If you are returning after a stint living abroad it may be a good idea to get your chequebook out and repair your state pension.

Getting into the Second State Pension

Why have just one state pension when you can have two? As well as the basic state pension there is the very intuitively titled second state pension or S2P for short. Put simply, the S2P provides a top up to your basic state pension. In return for higher NICs you get an extra state pension. The S2P isn't as large as the basic state pension but it can provide extra retirement income.

You contribute extra NICs in order to earn entitlement to the S2P. The S2P is income related which means the size of the eventual payment depends on your level of income during your time working and how long you contributed to the S2P for.

S2P is the replacement for the State Earnings Related Pension Scheme (SERPS). They are in essence the same except that under S2P people on low and modest earnings have more of a chance to build up a better pension. Under S2P rules the system 'credits' or 'bumps up' earnings for eligible groups to a flat rate of £12,100. In other words, if you earn under this amount, the S2P rules treat you as if you had earned £12,100.

SERPS morphed into S2P in 2002 so if you were working before that date then you are likely to receive some income from SERPS and some from S2P – unless, of course you were contracted out. There is more on this later in the chapter.

According to the Pension Advisory Service (Opas) a S2P/Serps member who has earned enough to pay the top rate of income tax since 1978 would be entitled to £69 a week extra pension if they retired tomorrow.

But most people aren't in the fortunate position to be top rate tax-payers for nearly thirty years. In reality, most people find that when it comes time to retire their S2P is worth perhaps no more than £10 or £15 a week.

Postponing your retirement in return for extra cash

Some people don't want to retire at 60 or 65. They enjoy their work and want to carry on for as long as possible. The government wants to encourage people to stay at work for longer – after all if they're at work they earn more and therefore pay more tax. To this end the government recently decided that it would pay people if they deferred collecting their state pension.

It has been calculated that someone deferring the basic state pension of £82.05 a week (2005–2006) for five years will see it rise in value to £112.80.

Alternatively, you can choose to receive a one-off taxable lump sum payment along with your normal pension.

You don't have to be a member of the S2P. You can choose to *contract out*. This means your NICS contributions that would normally go to the S2P go into another pension scheme – either a workplace or a personal pension.

If you contract out using a personal or stakeholder pension, HM Revenue and Customs (formerly the Inland Revenue) reimburses part of your NICS and these go into your private pension fund. This is invested and the idea is that you build up a replacement pension for the S2P you have given up.

The government sets the level of reimbursement that is paid into your pension scheme.

Contracting out was all the rage in the early 1990s. Millions left SERPS in the big hope that through investing their cash elsewhere they may get a better pension. However, contracting out hasn't turned into the retiring wealthy panacea many people hoped for. Some commentators say that many people who have chosen to contract out would have been better off remaining in the S2P. They argue that the S2P provides a higher income in retirement than if the NICs were paid into a personal pension which would then have to be invested and in turn buy an annuity. The advice from many money experts these days is if at all possible, stay contracted into the S2P.

 If you are a member of a workplace pension scheme you may find that you're automatically contracted out of the S2P. In other words the cash that would have gone into the S2P to provide you with a top up state pension is actually going into your workplace pension scheme.

If you're self-employed then at present you can't contribute to the S2P. However, the government has said that it wants to correct this anomaly and allow the self-employed to contribute to the S2P in future.

If you're self-employed you may be well advised to save and invest some extra cash to make up for the fact that you don't have any entitlement to S2P.

Making the Most of Company Pensions

When you start a new job your employer should give you details of the company pension scheme.

All firms that employ five or more staff have by law to offer access to a workplace pension scheme.

You have lots of different types of company pension schemes to get your head around, and some are more generous to employees than others. First up, two types of company pensions exist:

✓ **Occupational schemes.** Under this type of scheme the employer pays into a pension scheme open to all staff. If you join an occupational scheme you may be asked to make contributions. Crucially, these contributions are from your gross rather than your net salary. The idea is that your contributions when added to those of your employer result in a large enough pension fund being built up to provide you with retirement income.

✓ **Group personal or stakeholder pension.** This type of pension is cheaper for the employer as they are not duty bound to make contributions. Some employers still make contributions to a group personal or stakeholder scheme, but generally the level of contribution isn't as generous as under an occupational scheme. Again, though, ultimately the idea is to provide the employee with an income in retirement in addition to the state pension.

Some companies allow you to join the workplace pension from your first day, others ask you to serve a probationary period, for example six months.

No one can force you to join a company pension scheme. If you are not planning to be with the employer long, you may think that it's a waste of your time and resources to join.

If you leave the firm's employ within two years you can have your pension contributions refunded. However, these contributions are taxed and you can't get your hands on any money paid into your pension by your employer.

 With all company pension schemes, any contribution you make is shown on your pay slip. At the end of each year you should receive a statement telling you how much you have paid in and the size of your pension pot.

 With workplace pensions you usually have little say on how your money is invested. Your money is entrusted to an insurance company or pension fund management firm to invest on behalf of all members.

Understanding occupational schemes

Occupational schemes are meant to provide the employee with an income in retirement over and above the basic state pension. To this end the employer pays into an occupational scheme and employees are usually – although not always – asked to pay money in from their gross salary.

Occupational pension schemes break down into two distinct types:

- ✔ **Final salary schemes.** This type of scheme pays the employee a pension based on three factors: the length of service, the size of the member's salary at retirement, and something called the accrual rate – see below for more details. Final salary schemes are the grand-daddy of all workplace pensions and considered by many to be the most generous out there. However, many experts think this type of pension is in terminal decline, as outlined below.

- ✔ **Money purchase.** This is a simpler affair. You and your employer make contributions and this money is then invested. You are paid a pension according to the investment performance of the scheme.

A crucial difference between final salary and money purchase is who carries the can if investments go wrong.

Under a final salary arrangement, ultimately, if the money paid in doesn't perform well enough to meet the pension scheme promises, then the employer has to make up the shortfall.

On the other hand, under money purchase there are no initial pension promises. Instead the scheme member receives a pension based purely on how well the money paid in by them and their employer has fared once invested.

Both final salary pensions and money purchase pension schemes invest in similar kinds of things. They invest the bulk of their cash in a mix of bonds, shares, and property – just like private investors!

Looking at final salary schemes

Final salary schemes are considered very much the bee's knees of occupational pensions. Most experts agree that if you're offered the chance to join one you should, sharpish!

The main reason for the thumbs up to final salary schemes is that usually the employer contributes a lot of money to the pension. On average, an employer running a final salary scheme pays around 10 per cent of workers' salary into it. In effect, these contributions are deferred pay. If someone was to say to you, do you fancy an extra 10 per cent on top of your salary, what would you say?

One of the determining factors of the size of an employee's final salary pension is the *accrual rate*. Put simply, this is the proportion of final salary you get for each year's service with a company.

Take the example of Pauline. Pauline joined a company with a final salary scheme in 1985. She paid 5 per cent of her salary and her employer's contributions equated to 10 per cent of her salary. The scheme's accrual rate was $\frac{1}{80}$ of final salary. When it came time for Pauline to retire in 2005 she had built up a pension worth $\frac{20}{80}$ – or one quarter – of final salary. At retirement Pauline's final salary stood at £40,000, therefore her final salary pension would pay her £10,000 a year.

Just to put Pauline's good fortune into perspective for a moment: She would need a pension pot of around £150–180,000 to buy an annuity large enough to obtain an income in retirement of £10,000 a year.

Under the rules of most final salary schemes your pension entitlement rises each year, meaning that the amount of pension you're entitled to keeps pace with rising prices.

Final salary schemes offer members the chance to take a tax-free lump sum at retirement. However, doing so automatically reduces the amount of retirement income.

The fading away of final salary pensions

In recent years, employers have been fleeing final salary schemes at a rate of knots. They have rebelled against the high costs of final salary schemes and the fact that they are bearing all the risk if investments go wrong.

Some two thirds of final salary schemes are now closed to new people joining the company. Instead new workers are increasingly being offered access to a money purchase scheme.

This is bad news for workers because employers have been taking the opportunity presented by a switch from final salary to money purchase to cut the level of their contributions. A pension body recently revealed that firms that switched from offering final salary to money purchase had roughly halved the amount of cash that they were paying into their employees' pensions.

Of late, some final salary schemes have morphed into *career-average defined benefit schemes*. In plain English this means that instead of being based on length of service and final salary, retirement benefits are linked to length of service and the average salary of the worker throughout their time spent with the employer.

Having given final salary pensions the big up, there is a note of caution to be sounded. Recently some final salary schemes have failed to pay the pensions promised when the company backing them up has gone to the wall. The government has set up the pension protection fund (PPF) to prevent this happening in future. Under the PPF, final salary schemes pay an insurance premium and in return if they go belly up the PPF pays the pensions of scheme members. However, some experts suggest the PPF is under-funded and wouldn't be able to cope if a really big final salary scheme couldn't pay its members' pensions.

Exploring money purchase pensions

Money purchase pensions are far easier to get your head around than final salary. You and your employer make contributions into a pension scheme and this money is invested to provide a fund for you to live off in retirement.

Birth of hybrid schemes

There is a new kid on the pension block – hybrid pensions. As the name hints at, this type of pension combines some of the elements of money purchase and final salary schemes.

The most common hybrid is the *nursery scheme*. Here, you are a member of a money purchase scheme until you reach a given age, say 40, at which point you become eligible to join a final salary scheme. This type of scheme tries to offer the best of both worlds. First, if you're a young worker who stays with the company for only a short period, you benefit from the full value of your own and your employer's contributions.

But if you're an older worker, with the same company for many years, the final salary element of the hybrid pension means that you enjoy a degree of certainty. You know for a fact that at least part of your retirement income is dictated by how long your have worked with the company, your final salary, and the scheme's accrual rate – how much you get for each year's service.

The scheme member bears all the risk. If the investments do well then the size of their pension pot swells and this means that the scheme member is able to buy a larger annuity to live off in old age. On the flip side, though, if the investments do badly then there won't be as much cash with which to buy an annuity.

Your money purchase pension scheme may be set up so that you have some choice as to what investments your pension buys into. You may be presented with an array of funds to pick from. Some of the funds invest predominantly in shares, others bonds, while there may be an option to simply tuck the money away in a savings account.

The rule of thumb here is the older you are – and therefore the closer to retirement – the less risk you should take with your investment choice. See Chapter 10 for more on what types of investment are considered low-, medium-, and high-risk.

If you can't decide where to invest your pension money then go for the scheme's default option. By picking the default option you're signing over the choice of investments to the investment company managing the pension scheme. The usual pattern with a default option is that initially your money goes into riskier investments such as shares and then as you approach retirement you're shifted into safer investments like bonds and cash deposit accounts.

The size of the retirement income that your pension fund buys depends on two factors. First, how well your pension fund has performed. Second, the annuity rate on your retirement or, in other words, the price that you have to pay to secure a retirement income.

Weighing up group personal and stakeholder pensions

You may find that your employer doesn't pay into your pension. Instead they may offer you access to a group personal or stakeholder pension.

Your employer chooses the insurance company which runs the scheme and arranges for part of your salary to be paid into it.

Like a money purchase scheme, the size of your pension pot depends on the level of contributions and investment performance.

The advantage to you of signing up to a group personal or stakeholder pension rather than opening your own personal pension is that your employer should be able to negotiate lower initial and annual charges.

Some employers choose to contribute to their workers' group personal or stakeholder pension scheme; although unlike an occupational scheme they are not bound to do so.

Essentially there is only a hair's breadth of difference between group personal pensions and group stakeholder pensions. They both work on the same principle that the investment risk is borne by the scheme member rather than the employee. However, stakeholders are guaranteed to be low-cost and be super-easy to invest in.

  ✔ **Low cost.** The maximum management charge imposed on a stakeholder pension is capped at 1.5 per cent or 1 per cent if you joined before April 2005.

  ✔ **Hassle free.** You can invest anything from as little as £20 a month and there are no penalties for stopping making payments.

Stakeholder pensions are examined in greater detail in Chapter 7.

Death in service benefits

Some company pension schemes pay *death in service benefits*. This cheerfully titled benefit can provide your loved ones with a real financial pick-me-up if the worst happens.

In short, if you die before retirement then the pension scheme pays whomever you name as beneficiary a lump sum. This lump sum can be very large – sometimes as high as three or four times your annual salary. What's more, death in service benefits are paid free of Inheritance Tax. Check with your pension scheme to see if it pays death in service benefits.

However, stakeholder pensions have been a flop because employers don't have to contribute to them. Instead, all an employer has to do is offer access. Subsequently, many employees have figured that they aren't really worthwhile, preferring to spend their cash or invest it elsewhere.

Death in service benefits can be very lucrative, but you still may want to consider taking out life insurance that pays your loved ones on your death. You should strongly consider life insurance if you have large debts such as a mortgage that your loved ones may find difficult to pay if you died suddenly.

Giving Your Company Pension a Boost

You should receive a projection of how much your company pension is worth to you in retirement once a year. After seeing this projection you may decide that the pension you're on course to receive simply isn't good enough. Don't despair!

You may be able to boost your company pension by making what are called Additional Voluntary Contributions (AVCs).

You make AVCs via a separate scheme run by your employer.

This additional scheme is likely to be run on a money purchase basis. As a result, the size of the extra pension you get depends on how much you contribute and its investment performance.

Some generous employers offer to match the AVCs of their employees. Under such an arrangement if you make an AVC of £50 a month your employer also pays £50 a month into your pension pot.

You are allowed to pay a maximum of £215,000 or 100 per cent of your earnings into a pension each year. If you don't have earnings you're still allowed to pay into a pension, but your contributions are capped at £3,600 a year.

Exploring free-standing plans

AVCs aren't the only option for boosting your company pension. You can opt to make Free Standing Additional Voluntary Contributions (FSAVCs). FSAVCs work in the same way as AVCs, except that you get to decide the scheme provider.

FSAVC scheme charges tend to be much higher than with a company-run AVC. FSAVC charges are so high in fact that it has led to a dramatic tailing-off of their popularity amongst pension savers.

All money paid into an AVC or FSAVC comes from gross income, just like a standard company or personal pension.

Working Out that Pensions Are Only Part of the Answer

Pensions suffer from a bit of an image problem. Many people see them as boring and imposing a kind of financial straitjacket. After all, what other type of investment is there that bars you from accessing your cash until you're over the age of 50 or, in the case of the state pension, age 65?

But the tax breaks on offer through workplace and personal pensions – covered in this chapter and Chapter 7 – are unique and not to be sniffed at. What's more, with many company schemes the employer makes substantial contributions – miss out on these and you are in effect losing out on deferred pay.

As for the state pension, this can provide a useful financial backstop in old age – whatever else happens you know you have the state pension to fall back on.

But having put the case for pensions, it's now time for a reality check.

Pensions are all about the slow accumulation of wealth rather than stellar growth. Therefore, unless you're a fat cat company chief executive or high earning City whizz kid, you're unlikely to be able to invest enough cash into your pension to fund a really lavish retirement.

This book's title, after all, is not *Retiring Just Above the Breadline For Dummies*. To really get with the retiring wealthy programme you're going to need more than your pension. In fact, you're going to need a spread of investments such as shares, property, bonds, deposit savings accounts and even some left-field riskier plays.

Chapter 7

Hoarding Your Very Own Pot of Cash: Personal Pensions

*P*ersonal pensions – also called private pensions – can help you make the most of the whopping tax breaks available to you in saving for retirement. What's more, the rules governing personal pensions changed in April 2006, making them even more flexible.

Personal pensions are also portable – you can take them with you from job to job. You can even pay into one when you're out of work or self employed.

In this chapter, I take a long hard look at personal pensions so that you can decide what role they should play in your retiring wealthy plan.

Understanding What Personal Pensions Have to Offer

A personal pension is a scheme that you set up yourself rather than through an employer. You choose the provider – from literally hundreds – and have the option if things go badly to move your money to another provider.

The big idea of a personal pension is that the money invested grows sufficiently to enable you buy a large annuity – income for life – to tide you over in old age.

Millions of people have a personal pension and you can see why they are so popular when you consider what they offer:

- **Flexibility.** If you move job your pension moves with you. With a personal pension you get to choose where your money is invested, while under a company scheme the decision is made for you.

- **Choice.** Hundreds of pension providers exist – insurers, banks, investment houses, even supermarkets have got in on the act. You can scan the market and go for a provider that offers the pensions nirvana of low charges, high performance, and oodles of investment choice.

- **Tax-free lump sum.** You can take 25 per cent of your pension pot as a tax-free lump sum. Some people invest in a personal pension purely to scoop this tasty tax break. See Chapter 9 for more on the tax-free lump sum.

 You can choose to have some of your National Insurance Contributions (NICs) rebated by the government and paid into your personal pension. This process is called *contracting out*. By contracting out you lose entitlement to the state second pension (S2P), but the gamble is that the NICs invested in your personal pension will perform well enough to provide you with a larger income in retirement.

 A growing consensus exists that most people would be better off remaining contracted into the S2P rather than having NICs rebated into a personal pension. Many experts argue that the government rebate is too small and as a result it won't grow sufficiently within a personal pension to make up for the loss of S2P entitlement.

The Personal Pension Tax Break

By far the biggest thing that personal – as well as workplace – pensions have going for them is generous tax relief on contributions. This tax relief works as follows:

- **Basic rate taxpayer** – every 78p you invest is topped up to £1 by the government.

- **Higher rate taxpayer** – every 60p you invest in your pension is topped up to £1 by the government.

Personal pensions mis-selling

Not too long ago the sale of personal pensions was mired in scandal. In the late 1980s and early 1990s personal pensions were all the rage and wide-boy financial advisers persuaded hundreds of thousands of people in the UK to stop contributing to their workplace pensions and open a personal pension; back then you had to choose one or the other.

The financial advisers earned huge commission payments from persuading people to switch. But often this advice was lousy. People were invariably better off sticking with their workplace pension.

It's worth noting that it wasn't just fly-by-night financial advisers involved in the scandal but some big High Street banks and insurers. In short, the pension industry was up to its neck.

However, the industry regulator – now called the Financial Services Authority (FSA) – and the industry ombudsman got involved and ordered firms to make good their wrongs. As a result, the industry was forced to pay billions of pounds in compensation to the public.

See Chapter 5 for tips on how to spot a mis-sale and seek out a good financial adviser.

CHEAP CHIC A great plus point for some pension savers is that their contributions – provided they earn enough – may receive tax relief at a rate of 40 per cent, but when it comes time to receive retirement income from their pension they may only be earning enough to be taxed at the basic rate, currently 22 per cent.

Figuring Out Personal Pension Performance

Whether your personal pension will grow sufficiently large to provide the basis of a wealthy retirement depends on four factors:

✔ **How much you pay in over the years.** It's an investment truism that the more you pay in the more you should get out and this is never truer than with pensions. Contribution levels used to be tightly controlled, but now you can contribute up to 100 per cent of your income up to a maximum of £215,000 into a personal pension. You can read more about contribution levels later in the chapter.

✔ **When you start making contributions.** The younger the age at which you start a personal pension, the longer the money has to grow. It has been estimated that every £1 you pay into a pension in your 20s is worth £3 that you pay in during your early fifties.

✔ **Level of charges.** Your pension provider levies a charge for managing your pension. It may also levy charges if you stop contributing or want to transfer your pension pot to another provider. Think about it: Every pound you pay in charges is a pound that can be invested to help provide you with a wealthy retirement. Charges on personal pensions have been falling of late, but some investors who opened plans in the 1980s and 1990s are saddled with high charges.

✔ **Annuity rate.** Personal pension rules used to dictate that you have to use 75 per cent of your fund to buy an annuity – an income for life. In recent years annuity rates have fallen, which means that it has cost people more to secure a decent retirement income. If annuity rates fall further you may have to save more in your pension to enable you to buy an income which will allow you to enjoy the finer things in life in old age.

At retirement your pension provider offers to convert your pension pot into an annuity for you – that's nice of them, isn't it? No, it's not. You're likely to find that you can get a better annuity by ignoring your pension provider's generous offer and shopping around for an annuity. Choosing the right annuity is hardly glamorous – in the way that making a killing on the stock market is – but it's one of the most crucial financial decisions you can make. See Chapter 9 for more on buying an annuity.

A major plus point with annuities is that they guarantee an income for life and not just for a set period of time. It doesn't matter if you're lucky enough to retire at 55 and live to 100, you still continue to receive an income.

Weighing Up Personal and Workplace Pensions

So what's better – company or personal pension? Which type of pension promises the quicker route to a wealthy retirement?

The answer always used to be a company pension, for the following reasons:

✔ **Employer contributions.** Companies offering a pension scheme to staff often make contributions, which can help boost the size of the pension pot. It's unusual for an employer to make payments into a worker's personal pension plan.

✔ **Employers meet the cost.** The company bears the costs of administering the pension, while with a personal pension plan it's up to the saver. And as I mentioned earlier in this chapter, every pound disappearing in charges means a smaller pension pot. With company schemes the costs of administering the scheme is borne by the sponsoring employer.

Personal pensions were seen as bit of a poor relation to company schemes. If you were self-employed or didn't have access to a company pension then you would go for a personal pension plan, but otherwise forget it.

But the pension goalposts have been moved for a number of reasons. What's been happening in the world of company and personal pensions should make you question the 'company pension is always best' theory:

✔ **Lower charges on personal pensions.** The introduction of stakeholder pensions with their low charging structure led to a general lowering of charges across the whole personal pension sector – although being a member of a company pension is still the low-cost option. See more on stakeholder pensions below.

✔ **Falling away of employer commitment.** The company pension system has been going through turmoil in recent years, with many employers closing lucrative final salary schemes to new members and cutting the amount of cash they pay into their workers' pensions. See Chapter 6 for more on the growing woes of UK company pensions.

✔ **Greater flexibility.** In the past personal pension providers often levied penalties on savers who stopped making contributions. Nowadays, providers increasingly offer savers the chance to lower or stop contributions at will without penalty.

All in all, the gap between personal and company pensions has closed a little. This is due to personal pension providers pulling their socks up and employers cutting back on their commitments.

Having Your Pension Cake and Eating It

It's no longer a case of choosing a company or personal pension – you can have both!

It used to be the case that if you were paying into a personal pension and then decided to join a company scheme you had to stop contributing to your personal pension. As a result, your personal pension provider levied a penalty and the pension became *paid up* – barred from making further contributions.

Fortunately, the days of penalties and pension freezing are fast coming to an end. New pension rules from April 2006 allow you to have as many different pensions as you want all running alongside one another.

Let's see how this can work in practice. Ivan is self-employed and decides to open a personal pension. He pays into the scheme but after a few years decides to get a salaried job; in other words he becomes an employee.

Ivan's new employer offers an occupational pension scheme – a type of company pension where the employer has to make a contribution – which he decides to join.

In the past Ivan would have had to stop paying into his personal pension, but not any more. Instead Ivan pays money into his occupational scheme *and* his personal pension. This way Ivan is able to save really hard towards a wealthy retirement and make maximum use of the tax relief on pension contributions.

After ten years being an employee, Ivan decides to return to self employment. His occupational scheme won't allow Ivan to contribute once he has left the firm's employ. However, this doesn't bother Ivan, as he puts the money he would have paid into the occupational pension into his personal plan.

When Ivan eventually decides to retire, he has the income from his occupational scheme and his personal pension to rely on. And because Ivan was able to contribute into his personal pension over many years – rather than stopping when he was a member of a company scheme and then starting again – he has been able to build up a bigger pension pot.

One big advantage for Ivan of having both personal and workplace pensions is that he has reduced his risk. If one of his pensions underperforms then the other may ride to the rescue by performing well.

Some people with personal pensions may find that they still face penalties and having their pension paid up if they stop contributing. Best check with your pension provider what the rules of your scheme are.

Buying a Personal Pension

If you contribute to a pension for many years it can grow so large that it vies with your home for the prize of being your biggest asset. Therefore, it's key to get your choice of pension provider right.

So where to start? There are lots of free financial comparison Web sites such as www.moneynet.co.uk, www.moneysupermarket.com, and www.moneyfacts.co.uk which have all the performance info you need on all the different pensions on offer.

The Department of Work and Pensions Web site has lots of advice on what to bear in mind when choosing a pension. Check it out at www.dwp.gov.uk.

Pension providers produce what are called key features documents. These documents outline – in great detail – all you need to know about the pension on offer. These documents may be boring, but it's important to read them thoroughly. You are looking for the low-down on the following:

- ✔ The past performance of the pension fund.
- ✔ Details of the management charges.
- ✔ What happens to your scheme if you stop contributing.
- ✔ How much investment choice you get.

When it comes to choosing a personal pension, remember to pay particular attention to the charges. High charges can really damage the long-term growth prospects of your pension.

Buying a pension is a major decision. You may be best seeking independent financial advice.

The past performance of a pension fund is no guarantee that it will do well in the future.

Taking Control of Your Personal Pension

Some personal pensions give you the option of choosing where your pension is invested. You should look for a pension that gives you a say in where your money is going.

Usually the choice includes a mix of low-, medium-, and higher-risk investments, including:

- **Low risk** – cash deposit accounts, bonds, and government securities called gilts.

- **Medium risk** – with profit funds, which in turn invest in bonds, shares, and property.

- **Higher risk** – property investment funds and stock market funds including unit and investment trusts.

See Chapters 10, 11, and 12 for more on all the above investments.

When choosing where your pension fund invests, bear in mind your other investments. If, for example, you have a lot of money tied up in property, it may be best to avoid investing in property funds through your pension. Remember, the broader the spread of investments you have, the less likely you are to come a cropper!

Don't worry if you don't fancy taking control and choosing where your pension money is invested. Your pension provider may offer a *default* option. Under a default option your money will be invested for you, usually in low- and medium-risk investments of the providers' choosing. Be warned though, picking a default option may mean paying higher annual charges.

Being focused in rooting out a personal pension that offers low charges and flexibility should ensure that you don't make a bad choice. But, nevertheless, there may be a time when you decide that you want to transfer your personal pension to another provider – who may be offering lower charges or better investment choice – or even into a company scheme.

Not all company pension schemes accept transfers in of personal pensions. Check with your company pension scheme administrator before setting the pension transfer ball rolling.

Understanding the Effects of Charges

You may have noticed the words 'charges' cropping up a lot in this chapter. That is because the level of charges has a huge effect on your pension.

Pensions tend to be held for longer than other investments and savings – usually twenty or thirty years. As a result, even small differences in charges – say a quarter or a half per cent a year – can make a huge difference to the ultimate size of your pension pot.

The dramatic effects that charges can have are demonstrated in the following example.

Twin sisters, Imogen and Samantha, each open a personal pension at the same time but with different providers. Imogen's provider charges her 1 per cent per year to manage her pension fund. Samantha's provider charges her 1.5 per cent a year to manage her pension fund. The sisters both pay £100 a month into their pension funds for 35 years. Both pension funds grow at 7 per cent a year for the full 35 years.

When Imogen came to retire, her pension fund was worth £138,000 and over the 35 years she paid £34,000 in charges.

However, paying just 0.5 per cent more each year than Imogen in charges meant that Samantha's pension at the end of 35 years was worth £124,000 as she paid £48,000 in charges.

The message is keep an eagle eye on charges to make sure your pension provider isn't taking too big a slice of your retirement wealth.

Securing low charges is important, but it's not the be all and end all. You should also consider past performance, choice of investments on offer, and whether you can stop or vary contribution before choosing your pension.

The personal pensions market is very competitive and as a result charges have been falling in most of the industry during recent years. However, some horror pensions are still being sold that have very steep charges and penalties. Not too long ago I came across a pension which levied an annual charge of 2.5 per cent – two and half times the maximum allowed charges under a stakeholder pension.

The different types of charges you should keep a watchful eye on include:

- ✔ **Initial charge** – the fee for setting up the pension plan.

- ✔ **Annual charge** – the ongoing management fee.

- ✔ **Transaction charge** – a small, incremental charge levied for new investment by your fund.

- ✔ **Transfer charge** – the fee for transferring your money out of one pension and into another.

 Don't just look at one charge in isolation, look at the whole package. One pension may have low annual charges but hefty penalties for transferring out. Another pension may have slightly higher annual charges but impose no charges for transfer out. The latter may be the best choice, because if the pension underperforms it is easier for you to cut your losses and take your money elsewhere.

 Stakeholder pensions have some of the lowest charges in the pensions universe and you can stop contributing at anytime without fear that the fund will become *paid up.*

Staking Your Future on a Stakeholder Pension

Stakeholder pensions are a low-cost, easy to understand, flexible personal pension with no hidden costs. Stakeholder pensions offer the same tax benefits as a standard personal pension but with the added appeal of low charges and flexibility.

Stakeholder pensions are designed to be simple, easy to understand products encouraging low- to middle-income people to save more for their retirement. Generally, stakeholder pension funds tend to be a safety-first long-term investment.

For a pension to be called a stakeholder, it must conform to the following rules:

- ✔ The annual management charge is capped at 1.5 per cent a year and there are no other fees. (The charges cap is 1 per cent if the stakeholder was opened before April 2005).

- ✔ You can invest as little as £20 a month and can stop and then restart contributions at any time.

Limits to pension contributions

Up until recently a limit had been imposed on pension saving. This limit was an ultra-complex formula based on age. The good news is that this complex system has been swept away and replaced with something a lot easier for savers – and money experts – to get their heads around.

You may now contribute up to 100 per cent of your annual income into a pension, up to a maximum of £215,000. In addition, non-taxpayers are able to contribute up to £3,600 a year into a pension scheme.

From April 2006, you're also able to contribute to any number of pensions at the same time.

However, the total value of all your pensions must not exceed £1.5m, rising to £1.8m in 2010. You are allowed to save over this threshold, but if you do the tax system becomes punishing rather than generous, so it's best to keep below the lifetime limit.

A strong case exists for investing in a stakeholder pension rather than a standard pension as the charges are lower. However, you may consider going for a standard pension if the charges are just a little over 1 per cent and the fund offers a wide range of investments for you to choose from.

Although stakeholders haven't caught the public imagination, they have had a marked impact on the rest of the personal pensions universe. Standard, non-stakeholder, personal pensions have often cut their charges to compete with stakeholder schemes; this can only be good for investors.

Even if you are a non-earner you can pay into a stakeholder pension. Some wealthy parents and grandparents have opened and paid into stakeholders in the name of their children or grandchildren with the idea of giving their long-term pension saving a kick-start.

Chapter 8

Taking Control with a Sipp

*P*ensions are supposed to be impenetrable products. You hand over your cash each month and a huge hulking insurance company invests it on your behalf. You have very little say in where your money goes and just hope that everything will be well and you will have a tidy pile of cash to live off in retirement. In short, the one word you don't associate with personal pensions is control.

But *Self Invested Personal Pensions* (Sipps) are all about control. You get all the tax breaks of a standard pension but *you* make the investment decisions.

In this chapter, we explore Sipps, what they are, and what role they can play in your retiring wealthy plan.

Introducing Self Invested Personal Pensions (Sipps)

Think of a Sipp as a shopping trolley, in which you hold lots of different investments. You get tax relief on your contributions, like a personal or workplace pension. Tax relief is not to be sniffed at; it can give your pension fund an enormous boost.

If you're a basic rate taxpayer for every 78p you pay in your pension fund the government adds another 22p. If you're a higher rate taxpayer for every 60p you pay in, the government adds another 22p initially and then you can claim a further 18p through your tax return. In addition, all income and growth on investments held in a Sipp is tax free.

You can contribute to a Sipp even if you're not earning an income. You can pay in at least £2,808 per year, which with basic rate tax relief is boosted to £3,600. This means that children, retired people, and non-working carers can contribute to a Sipp.

Using a Sipp as your pension plan offers several advantages:

- **More control:** You make the investment decisions rather than some highly paid pension fund manager. Whether or not you retire rich or not is down to you. What you say goes and that can be very empowering.

- **More choice:** Sipps allow you to pick from lots of different investments allowing you to build up a diversified investment base while taking advantage of the tax relief available on pensions.

- **More fun:** Building your pension pot can become a bit of a hobby. Weighing up different types of investment and deciding what funds to commit requires research, time, and know-how. Sipps are a good way of expanding your personal finance knowledge – which you can also do by reading this book, of course!

But inevitably Sipps also have a downside. These are the sort of problems you need to consider:

- **Making the wrong choices:** You may not have huge faith in pension fund managers, but who is to say you'll do any better – in fact you may do a lot worse. In fact your understandable desire to get things right may cloud your judgement resulting in you putting your money into investments that are too risky or too safe. Can you really be dispassionate and think clearly when your retirement wealth is on the line?

- **Being time consuming:** You may set out on a Sipp full of enthusiasm but do you have the time to keep at it year in year out? You need to track your investments to see how they are doing, whereas with a standard personal pension you leave the fund manager to get on with his or her job. Pension saving is not a fad, it is a long-term commitment.

The Sipps revolution that never happened

Exciting is not normally a word you associate with pensions. But for a few months in 2005 pensions got just a little bit, well, exciting. The reason? The government announced that from April 2006 it planned to allow people to hold residential property and collectables, such as fine wine and classic cars, in their Sipp. It took potential buy-to-let investors and collectable enthusiasts about a nano-second to see the pound signs floating in front of their eyes. They were looking at the delicious prospect of getting tax relief on their investments just as long as they held them in a Sipp. The press reported that thousands of investors were poised to open a Sipp to take advantage of the fab tax breaks.

Facing the prospect of giving away lots of money in tax relief, the government got spooked and in late 2005 effectively reversed its decision to allow people to use their Sipps to invest in buy-to-let and collectables.

✔ **Carrying high charges.** Bizarrely, Sipps can sometimes be as expensive as a standard personal pension. The Sipp providers argue that fees are high due to 'administration costs'. But you may find it odd that you're being asked to shell out when it's you making all the tricky choices, such as where to invest. The good news though is that the Sipps market is becoming more competitive and charges are falling fast.

 Sipps are generally a higher risk option than a standard personal pension run by an insurance company. Personal pension funds are huge business – some are worth many billions of pounds – so are managed by professionals to achieve growth without putting financial security at risk.

 Sipps are not to be entered into lightly, they can be costly and if things go wrong you have no one to blame but yourself. You may want to seek financial advice from a qualified professional before starting a Sipp. See Chapter 5 for more on how to find a good adviser.

 You are allowed to invest in property through your Sipp. You can invest directly in commercial property or through a property investment fund. These funds pool investor cash to buy up property. Borrowing up to 50 per cent of the value of your Sipp to fund a commercial property purchase is allowed; so, if your Sipp has £100,000 in it you can borrow £50,000. Just remember, if you borrow and are unable to keep up with repayments the commercial property may be repossessed by your lender.

Moving out of the Sipps fast lane

In all the excitement about the freedom offered by Sipps it can be easy to forget the fact that it's just another personal pension and still subject to strict rules on access to funds.

Sipp investors can't access their pension fund until they are at least age 50, rising to 55 in 2010.

They can only take 25 per cent of their fund in cash at retirement. The remaining money usually goes towards buying a retirement income – called an annuity.

Annuity rates have been falling for the past decade, so are becoming less popular. They are also an ultra-safe investment, which maybe a bit hard for someone who has been managing their own Sipp to deal with. Using cash from a Sipp to buy an annuity has been likened to being made to sell a Ferrari and buy a Morris Minor! Check out Chapter 9 for more on how annuities work.

If you own shares in a non-stock market listed business or one listed on OFFEX – which simply means *off exchange*, a sort of baby stock market for fledgling firms – then you can put these into your Sipp too.

This can be very handy as any dividend that you receive slots into your Sipp tax free and what's more if you sell your shares you'll do so free from Capital Gains Tax (CGT).

Looking at Sipp Investments

Sipps allow you to divide your pension pot into many different types of investment. These investments range from the quite risky – single company shares – to the ultra safe – government gilts.

Most but not all the traditional Sipp investments involve the stock market in some way. Your choices are as follows:

- ✔ **Collective investment schemes:** These pool investor cash to buy a range of shares and sometimes other investments such as bonds. Qualifying collective investments include unit trusts (also called OEICS), investment trusts, and with-profit funds. See Chapter 12 for more on unit and investment trusts and Chapter 11 for the ins and outs of with-profit funds.
- ✔ **Single company equities:** You can invest in any share on any stock market throughout the world through a Sipp. See Chapter 12 for more on picking shares.

✔ **UK government gilts:** You lend the government cash and in return it promises to pay back the loan plus a regular rate of interest, which is usually fixed at the outset but can be linked to the level of inflation.

✔ **Corporate bonds:** Essentially, these work the same as gilts only they tend to have a shorter lifespan and are a little riskier as companies are more likely than the UK government to go bust.

✔ **Shares futures and options:** Put simply this is the right to buy or sell a quantity of shares at a specific date in the future. Futures are high risk and very specialist and are looked at in Chapter 17.

✔ **Permanent interest bearing shares (PIBS):** These are shares issued by building societies which normally pay a fixed rate of interest. Pibs are a safe but very little known investment. All in all, the corduroy jacket of investing – not very sexy!

✔ **Cash deposit accounts:** These need little introduction, being a standard savings account in which your money earns interest and the capital is safe. The nitty gritty of savings accounts is explored in Chapter 10.

✔ **Traded endowment policies:** These are second-hand endowment policies that are yet to mature bought through a traded endowment broker. The investment is indirectly related to the stock market because at least part of the underlying performance of the endowment will be reliant on share price growth.

✔ **Commercial property:** Some Sipps allow you to hold commercial property such as offices, warehouses, and retail outlets. A Sipp can also invest indirectly in property through a property unit trust. See Chapter 15 for more on investing in commercial property.

The investments to consider for your Sipp depend on your age, approach to risk, and the size of your fund. If you don't have a lot of money in your Sipp, or you are near your planned retirement date, you're best going for safer investments, such as collective ones. On the other hand, if you have a large fund or are quite young you can afford to take some risks. See the section 'Building a Balanced Sipp Portfolio' later in this chapter for more on high-, medium-, and low-risk Sipp investments.

Some Sipp providers offer you a wider range of investment choice than others. The Sipp provider tries to strike a balance between breadth of choice and the need to keep down its administration costs.

Any investments held in a Sipp aren't strictly yours. Everything is legally owned by the Sipp pension fund, overseen by a scheme trust. The Sipp provider acts as the trustee.

Keeping Your Sipp in the Family

Family members, friends, and even business partners can have what is called a *linked Sipp*. They all have their very own ring-fenced Sipp pension pot with the same provider but have the ability to pass on the cash they have invested to the other linked Sipp members when they die.

The Inheritance Tax (IHT) implications of a linked Sipp are yet to be finalised – the Treasury is still umming and ahhing over this one. But if the money held in the linked Sipp goes to the other Sipp members free of IHT, it may prove to be a real boon for those with large estates looking to minimise any eventual IHT bill.

 In the 2005–06 tax year, IHT at 40 per cent is charged on estates worth in excess of £275,000 (rising to £285,000 in the 2006–2007 tax year). However, transfers between spouses, and to exempt beneficiaries such as charities, are free of IHT.

Choosing the Right Sipp Provider

You need a Sipp provider to oversee your investments. Insurance companies offer Sipps as do some large Independent Financial Advice firms.

Your Sipp can eventually be worth a lot of money, so you have the right to demand the best. Only consider Sipp providers that offer you the following:

- ✔ The ability to make new investments by phone, post, and online.
- ✔ Lots of free information such as regular updates on how your Sipp is doing and analysts' reports.
- ✔ As varied a range of investments as possible.
- ✔ Access to independent financial advice if you need it.

There are three areas you need to bear in mind when choosing a Sipp provider:

> ✔ The level of service on offer.
>
> ✔ The level of charges.
>
> ✔ The range of investments.

There are lots of providers out there each claiming to be the best. It maybe best to see an independent financial adviser (IFA) who'll look at the whole market and recommend the one that's right for you. Chapter 5 shows you how to find a good IFA.

Provider services

The Sipp provider will offer either an advisory or execution only service.

> ✔ **Advisory service:** Under this arrangement you will receive advice on which investments to put into your Sipp. But the final decision on whether to act on the advice offered is up to you.
>
> ✔ **Execution only:** You call all the shots from start to finish, and your Sipp provider follows your instructions to the letter.

From time to time the Sipp provider will send you a statement detailing how your Sipp investments are performing – usually once a year.

Keep your Sipps statement safe; you will need it if you fill in your tax self assessment form.

Sipp charges

Sipp charges break down into two different types:

> ✔ **Upfront charges:** This is an initial setting up fee often several hundred pounds.
>
> ✔ **Ongoing charges:** The provider may levy an annual charge for managing the fund as well as a transaction fee for each new investment made.

For example, if you buy shares to put in a Sipp the provider will charge either a flat fee or a percentage of the money being invested.

High annual charges can eat into the performance of your Sipp investments.

Changing Sipp provider

There really are only a couple of reasons to transfer any sort of pension, including a Sipp, between providers and they are the following:

✔ **The new provider charges less:** It may cost you cash to move so make sure that the provider you're switching to is offering enough of a financial incentive in the way of lower charges to make this worthwhile.

✔ **The new provider offers more choice:** Not all providers may offer the range of investments that you require. Diversity is very important to building a success-ful SIPP.

If you transfer your pension to another provider you may find that you have to pay a penalty.

Some providers offer what are called 'free Sipps' but nothing in life, apart from fresh air, is free. The providers of 'free Sipps' may not levy an upfront charge but this is on the proviso that you invest some of your Sipp money in a fund that they run. These funds come with guess what? Charges!

Range of investments

Not all providers will offer access to the full universe of Sipp quali-fying investments. They may for example only be able to offer access to shares in the UK's largest companies, leaving out all the medium and small companies.

The greater the range of investments on offer, the more flexibility you have. Flexibility is a good thing as it makes it easier for you to diversify your investments.

Building a Balanced Sipp Portfolio

You should look to build a Sipp which includes low-, medium-, and even some high-risk investments. The idea is that if all goes wrong with your high-risk investments then the safe low-risk investments give you a good fall-back position. If you have all your money in high-risk investments and they go wrong you can conceivably lose everything.

Table 8-1 categorises Sipp investments by degree of risk.

Table 8-1	How Risky Is Your Sipp?
Low risk	
Deposit savings	
UK government gilts	
Permanent interest-bearing shares (PIBS)	
Medium risk	
Gold bullion	
Bonds and other fixed interest securities	
Collective investment funds such as unit and investment trusts	
Traded endowment policies	
Commercial property	
High risk	
Individual company shares	
Share futures and options	
Private company and Offex shares	

Your pension is likely to be vital to your retiring wealthy plans, so don't take too many risks with your choice of investment. The closer you are to retirement the less investment risk you should take.

Some share investments are obviously riskier than other. Shares in a multinational such as Tesco or BP are less likely to nosedive than say shares in an Internet company.

When deciding which types of investment you should put into your Sipp, look at the investments you already hold. If you have lots of cash in savings deposit accounts you can probably afford to intro-duce a little risk into your Sipp by buying shares.

To Sipp or Not to Sipp

Sipps aren't for everyone. They are expensive and require a good deal of financial knowledge to manage effectively. You have to be confident that you know what you are doing and are up to the job.

Also Sipps involve a lot of work. Ask yourself whether you have the time to keep an eye on how your investments are performing.

Sipp charges can be high, so it may not be worth you opening one if you don't have a large amount of cash to invest or are on a low wage. If you don't have much cash then you may be best going for a low-cost personal pension called a *stakeholder*. See Chapter 7 for more on this type of scheme.

If you have any doubts about your ability to manage your Sipp you may be best sticking to a personal or workplace pension, particularly if your employer makes a contribution.

You can open a Sipp even if contributing to a company pension scheme as well. Having more than one pension on the go gives you greater investment diversity.

Chapter 9

Working with Your Pension

● ●

In This Chapter

▶ Delaying your state pension

▶ Investing a lump sum

▶ Buying an annuity

▶ Making the most of small pensions

▶ Working beyond retirement age

▶ Assessing pension alternatives

● ●

*I*n this chapter, I show you how to work with your pensions –
state, workplace, and personal – so that they produce the most
bangs for your buck.

Take a peek at the pension management tactics outlined in this
chapter and you'll have an A1 chance of being able to kick off your
shoes and enjoy a wealthy retirement.

Delaying Your State Pension

As people get older many choose to turn a blind eye to birthdays –
personally I have been 'around' 30 for a good five years now.

After all, age isn't important, it's how young you feel that counts.
One birthday, though, that people don't tend to forget is the one
that entitles them to a state pension – currently 65 for men and
60 for women. Some can hardly wait to take that trip to the Post
Office and collect the pension that years of hard work and National
Insurance contributions have entitled them too. But hold on a
minute! Don't go beating that post office door down yet. The government is now paying people to take their state pension at a later
date, which is called deferral.

In return for agreeing to forgo receipt of the state pension you will receive either of the following:

- ✔ The amount you deferred as a taxable lump sum payment.

- ✔ A higher income from your state pension when you do eventually collect it.

The size of the payment you receive for not taking your state pension depends on the length of time that you have been making National Insurance contributions. If you have saved enough to earn a full basic state pension you can expect to receive top whack for deferral. If, on the other hand, you have a patchy NIC record – not enough to earn a full basic state pension – it follows the deferral payment will be lower too.

Doing the state pension deferral sums

If you defer taking the full basic state pension – currently £82.05 per week for a single person in the 2005–2006 tax year – you may choose either of the following payments (depending on how long you defer for):

- ✔ A taxable lump sum equivalent to your state pension for the amount of time you have decided to delay claiming the state pension (which must be for at least 12 months) plus interest set at 2 per cent above the Bank of England base rate

- ✔ A higher level of pension income when eventually you do decide to collect your state pension. You earn state pension at an extra 1 per cent for every five weeks you put off claiming (equivalent to about 10.4 per cent for every year you defer)

If you want to gain extra pension income you have to defer for at least five weeks, but if you want to scoop the lump sum you must defer for 12 months. You are free to defer taking your state pension for as long as you want – a five year limit used to exist but this has now been removed.

But face facts, the government would not be offering this if it didn't make financial sense for it to do so.

The government employs a whole army of actuaries. The jolly job of a government actuary is to calculate how long the population is likely to live. These stats are used to set the maximum deferral payment. The law of averages suggests that sufficient numbers of people die before collecting their deferred state pension to make it worth the government's while.

By choosing to defer you are in effect gambling that you will be one of the lucky ones to make it through to collect your enhanced state pension or get time to spend your lump sum payment.

 The lump sum for delaying taking the state pension is only payable after you start to collect your pension. So delay taking the state pension until age 70 and you will only receive your payout at age 70, not at the time you decide to delay.

Asking the key question: Can you afford to defer?

Regardless of all this grim reaper talk, the bottom line with deferral is that you have to be able to afford to do without your state pension. It makes no sense to live on out-of-date own brand spaghetti hoops for five years just so you can collect a higher state pension.

In truth, you have to have either of the following to be able to defer your state pension:

- **The ability to carry on working.** Many people simply hate the idea of giving up work and as long as your health and your employer allow you to, then why not carry on earning?

- **Enough money tucked away.** Hopefully if you follow the tips in this book you'll be able to build a big enough cash pile to allow you the option of deferral.

 Women generally live five years more than men. It may be morbid, but this gender longevity gap should play a part in your deferral decision. Odds are higher that you live long enough to collect your deferred state pension if you're a woman than if you're a man.

 Be sure you can afford to do without your state pension before going for the deferral option. You do not want to leave yourself short today in a bid to collect a higher pension tomorrow.

Investing a Lump Sum at Retirement

Retirement often coincides with the receipt of a cash lump sum. This lump sum can take different forms, including:

> ✔ A payment from your employer for taking early retirement.
>
> ✔ A tax-free lump sum taken when you collect your pension.

This retirement cash lump sum can be worth a lot of money and what you do with it can have major implications for how comfortable or uncomfortable your old age is.

If you want to know if your occupational pension scheme offers a lump sum, check out the members' handbook. For more on the ins and outs of occupational pensions see Chapter 6.

You can spend your lump sum on whatever you please – fast cars, luxury holidays, even miniature golf, the choice is yours – or invest it in order to produce an income or with the idea of it growing into a larger cash pile later in life.

Most people, to be honest, choose to spend a bit and save a bit of any lump sum they receive.

As far as personal pensions go you can take up to 25 per cent of your pension pot as a tax-free lump sum; in most circumstances the rest of this cash is used to buy an annuity – an income for life – by age 75. This lump sum can't be any larger than 25 per cent of the lifetime limit on a pension fund – £1.5m from 2006 rising to £1.8m in 2010.

There are advantages to investing your lump sum, such as:

> ✔ **Higher growth.** Money invested in a pension tends to grow rather slowly. You can take your lump sum and invest it somewhere where there is a better chance of higher returns, for example the stock market.
>
> ✔ **Tax efficiency.** Income from an annuity is taxable but income from some other types of investment – such as cash ISAs – is not. Therefore, it may be a smart tax ploy to plough as much of your pension pot as possible into an investment which produces tax-free income.

Be careful of sinking a substantial part of your lump sum into risky investments such as company shares. After all, stock markets have a habit of going down as well as up. The golden rule is only ever invest in medium- and high-risk investments if you can afford to lose your cash. See Chapter 10 for more on telling a low from a high-risk investment.

Just because you're allowed to take *up to* 25 per cent of your pension as a lump sum doesn't mean you *should* do it. You may be best taking nothing at all or just 5 or 10 per cent of your pension as a lump sum and leaving the rest to buy an annuity. See later in this chapter for more on buying an annuity.

Getting It Right: Buying an Annuity

An annuity is a guaranteed income that is meant to see you through your autumn years until it's time for your appointment with the big fella in the sky.

You give an insurance company your pension pot and – *shazzamm!* – it converts the cash into an annuity for you to live off.

Buying an annuity is one of the most important financial decisions you can make. But many people spend next to no time deciding which annuity to buy. This laziness – for want of a better word – makes some pension providers very happy, because it means they can get away with a great big confidence trick.

The con works like this. When you decide you want to retire and collect your pension your pension provider – invariably an insurance company – tells you how much money you have in your pension pot. More often than not they offer to magically convert this pension pot into an annuity, saving you the hassle of shopping around. But you can nearly always get a higher annuity by exercising what is called the *open market option*. This simply means you have the right to take your pension pot and shop around for an annuity.

Hundreds of companies offer annuities and the amount of income they offer can vary wildly, sometimes by up to 20 per cent. If you look on the bright side you may spend 30 years or so retired, so get your choice of annuity wrong and you can be missing out on tens of thousands.

Once you've signed up to an annuity that's it, you can't switch from one provider to another. One way around this problem is to buy a limited period annuity rather than a lifetime annuity. From April 2006 this type of annuity allows you to buy an annuity to provide income for a limited period of time, say five years, allowing you to shop around for a better deal on a lifetime annuity later on.

Shopping around for an annuity can be a long job if you do it alone. An independent financial adviser can help you find the right one for you. You can also check out the annuity bureau Web site www.annuity-bureau.co.uk which collates all the available annuity rates on offer.

Understanding annuity calculations

Your retirement income depends on the size of your pension pot and the annuity rate offered by the insurance company. Simple enough you may think, but the complexity kicks in when you look at how the annuity rate is calculated.

Annuity rates are calculated on a case-by-case basis as the insurance company's aim is that your pension pot runs out at the same time as you die. If you outlive the insurance company's predictions then it loses out as it continues to pay an annuity income. On the flip side, if you die before your pension pot runs out the insurance company makes money (although there are some annuities which allow you to sign over your annuity on death, see later in this chapter for more).

The insurance company makes some assumptions as to your mortality and how long the annuity income is therefore likely to have to be paid based on the following criteria:

- ✔ **Age.** The older you are when you buy an annuity the better the rate you're offered. This is because the insurance company calculates that it needs to pay an income for fewer years.

- ✔ **Gender.** Women live on average 5.2 years longer then men. This is great in all other respects apart from the fact that this means they get a lower annuity rate. Recently there were moves by EU commissioners to equalise the annuity rates of men and women, but this has come to nothing so far.

- ✔ **Lifestyle.** If you're a smoker or a heavy drinker then the insurance company figures you won't live as long, therefore it pays a higher annuity rate.

- ✔ **Health.** If you have health problems such as heart disease or a degenerative condition you can get an impaired life annuity. The annuity on offer is far more generous than for someone who is in rude health.

The annuity income you can expect in retirement is based on a prediction of how long you're likely to live.

To illustrate how annuity rates work in practice, take the example of Mark and Philippa. Both have a pension pot of £100,000 and are looking to buy annuities on their 65th birthdays.

Mark as a man is likely to live five years fewer than Philippa therefore he stands to get a higher annuity rate. However, while Mark survives on tofu and runs marathons, Philippa is a lifelong smoker with a heart condition. Therefore the insurer cuts Philippa's life expectancy by three years. Mark still gets a higher annuity rate as he is predicted to die two years earlier than Philippa.

Some insurance companies specialise in annuities for impaired life and smokers. Best go see an independent financial adviser for more on choosing one of these annuities.

Interest rates have a major influence on annuity rates. This is because insurance companies invest the money they receive from people buying annuities. Insurers invest this money in low-risk investments such as government bonds, known as gilts, which are very sensitive to interest rate moves. If interest rates decrease the return on investment also falls and this means the insurance company is less able to afford to offer high annuity rates.

Choosing a level or rising annuity

Whether you go for a level or rising annuity can have a major impact on your financial position in retirement. The differences between these types of annuities are as follows:

- ✔ A level annuity is fixed for life so you get the same amount until you die.
- ✔ A rising annuity starts off lower then a level annuity but increases each year to keep pace with inflation or by a pre-set percentage.

To illustrate the differences between these two types of annuity let's look at Mark and Philippa again.

Mark uses his £100,000 pension pot to buy a level annuity. The insurance company offers him an annuity rate of 7 per cent. Mark's income for his annuity is £7,000 a year. He's very happy with this for a few years, but then he notices that his income is buying him less in the shops because prices are rising but his income isn't.

Philippa on the other hand uses her £100,000 pension pot to buy a rising annuity. Philippa was in line for a slightly lower annuity than

Mark anyway, because of their respective life expectancy calculations. However, this difference is exacerbated because Philippa wants to buy the guarantee that her income will rise to keep pace with inflation each year. At first Philippa earns far less than Mark but over time her income increases at least in line with prices and ultimately overtakes his.

Level annuities offer jam today and you can budget easily as you know exactly what is coming in. Rising annuities, on the other hand, offer the security that if you enjoy a long life then your income should increase in line with prices or by a set percentage.

If you buy a level annuity and inflation takes off you may find that the buying power of your income shrinks alarmingly.

You can buy an investment-linked annuity. Your pension pot is invested in a range of different low- to medium-risk investments and your income rises or falls in line with their performance. However, investment-linked annuities should be approached with caution as there is the potential for big falls (as well as rises) in income.

You have the option of buying a *limited period annuity*. This product provides an income for five years. At the end of the five year term you can either buy an annuity to last your whole life or another limited period annuity.

Figuring out when to buy an annuity

It used to be the case that like night follows day retirement would prompt the purchase of an annuity. However, times have changed and many people hold out to the last possible moment before buying an annuity – new pension rules have dispensed altogether with the requirement to buy an annuity by age 75.

Delaying buying an annuity can have the following advantages:

- ✓ **Higher income.** The longer you leave it the higher the income you should get because the insurance company calculates that you're likely to draw an income for less time.

- ✓ **Investment performance.** By delaying buying an annuity you give your pension pot more time to grow. When eventually it's time for you to take the plunge then you may find you have a larger pot enabling you to buy a bigger annuity. An alternative to this strategy is to buy an investment-linked annuity, see earlier in this chapter for more.

The 'longer you leave it the higher income you should get' theory doesn't always stand up. If interest rates fall sharply while you're delaying buying an annuity the insurance company reduces the annuity rates it pays to reflect the fact that the return it gets from investing the money you use to buy an annuity has fallen.

You should only consider delay buying an annuity if you have enough money coming in from other sources to live off. The delay option should only be considered under the following scenarios:

- ✔ You continue to work and earn beyond age 65, in other words you haven't fully retired yet.

- ✔ You have substantial savings and investments you can live off without need to use your pension to buy an annuity.

From April 2006 you can cash in a pension fund worth up to £15,000 at retirement. You can take 25 per cent as a tax-free lump sum while the remainder of the fund is taxed as earned income. Therefore if you're a basic rate taxpayer you pay 22 per cent but if you're a higher rate taxpayer you're taxed at 40 per cent.

Checking out income drawdown

There is one way to delay taking an annuity and yet still get an income from your pension. After you have taken your tax-free lump sum you're allowed to take an income from your pension fund. So instead of using your pension pot to buy an income – an annuity – you simply draw an income direct from your pension pot.

This process is called *income drawdown*. The amount of income you can draw from your pension pot is strictly limited by HM Revenue and Customs. The maximum amount of income you're allowed to draw each year is roughly equal to what a single-life level annuity would pay (see below for more on single-life annuities).

The big idea is that your pension fund remains invested and you simply cream off the growth to give you an income. Ultimately, when you do buy an annuity not only should your pension fund be the same or higher than it was when you started the drawdown process but it should buy you a bigger annuity because you're older.

Sometimes you'll find income drawdown referred to by pension industry insiders as an *unsecured income*.

Here's an example of how income drawdown can work.

Herdeep has a pension pot worth £500,000. If at age 65 he were to buy an annuity his insurance company would pay him 6 per cent, equivalent to £30,000.

However, Herdeep decides to go for income drawdown and receives an income equivalent to 6 per cent of his total pension for the next ten years. At age 75 Herdeep buys an annuity. His pension pot has been eroded a fraction to provide him with an income but is still worth £480,000. Now because he is a lot older and only likely to live a few more years his annuity rate has risen sharply to 8 per cent, equivalent to a whopping £38,400 a year.

If you want to draw an income from your pension fund then your pension provider levies a charge. These charges can be high so best be 100 per cent sure that it's worth it.

Income drawdown comes with a major health warning. If your pension fund falls in value – as can happen due to say a stock market crash – then there won't be any investment growth from which to draw an income. Therefore, any income you draw will come direct from the capital value of the fund. A few years of investment under-performance combined with income drawdown can see your pension fund fall in value alarmingly.

Income drawdown is a bit of a gamble and for this reason most money experts reckon that unless your pension fund is worth more than a cool £250,000 you shouldn't consider it.

You don't have to wait until age 65 to start income drawdown, you can do it from age 50 if you want.

Review your decision as to when to buy an annuity at least once a year.

Making sure your annuity survives you

Under a *single-life annuity* when you die your annuity dies with you.

This isn't much good if you're married. You may, therefore, consider buying a joint-life annuity. Under a joint life annuity when you die part or all your income passes to your spouse.

Of course, in order to pay for this, you have to accept that your annuity rate will be lower than it would have been if you'd purchased a single-life annuity.

An end to annuities?

From April 2006 it is possible to avoid buying an annuity altogether. New pension rules allow the drawing of an *alternatively secured income,* also called an *alternatively secured pension*. Put simply this is the continuation of income drawdown beyond age 75.

However, the maximum income that is allowed to be withdrawn will be 70 per cent of a single-life level annuity rather than the 120 per cent of a single-life level annuity allowed up until age 75. This has the major advantage that if you were to die then the pension fund can pass to a spouse.

Nevertheless, the drawing of alternatively secured income should only be considered by people with large pension pots.

The greater the proportion of your annuity income that passes to your spouse the more it is going to cost you.

From April 2006 there is a way to pass on your pension fund even after you've used it to buy an annuity. Under a value-protected annuity, if you die before age 75, what's left in your pension fund goes to your named beneficiary, usually a spouse. However, there is a one-off tax charge of 35 per cent levied on the residue of the fund. A value protection annuity is only available up to the age of 75.

Making the Most of Lots of Little Pensions

It's likely you have more than one pension fund, and you may in fact have lots of small pensions. What to do with these little critters?

You have the following options:

- ✔ Transfer all into one pension.
- ✔ Cash them in.
- ✔ Leave them where they are.

Taking the pension transfer option

The attractions of pension transfer are plain to see. You put all your pensions under one roof, at a stroke easing your administrative burden. What's more, if you're in luck, your one super-charged pension may perform well.

However, often pension providers levy a charge for transferring funds. Some providers even charge you for transferring funds *into* a pension. Sometimes working with your pension can be a bit like living life as a pelican – everywhere you look you're confronted with a bill!

Cashing in your pensions

If you're a member of an occupational scheme for less than two years you're allowed a refund of your contributions – although not your employers' contributions – but the fund is taxed at a rate of 35 per cent.

Leaving your pensions alone

This may well be the best option. By leaving your pension schemes intact you avoid having to pay transfer charges and you benefit from investment diversity.

Most money experts agree that it's usually a bad idea to transfer from a company pension into a personal pension scheme. Often company pension schemes come with the guarantee that you receive a percentage of final salary for each year of service. What's more, some schemes even guarantee your spouse a pension on your death. Under a personal pension the size of your pension pot relies on investment performance – there are no guarantees. For the low-down on the different types of workplace pensions see Chapter 6.

Executing a Pension Transfer

Pension providers used to impose all sorts of penalties on investors for transferring their pension fund out. Put simply, they figured that if they made it difficult and expensive for people to transfer their pension they wouldn't bother. However, thankfully, those days are disappearing fast and it is now relatively easy and inexpensive to transfer a pension.

But just because it's getting easier to transfer a pension doesn't mean necessarily that you should ever do it.

You may choose pension transfer under the following circumstances:

✔ Your current pension is underperforming and you think you're better off if the money is invested elsewhere.

✔ Your current pension is small and you feel for ease of administration it would be worthwhile transferring it into a larger pension fund that you already hold.

✔ You have spotted a top-drawer pension which offers the panacea of investment choice and rock-bottom charges.

The older your pension plan, the more likely the provider is to charge a hefty fee for transfer out. Always check with your pension provider how much it costs to transfer your pension.

Some with-profits pensions levy a *market value adjuster* (MVA) on the funds of investors looking to transfer out. The insurance industry, which runs with-profits funds, tries to deny it but MVAs are nothing more than a pension penalty with a fancy name. Unfortunately it's hard to avoid exposure to this charge as most with-profits funds reserve the right to impose an MVA at any time.

Stakeholder pensions – a type of low-cost personal pension – as a rule don't charge their savers for transferring funds out. Stakeholder pensions are the easiest and cheapest type of pension to own. See Chapter 7 for the low-down on stakeholders.

If you decide that a pension transfer is the way to go simply follow the easy procedure below:

✔ Ask the provider of your pension for an estimate of how much your pension is worth if you transferred it out – this is called the transfer value. Pay particular attention to any penalties.

✔ Inform the providers or scheme administrator of the pension you'd like to transfer into. They should send you some forms to get the pension transfer ball rolling.

✔ The scheme you're transferring into should now contact the scheme you're leaving and between them they will sort out the transfer.

If you're transferring a pile of cash from one personal pension into another then it should be a cinch for the schemes to come to an agreement over the transfer value. But if you're transferring into or out of a final salary pension scheme – where benefits relate to final salary and number of years' service – then actuaries of the accepting and crediting scheme may have a job reaching agreement as to the right level of transfer value.

Dangers of Unlocking Your Pension

If you've ever watched daytime TV – and let's face it we've all watched an episode of *Trisha* at some low point in our lives – you've probably seen an advert from a firm offering to unlock your pension.

Unlocking a pension is advertising speak for taking pension benefits before you retire. If you're over 50 you may be able to draw benefits from your pension. However, according to no less an important body as the Financial Services Authority (FSA), the City regulator, it is rarely in your long-term interests to unlock a pension. Now the FSA, in my experience, is a rather staid safe organisation that doesn't like saying boo to a goose, so for it to say something is rarely in your long-term interests you know it's got to be a bad idea – in fact a monumentally bad idea.

Here are some reasons why, when you see those pensions unlocking adverts, you should simply switch over:

- ✔ If you draw pension benefits early you will have less – much less – to live on in retirement.
- ✔ If you're in money trouble then by unlocking your pension you may automatically bar yourself from state benefits.
- ✔ By drawing your pension you may lose in death-in-service benefits.
- ✔ Drawing your pension early may result in penalties being levied by your pension provider, further depleting your money pile.
- ✔ Daytime TV, which features the adverts, isn't good for your soul (I just threw that one in).
- ✔ And if that isn't all bad enough, firms offering to unlock your pension will no doubt charge you a great big fee for the privilege!

Check out the Financial Services Authority Web site for more on the dangers of pension unlocking – www.fsa.gov.uk. And if you're having money problems then you should go see your local Citizens Advice Bureau. Check out your phone book for the nearest branch or the CAB Web site on www.nacab.org.uk.

Keeping an eye on the creep of pension credit

Back in 2003 the government introduced pension credit. The idea was to boost the incomes of Britain's poorest pensioners – great, you may think. However, the government soon realised that people who had built up a small pension pot felt a bit miffed. After all they had made sacrifices during their working life to put money aside only for the government to come along and boost the incomes of those who hadn't put anything away.

So the government decided to 'reward' pensioners with small pensions by allowing them to claim a credit of 60p for every £1 of pension income – other than the state pension – up to £150.55 for single people and £220.83 for couples in the 2005–06 tax year.

Therefore we have an income element of pension credit – available to pensioners with very few means – and the savings element of pension credit – available to people with small pension pots. How does this affect your plans?

The government has said that it intends to raise these two credits in line with earnings for the next few years at least. This means that over time more and more pensioners are going to be able to claim pension credit. Some economists have suggested that eventually two thirds of pensioners may be able to claim either the income or savings element of pension credit.

Now some suggest this is a disincentive for people to save – they will either choose not to bother and rely on the income element or see the reward for saving as too small.

The government has recently woken up to these possibilities and has hinted that the pension credit may not be here to stay. Therefore, unless you are very close to retirement, you should not bank on the pension credit. Anyway, if you're serious about retiring wealthy you should be aiming to build up a cash pile so big that you'll be too busy sunning yourself on a beach to give a second thought to pension credit.

Keeping Your Nose to the Grindstone: Working Beyond Retirement

Some people can't wait to leave the world of work, but others find their job gives their life extra meaning. These people love the cut and thrust of the workplace and the camaraderie, although they probably draw the line at the work's canteen.

If you love rather than loathe work then as far as building up a big cash pile is concerned you should be quid's in. Put simply, the longer you work the more money you should accumulate for when you eventually decide to retire.

Here are some ways you can benefit from carrying on working:

- ✔ You can defer taking the state pension in return for a lump sum or higher pension income.
- ✔ You can continue to work for your employer while drawing your pension from the employer's workplace pension scheme.

If you have already paid enough National Insurance Contributions (NICs) to earn a full state pension you don't have to keep contributing after age 65 for men and 60 for women. You can save up to 11 per cent of your salary by not paying NICs.

Your pension and retiring abroad

Lots of us – me included – fancy spending a large chunk of our golden years in sunnier climes. But before selling your home in Luton to take up residence in Lisbon or trading Tamworth for Torremelinos, you need to give some thought to what you're going to live on when you get there, in other words, your retirement wealth pot.

If you leave the UK permanently (in tax parlance this is called *becoming non-resident*), you are no longer liable to pay tax on any overseas income, but you'll have to pay tax on this in your new country of residence. But income earned in the UK may be taxed in the UK and in your new country – two tax hits, ouch! Yet don't despair, if your new country of residence has what's called a *double taxation agreement* with the UK then you'll only have to pay one lot of tax on your income deriving from the UK – now that *is* a relief! Countries that have such agreements include: Australia, France, Ireland, New Zealand, South Africa, Spain, and the US.

If you receive a pension from the UK civil service or armed forces then that is taxed in the UK.

It's always worth bearing in mind that most western countries have higher taxes than the UK – you knew there was a reason why you put up with the awful weather!

The position with the UK state pension is even more complex. If you retire to an EU country the government will increase your pension every year, normally in line with UK inflation. However, if you retire outside the EU you may find that your state pension payments do not increase every year. This probably doesn't make much of a difference over one or two years but over 10, 15, or 20 you find your UK state pension buying you less and less.

For more details on your pension rights when retired abroad call the HM Revenue and Customs centre for non-residents on 0845 0700 040.

You may prefer a gradual retirement. This may involve you working part-time. Some pension schemes allow you to draw on a part of your pension while leaving the remainder untouched, helping you to augment the income that you earn from work.

Assessing Pension Alternatives

Lots of people don't like pensions and you can kind of understand why. Pensions are not very flexible – you normally can't get your money out until you're at least 50. What's more pensions with their promise of a steady income a long time into the future are hardly the stuff of seat-of-the-pants excitement.

Yet in one way pensions are risky. You can die before being able to cash in your pension. Think about it: You contribute for years and years only to get run over by a bus on the morning of your retirement from work – how very annoying!

If you simply can't abide pensions then you want to cast your eye over the alternative tactics you can deploy to reach your retiring wealthy goal:

✔ Instead of saving in a pension invest in property. This can offer the twin benefits of capital growth and investment income. See Chapter 15 for how to buy-to-let your way to a wealthy retirement.

✔ Make sure you use your full tax-free savings allowances. You're allowed to save up to £7,000 a year in a Maxi Individual Savings Account (ISA) tax-free. Over many years you can build up a tidy nest egg by using ISAs. What's more, you're free to spend any money in an ISA as you want and don't have to use any of it to buy an annuity. See Chapter 10 for more on tax-free savings.

If you're a UK taxpayer then you're building up entitlement to the UK state pension. Even if you hate pensions with a passion you shouldn't ignore your state pension – it can provide a useful base income in retirement. See Chapter 6 for more on the basic state pension.

Paying Extra: Boosting Your State and Work Pension

Your can boost the value of your state pension in the following ways:

✔ Making up any shortfall in your National Insurance Contribution (NICs) record to ensure your entitlement to a full basic state pension.

✔ Contributing to the State Second Pension (S2P), which pays a pension in addition to the basic state pension.

If you have a workplace pension you may be able to boost its value through the following ways:

✔ Making Additional Voluntary Contributions (AVCs) into a money purchase pension from your pre-tax salary.

✔ Increasing the level of contributions into your workplace pension.

If you're a member of a final salary pension scheme it may not be possible for you to increase your contributions – contributions levels are likely to be set by the scheme trustees at a percentage of salary. However, you're free to make AVCs or to open a separate personal pension into which you can make contributions. See Chapter 6 for more on final salary pensions.

Boosting a personal pension is a doddle – all you have to do is up your contributions. From April 2006 you're allowed to contribute 100 per cent of your income up to a maximum of £215,000.

Keeping Track of Your Pension

If you want to manage your pension affairs effectively it's essential to have a handle on where your money is invested and how well it's performing.

Every year, take a few hours to review your pension provision. Here's how to do it:

✔ Get a state pension forecast from The Pension Service, Tyneview Park, Whitley Road, Newcastle upon Tyne, NE98 1BA. You can also get a forecast online at www.thepension service.gov.uk/atoz/atozdetailed/rpforecast.asp.

✔ If you have a personal/workplace pension then you should get an annual statement telling you how much it's worth and how much you can expect it to be worth in retirement.

Part III
Building Up a Nest Egg: Saving and Investing

"Just _who_ recommended this financial advisor to you, Norman?"

In this part . . .

You can use the information in this part to really grow your wealth. I show you how you can make a little stretch a very long way through compound interest and long-term investment strategies. Included in this part is the full low-down on savings accounts, National Savings, bonds, and share investing. In fact, reading the chapters in this part makes you *au fait* with some of the most common and important savings and investment products you can use to make your retiring wealthy dream come true.

Chapter 10

Starting Out on Savings and Investments

. . . .

In This Chapter

▶ Being comfortable with risk

▶ Checking out low-, medium-, and high-risk savings and investments

▶ Building your low-risk base camp

▶ Homing in on National Savings

▶ Shopping around for a savings account

▶ Making the most of ISAs

. . . .

*I*n this chapter, I run through some of the core savings and investments available.

They may not be exotic but they really have their uses, providing you with a money base camp from which you can strike out for the retiring wealthy summit!

Knowing Your Risk Profile

Before making any investment – whether you're putting money into a building society savings account, purchasing shares, or buying bonds – it's crucial to ask yourself what you are truly looking to achieve.

Yes, you want to turn a little money into a lot – we all want that – but think again! There are probably some caveats you'd like to throw in.

You may think: I'd like to turn this £10,000 into a cool million but I don't fancy losing my original stake as I'd like to take the family to Florida this year. Life is chock full of priorities and you have to invest accordingly.

Investors can be broken down into three distinct groups according to how much risk they are ready, willing, and able to take on:

- ✔ Risk-takers.
- ✔ Middle-of-the-roaders.
- ✔ Safety-firsters.

Which one best describes you? Perhaps even a combination of all three.

Taking risks

Risk-takers are the real fly-boys and girls of the savings and investment world. They tend to be single-minded about their approach to money. They are willing to risk it all in the pursuit of turning their small pot of cash into a money mountain. This doesn't mean that they take stupid risks – beating on the door of the local casino every evening, for example – but when they do see an opportunity they go for it hook, line, and sinker. Their mantra is: 'You have to speculate to accumulate.'

Risk-takers may find that they go from rags to riches and back to rags again several times during their lives.

If you watch the movies or read the newspapers you can be forgiven for thinking that lots of investors are risk-takers, but in reality such people are few and far between.

The people most likely to be risk-takers are younger people with time on their hands to pick themselves up and dust themselves off if their investments go wrong.

Staying in the middle of the road

Middle-of-the-roaders want to make money just the same as the single-minded risk-takers, but they don't want to risk all in the pursuit of a whopping investment return. They are willing to take some risk and even possibly lose a substantial amount of money in the pursuit of wealth, but they also want to be sure that, if everything goes wrong, they have a backstop in place. A large percentage of people can be categorised as middle-of-the-roaders.

Those most likely to be middle-of-the-roaders are people in their 30s and 40s hoping to give their wealth a little pizzazz to push towards a level that can provide a comfy retirement. However, they still want to make sure that their current responsibilities such as paying the mortgage and children's education costs are met in full.

Putting safety first

Safety-firsters would obviously love to make lots of cash from their savings and investments but realise that to do so they will have to take risks – risks they are not prepared for. They believe the safe slow accumulation of wealth over time is preferable to the seat of the pants existence of the risk-takers. They don't ask much, just to get rich slowly!

Having read all three of these descriptions you probably recognise yourself in them either today or in the past. The truth is that few investors stay a risk-taker, middle-of-the-roader, or safety-firster all their life. As life's priorities change so does your investment outlook.

Therefore, it's a smart ploy before you start saving and investing to assess where your life is at, what responsibilities you have, and what you're looking to achieve.

Getting the Investment Balance Right

Determining what kind of savings or investment product you should go for is important – high-risk, medium-risk, or low-risk. If you go to see a financial adviser or independent financial adviser (IFA) they will go on about having a balanced approach to investment. Essentially this means having the right proportion of high-, medium-, and low-risk savings and investments for your personal circumstances.

If you'd like to know the right level of risk for you the Financial Services Authority (FSA) – the body which regulates the financial industry – has a free online test you can take. Check out www.fsa.org.uk for more details.

If you go to see a financial adviser or IFA they're duty bound to do a risk assessment on you. This doesn't mean talking to you and deciding whether you're to be trusted with sharp objects, it simply means assessing whether you have the financial security to cope if the investment they recommend goes pear-shaped. In the past, many financial advisers and IFAs have been found guilty of recommending investments which were too risky for the investor. This process is called mis-selling. See Chapter 5 for more on mis-selling and how financial advisers and IFAs work.

Telling High Risk from Low Risk

If a stranger sidled up to you in the pub and offered to be back next week with £10 if you give him £5 today, you'd be justified to view this as a risky – one can say foolhardy – investment. But not all savings and investment products are as simple as the lend-me-a-fiver routine in the pub.

High-, medium-, and low-risk savings and investments all have individual characteristics which mark them out as such. Know the tell-tale signs and you will be able to judge high-risk from low-risk products.

Some financial firms brand their products as high-, medium-, or low-risk investments. Don't just take their word for it. There have been many mis-selling scandals where a firm has said something is low-risk in marketing literature only for it to prove a highly dangerous investment, which ends in tears for those investors who believed the hype.

Understanding low-risk investments

Low risk does exactly what it says on the tin – your money grows (probably not very fast) but is always safe.

In general, all low-risk investments should share the following characteristics:

- ✔ **The original investment is guaranteed:** Products such as deposit savings accounts promise to pay back all the original stake plus interest.

- ✔ **The institution offering the investment or savings is trustworthy:** It stands to reason that £500 paid into a savings account with a High Street bank or building society is less at risk than the same amount held in a savings account with a bank offshore.

- ✔ **Returns tend to be steady if unspectacular:** Most low-risk investments have a guaranteed rate of return which you know at the outset. This is true of most National Savings products for example.

Typically, low-risk investments include:

- ✔ Deposit savings accounts.
- ✔ National Savings investments and savings accounts.
- ✔ Government bonds.
- ✔ Some blue-chip company bonds and life insurance bonds.

Deposit accounts and National Savings are examined in detail later in this chapter, while bonds are the focus of Chapter 11.

All major UK banks and building societies are members of the Financial Services Compensation Scheme. The scheme guarantees to refund depositors their money should the bank or building society go bust. Bear in mind though the scheme will only pay a maximum of £31,700 to savers.

Some low-risk savings accounts promise to pay a higher rate of interest as long as you agree to leave your money alone for a set period of time, anything up to say five years. This is all fine and dandy unless an emergency strikes and you need the cash quickly. We examine the option of going for higher interest at the expense of tying up your money later in this chapter.

Understanding medium-risk investments

Under a medium-risk investment you accept that you may lose a fair bit of your original stake but in return, if things go right, then your money will grow faster than if you stuck to low risk.

Medium-risk investments share the following characteristics:

- **You may lose part of your stake:** To accumulate you need to speculate – a little. However, in reality, a medium-risk invest-ment is unlikely to shrink to nothing.

- **They are usually meant for the medium or long term:** Medium-risk investments are likely to go through periods of underperformance and outperformance. This means that they should be allowed to run for at least five years allowing the peaks and troughs of underperformance and outperfor-mance to be smoothed out.

- **They are often related in some way to the stock market:** Most medium-risk investments depend for their growth on share price increases or companies paying dividends.

Medium-risk investments should not be embarked upon unless you're happy to leave your money in place for a minimum of five years.

Typical medium-risk investments include:

- Some collective stock market investments such as unit trusts or investment trusts.

- Some bonds issued by large- and medium-sized companies.

- Deposits held in offshore accounts.

> ✔ With-profits bonds issued by insurance companies.
>
> ✔ Guaranteed bonds which invest part of your money in the stock market and the rest is held in a deposit account.

Most medium-risk investments are usually managed on a day-to-day basis by a financial institution. For example, a fund investing in a basket of shares needs someone to decide which shares to invest in. This doesn't come free and investors are often asked to pay an initial charge and ongoing fees.

Some investments move from medium to high risk and vice versa over time. For example, an investment in a fund which invests in UK property may have been considered medium risk when property prices were rising sharply, but now that prices have stagnated or are fallen in some areas (at the time of writing) the same investment may be viewed as high risk.

Understanding high-risk investments

These types of investments are real seat-of-the-pants stuff. In many respects they are akin to gambling in that you risk losing your entire stake all in the hope of making a killing.

High-risk investments usually have the following characteristics:

> ✔ **They can be short term in nature:** Taking a risk often means exploiting a market opportunity. Investments can be made and then sold again a few minutes later. This though isn't always the case, if an investment proves a winner you may carry on with it, sitting back and simply enjoying watching the cash roll in.
>
> ✔ **There are no guarantees:** Put simply, you can lose all your original stake and with investments such as spread betting you can lose far more besides.
>
> ✔ **They depend on market moves:** High-risk investments are usually wedded and chained to growth or otherwise in the stock market or commodity markets. Your fortunes may be linked to those men and women you see on the TV news in those bright coloured jackets tick tacking on the dealing floor – yikes!

High-risk investments usually run for the short term but not always. Some high-risk investments work by tying up your money for a long time while in return giving you the chance of making a real killing when your investment matures. For example, venture capital trusts (VCTs), where you invest in a fund which in turn invests in start up firms, offer the prospect of stellar growth but only if you tie up your money for many years. See Chapter 17 for more on VCTs.

Typical high-risk investments include:

- ✔ Direct investment in shares of medium-size and small companies.
- ✔ Derivatives and other specialist stock market or commodity investments.
- ✔ Bonds issued by smaller or start up companies.
- ✔ Spread betting and venture capital trusts.

It's fair to say that the risks associated with some investments defined here as simply high risk can vary wildly. Direct investment in shares is deemed to be high risk but it's undoubtedly far riskier to invest in the shares of a start up Internet firm than it is in say a medium-sized company employing a few thousand staff.

Some investments disguise themselves as high risk but may just simply be a con. There are a plethora of dodgy unregulated firms out there offering equally dodgy investments.

Whether a savings or investment is high-, medium-, or low-risk partly depends on your personal and financial circumstances. For example buying £100 worth of shares is not really risky for a millionaire but can be considered highly risky if the £100 came from someone who only had a few hundred pounds to call their own.

Being ultra cautious may mean little or no reward

There is a trade-off between risk and reward. Generally, low-risk investments offer the least reward.

Take the experience of two brothers, Sanjeev and Husnan. Back in 1994 both Sanjeev and Husnan were each given £100 to invest by their father. Sanjeev went down the ultra cautious route and decided to save his £100 in a building society savings account. By 2004 his £100 had grown into £170. After rising prices were factored in Sanjeev's return looks even more miserly. On the other hand, Husnan invested his £100 gift into a basket of UK company shares. By 2004 Husnan's original £100 had grown into £365, so even after rising prices were factored in he made a nice tidy pile.

If you decide to go down the ultra cautious route you're unlikely to enjoy high returns, in fact the best you can hope for is to do a little better than inflation and get rich slow.

Taking an ultra cautious approach to savings and investments is not a passport to retiring wealthy unless you can think of some way of maximising your revenue streams.

The older you are the more sensible it is to be a safety-first investor. Risking all in your golden years can mean losing it all and you may not have time to make the money back.

 Most financial advisers and IFAs recommend that as you get older you shift out of high-risk to low-risk investment. In fact, it's pretty common for financial advisers and IFAs to tell their clients to sell up risky investments as they get older – even if these investments are performing well – in order to collect the profit and reduce risk.

Building Your Savings and Investment Base Camp

So you can spot your low-, medium-, and high-risk investments and you've taken on board the pros and cons of each. Now what do you do with your knowledge?

The key to being able to retire wealthy isn't really about taking silly risks – putting everything on black in the casino. Unless you're very lucky – and luck has a huge hand to play in high-risk investing – that way retirement poverty lies, not wealth.

A good plan is to build a nest egg of savings and investments which gives you the confidence – the bedrock if you like – to take a few risks to achieve better returns.

Think of your retiring wealthy project as trying to scale a tall mountain. You need to have provisions in place and a base camp before making a bid for the summit.

Low-risk savings and investments make up your retiring wealthy base camp.

 If you'd like to know what are the highest paying savings accounts log onto www.moneyfacts.co.uk for an up-to-date list.

 You may have to pay tax on any growth in your savings and investments. If you're a higher rate taxpayer you may end up paying 40 per cent of whatever you earn through your savings account or investment to HM Revenue and Customs. This is despite the fact that you may already have paid tax on the money when you earned it in the first place. See later in this chapter for ways to save and invest tax efficiently.

Beating the inflation rap

As a saver or investor the absolute bottom line is to secure a return which beats the rate of retail price inflation (RPI), currently between 2.5 and 3 per cent. Fail to beat this level of return and you actually lose money on your savings and investments in relative terms.

It's actually easier than you think for your savings and investments to fail to beat RPI. The investment may perform poorly for a start. For example, in 2002 shares listed on the London Stock exchange lost close to a quarter of their value at the same time RPI increased by around 3 per cent. So people who invested in shares during that time were hit with the double whammy of seeing their investment lose money while the cost of living grew.

Surprisingly, there are literally dozens of bank and building society savings accounts out there which pay a lower rate of interest than the RPI. Why do customers stick with these poor paying accounts? The answer is that they have taken their eye off the ball and they are actually getting poorer as a result. If you know someone in this position, buy them a copy of *Retiring Wealthy for Dummies* and get them to mend their ways!

Not only should you be looking to beat RPI you should also be aiming to achieve a little bit extra as a reward for not having spent the money in the first place.

Homing in on National Savings

National Savings are government run, have been around for donkeys' years, and are widely seen as the safest way to save and invest. They are guaranteed by the UK government and the money is used to bolster the public finances.

But safety comes at a cost: National Savings generally don't pay a high rate of interest.

The first National Savings account was introduced in 1861, the catchily titled *ordinary account* – those crazy Victorian marketing men! The ordinary account was still on sale until 2004.

Choosing the right National Savings for you

National Savings offer lots of different products, outlined in Table 10-1.

Table 10-1   National Savings Products

Product	Advantages	Disadvantages	Who do they best suit?
Premium bonds			
The most famous and fun National Savings investments. You buy bonds in £100 blocks and these are entered into a monthly prize draw. Prizes range from £50 up to £1,000,000 and are paid tax-free. You don't earn interest but you can surrender your bonds at anytime to receive your original stake back. The maximum you are allowed to invest is £30,000.	You can dip in and out of Premium Bonds very easily. You can buy them over the phone, Internet, or at the Post Office. They are fun and offer the chance of scooping a mega prize. There are no penalties for surrendering your bondsand getting your money back.	Premium Bonds aren't a standard investment. You are gambling not with the original stake but with the interest you can have earned if you'd put your money in a mainstream savings account or investment. You may never win!	Just about anyone who likes the idea of mixing investment with fun! The fact that you are leaving everything to chance means that this shouldn't be the mainstay of your retirement pot. Then again, if your Premium Bond was to scoop the £1,000,000 jackpot tomorrow then in one big leap you're across the retiring wealthy finishing line.
Fixed rate and capital bonds			
You agree to hand over your money. In return, at the end of three or five years, you get your money back plus a pre-agreed rate of interest.	It does exactly what it says on the tin and the return is guaranteed while the capital is not in jeopardy. You get your original stake plus a tidy sum in interest – what can be simpler? Interest is reinvested in the capital bond each year, which means that you don't touch the interest until the three or five year term is up.	In order to get the rate of return on offer you have to agree to tie up your money for a three or five year period. This is a long time, so you shouldn't agree to it unless you know you will not need the money in the interim. In addition, interest rates and inflation can rise sharply while your money is tied up. If this happens you may have been better off putting your money into an investment linked to the rise in prices. See below for more information.	Savers who want to know exactly what the investment return will be.

Product	Advantages	Disadvantages	Who do they best suit?
Income bonds			
Pay a regular income. Interest is paid gross though it is taxable. The interest rate is variable which means it moves up and down. People buying an income bond agree that they will give up to 90 days notice before before taking their money.	The payment of a regular monthly income allows the investor to plan. They can use this income to live off or meet a specific regular expense such as paying for a child to go through college.	Not very useful for people looking to build up a retirement pot as the original sum invested does not grow. The sole purpose of this investment is to provide an income.	Interest is paid gross which makes this investment ideal for non-taxpayers, such as pensioners earning too little money to pay income tax – £4,895 in the 2005–06 tax year.
Index linked savings certificates			
Offer to pay a rate of interest in excess of the retail price index (RPI). The investment grows a little faster than prices over the long term. Normally only available for a limited period – once they're gone they're gone, so if you see a good deal you have to go for them in double quick time.	Tax free and can be held by anyone. Linking returns to inflation guarantees the investment will not be eroded by inflation.	Normally only pay a little bit more than inflation. You can usually find a higher rate of interest elsewhere. Again you have to tie your up for a set period of time and if you want it back early you will be penalised.	Higher rate tax-payers who want to earn interest free of tax. People who want to be sure that their savings will earn more than inflation.

(continued)

Table 10-1 *(continued)*

Product	Advantages	Disadvantages	Who do they best suit?
Fixed interest savings certificates			
Essentially the same as index linked savings certificates, except that a guaranteed rate of return is provided rather than one linked to increases in prices.	Tax-free and can be held by anyone. The fixed rate on offer may well beat price inflation comfortably.	You have to tie your money up for a set period of time and if you want it back early you will be penalised. There is no automatic guarantee that your savings will grow faster than inflation.	Higher rate taxpayers who want to earn interest free of tax.
Standard savings accounts and cash ISAs			
The National Savings version of savings account. You can manage the bank or building society your savings account at Post Offices. National Savings also offers an ISA savings account. With this type of account interest earned is tax-free.	Interest accrues over time and you can withdraw your cash at reasonably short notice. They can be very easy to manage.	You can get a higher rate of return by going to a bank or building society. In reality a bank or building society is as safe a home for your money as National Savings.	Targeted at everyone. Literally millions of Britons have these types of savings account.

All National Savings and Investments are *capital secure*, which means that no matter what happens you are guaranteed to get back your original investment at the very least.

Some National Savings products such as index-linked and fixed-rate savings certificates pay interest free of tax.

Some people in the press and financial advisers are critical of National Savings. They argue that higher returns can be had elsewhere. Nevertheless, National Savings are the UK's favourite investment choice. The security that they offer appeals to young and old alike.

You can check out National Savings and Investments products at www.nsandi.com.

Using National Savings in your big plan

National Savings are government run and have never been very generous – no surprise there! If you're looking to make your fortune in quick time then National Savings are not the place for all your money.

But they do have some key advantages that should make you consider them as a something to form part of your investment base camp:

- ✔ They are rock solid and safe.
- ✔ All investments are capital protected – you get back every penny you invest.
- ✔ Some investments are guaranteed to beat inflation.
- ✔ There is the chance to win very big indeed through Premium Bonds.
- ✔ Some investments such as cash ISAs and savings certificates pay interest tax-free.

Shopping Around for a Savings Account

National Savings aren't the only investment you should consider for your retiring wealthy base camp. Banks and building society savings accounts offer nearly identical security and often pay a higher rate of interest.

There are hundreds of accounts to choose from but stick to the ones that pay the highest rate of interest as this way your pot of money will grow fastest.

Banks and building societies offer stepped interest rates. This means the larger the amount of cash you put into the account the higher the rate of interest you earn.

It's unlikely that the bank you have your current account with will offer the best rate of return so you need to shop around for a savings account.

Fortunately, there are lots of free financial comparison Web sites to help you track down the highest paying account. These include:

- www.moneyfacts.co.uk
- www.moneysupermarket.com
- www.moneynet.co.uk
- Best buy tables in national newspapers and on Ceefax page 251

Some account providers offer the facility for you to bundle your accounts together with those of family members in order to earn a higher rate of interest. For example, if you and your mother have £5,000 each in separate accounts with the same provider bundling can help you earn the rate of interest that would normally only be paid on balances of £10,000 or more. Crucially, in all ways apart from calculating interest, the accounts remain completely separate.

Notice account or instant access?

Choosing a savings account is not just a matter of picking the one that pays the highest rate of interest. Some accounts ask you to give notice when you want to withdraw cash or close the account.

It's a little like giving notice at work: You have to stay committed for a pre-agreed period of time, but there's nothing to stop you spending the day surfing the net and making hourly trips to Starbucks!

The length of notice on a savings account may vary from 30 days right up to a whopping 180 days. You can get out of this notice period and get your money straight away but you will have to pay a penalty of loss of interest.

Instant access means that there is no penalty for getting your hands on the money in the account.

Very few accounts are genuinely instant access. For example the account may be managed over the phone or Internet and it may take a few days to electronically transfer money from the savings account to a current account. It usually takes between three and five days for money leaving a savings account to appear in your current account.

It used to be the case that notice accounts rewarded loyalty by paying higher interest than instant access. But in recent years banks and building societies have been competing for instant access account business. As far as they are concerned instant access is cheaper and easier to administer. Many of the highest paying accounts these days are instant access. So why agree to a notice period?

Jumping through the identity hoops

The days when you could simply trot up to your nearest bank or building society, slap some notes on the counter, and open a savings account are long gone. These days, banks and building societies want to see two or three pieces of ID before they let you open an account.

The idea is to deter money laundering – for one thing the ink can run! – by making it easier for the authorities to know what money belongs to whom.

You need separate ID that proves who you are and where you live.

- ✔ ID that proves who you are includes passport, photo driving licence, firearms certificate, police warrant card, birth certificate, pension book, or armed services ID.

- ✔ ID that proves where you live includes utility or council tax bill, credit card or bank statement, tax notification from HM Revenue and Customs (formerly the Inland Revenue).

Most banks and building societies insist that the ID proving address is very recent, within the last three months. Some bizarrely insist that if it's a bill it has been paid – there is no way of proving this so they just end up taking your word for it!

Banks and building societies are free to choose which ID they accept or don't accept, so you may find that one will agree to a firearms certificate while the one next door won't. Check with the bank or building society which ID is acceptable. Some tend to be flexible, others act like real 'jobs-worths'.

National Savings and Investments don't automatically require people opening new accounts to produce ID.

Financial advisers still try and encourage people to open notice accounts because having to give notice discourages people from dipping into their savings for non-emergencies.

Being prepared to move your money regularly means that you are better able to take advantage of the best offers in the marketplace. The savings market is very competitive and you should look to exploit this fact to the max by being what is commonly called a 'rate tart', ready to move your cash to the account provider paying the highest rate of interest. So keep a close eye on the interest rate on your account!

Letting compound interest work its magic

Interest rates paid on savings accounts are a million miles away from being sexy. The prospect of earning £4 or £5 in interest for tying up a £100 in a savings account for an entire year hardly sets the pulse racing!

But over the long term something great happens to savings. Interest adds up – it compounds – and over the years a little pile of cash can turn into a mountain.

Take £100 earning 5 per cent interest a year. This will double to £200 not in 20 years but in fewer than 15 because of compound interest. See Chapter 3 for more on compound interest.

Making the Most of ISAs

When it comes to building up a retirement pot one of your big enemies – surprise, surprise! – is HM Revenue and Customs.

Savings are taxed at a minimum 20 per cent, while profits made from share investments are subject to Capital Gains Tax. Any way that you can use to protect your savings and investments from tax needs to be grabbed with both hands.

Reducing your tax bill is the subject of Chapter 21, but as far as your savings and investments are concerned there is one quick fix to diffuse the tax bombshell. You can wrap your savings in what is called an Individual Savings Account or ISA for short.

Strings on the ISA tax break

Sadly there is no such thing as a free lunch – believe me I have looked everywhere for one!

ISAs offer a valuable tax break but there are rules:

✔ Once your money has left an ISA it can be subject to tax as normal.

✔ Annual ISA limits are just that – once you've reached them you can't invest more until the following tax year.

✔ You have to be over 18 to open one and supply appropriate ID. See 'Jumping through the identity hoops' earlier in this chapter.

Putting your money in an ISA means it can grow free of tax. This is of most benefit when it comes to money held with a bank or building society as this automatically attracts tax.

Usually when money is invested in say bonds or shares it only attracts tax when it is taken out of the investment, and then only if the profit made means that the investor has enjoyed capital gains above the annual Capital Gains Tax (CGT) limit (£8,500 in the 2005–06 tax year).

There are two types of ISA, which both sound like two old British cars – Mini and Maxi. The rules governing Mini and Maxi ISAs are as follows:

✔ **Mini ISAs:** With mini ISAs you can invest your money in any of the following in any one tax year: Cash up to £3,000; stocks and shares up to £4,000. You can choose a different ISA manager for each mini ISA you take out if you want.

✔ **Maxi ISAs:** With a maxi ISA you can invest up to £7,000 a year in stocks and shares or in a collective investment such as a unit or investment trust.

You can use your annual ISA limits to build up a tidy nest egg in just a few years. If you save the maximum amount of money in an ISA for 20 years you would have put away £140,000, all growing tax-free.

Dividends earned from shares held in an ISA are taxed at a rate of 10 per cent. If you're a higher rate taxpayer this represents a saving because normally dividends would be taxed at a rate of 32.5 per cent.

You can only pay into one maxi ISA in a tax year and all your investment must be held with the same ISA manager.

Making sure you make use of your annual mini cash ISA limit is a bit of a no-brainer. ISAs are popular and banks and building societies often save some of their best offers to attract people looking to open an ISA.

Chapter 11

Exploiting Bonds to Boost Your Wealth Prospects

*Y*ou may not have heard a great deal about bonds. Unlike the property market, they aren't a big topic of conversation at dinner parties. And at first glance they don't offer seat-of-the-pants style get rich quick potential like shares.

Bonds also don't have films made about them like Wall Street. When Michael Douglas's character Gordon Gekko said 'Greed is good' he wasn't talking about thirty-year index linked government gilts, I can tell you!

But this doesn't mean you should leave bonds in the investment equivalent of the remainder bin – not at all. Particularly in recent times, they have become much loved by investors in the know. When stock markets stumbled bonds continued to stride forwards.

The name bond gives a clue to the inner beauty of this investment: They can offer a high degree of security, something certainly not to be sniffed at as you make your way up the retiring wealthy path.

In this chapter, I outline everything you need to know to become a bond investor.

What Is a Bond?

A *bond* is a loan made by the investor to a company or country's government called the bond issuer.

The bond issuer agrees to pay regular interest to the bondholder and then to repay the original investment on a set date in the future. On this date the bond is said to have *matured* – which doesn't mean that it can vote or go to the pub!

The big thing about bonds is that they offer investors certainty. No wonder such investments are often referred to as *fixed interest* or *fixed income*.

But that's not all that bonds are about. A market exists to buy and sell bonds after they have been issued. This second-hand bond market is absolutely huge with pension funds and insurance companies its major players, selling and buying billions of pounds worth of bonds every day.

 Bonds fit into three main categories according to how long they have left until they mature. A bond that has less than five years to maturity is known as a *short*, from five to fifteen years it's a *medium*, over fifteen and it's called a *long*.

The value of a bond can vary widely during its lifespan. See later in this chapter for more on what determines the price of bonds on the bond market.

Nevertheless, the amount the bondholder gets back on maturity or the interest paid do not alter (apart from bonds that link their interest payment to the inflation rate called *index-linked bonds*).

Pricing bonds

Unlike company share prices, which can move sharply for the most obscure reasons, the price of a bond is determined by three factors:

- ✔ **Interest rates in the economy:** Investors buy bonds for the interest on offer. It's only worthwhile purchasing them if the rate on offer is better than that available through a bank or building society.

- ✔ **The credit rating of the bond issuer:** How safe is the country or company issuing the bond? See later in this chapter for more on credit ratings.

✓ **The length of time before maturity:** The longer there is to go before maturity the greater the risk of an interest rate change or the issuer defaulting. Longer-dated bonds should pay a higher rate of interest to compensate investors for the increased risk.

Rising interest rates and inflation can catch bond investors out. Say an investor buys a long bond. A few years down the line interest rates may rise in the economy and a better return on the money may be available from a bank or building society account. If the investor then tries to sell the bond on, they will not get a high price for it.

Some government bonds promise that regular interest payments match or beat the rate of inflation rather than just pay a pre-set rate of interest. These index-linked bonds or gilts are ultra-safe as the investors' returns can never fall behind price growth – something that can happen with a standard bond or gilt. But there's a catch (you knew there had to be one) – the interest rate starts off much lower than a standard bond or gilt because no risk pricing is built in. In other words, the issuer pays no extra interest to compensate the investor for the risk that prices and interest rates in the economy will rise sharply during the life of the bond or gilt.

If you buy bonds issued by a foreign government you are taking a currency risk. If your money grows in value against the pound while it is tied up in a foreign currency then you'll lose out. For example, if you invest £100 in US Treasury bonds for 10 years during which time the pound halves in value against the dollar, you only get back £50 when the bond matures.

Some bonds issued by the UK government during the First and Second World Wars had no redemption date. These *war bonds* keep running and running until the government decides that it wants to pay back the original capital invested.

Buyer's guide to government bonds

If you're patriotic the following sentence may make you puff your chest out in pride: Bonds issued by the UK government are amongst the world's safest investments. The government issues what are often called *Treasury Bonds* or *gilts* to raise money for public spending. Pension funds and insurers lap them up because they know that no matter what else happens the UK government will pay out at maturity.

But as with everything else in the investment universe this security comes at a cost. The interest rate available on government bonds is often pretty low. But nevertheless you may consider that a sacrifice worth making.

Why buy bonds?

Well, to make money, of course! But bonds offer more than just a steady supply of readies. Buyers can enjoy the following extra benefits:

- **They balance an investment portfolio:** Bonds are a middle-of-the-road, medium-risk investment. Usually bonds pay a higher rate of interest than savings accounts without being as risky as investing in shares.

- **They offer certainty:** The fact that bonds have a date when they pay out means that investors can plan their finances for the arrival of a nice fat cheque at a specified date in the future.

 People often use bonds when they are saving for a particular expected future event such as paying for children to go to university or their own retirement.

Comparing Bonds and Shares

Companies issue both shares and bonds to raise cash for investment. Shareholders buy a part of the company, while bondholders buy a promise to have their investment repaid plus interest at a future date. But the differences between bonds and shares don't end there, as Table 11-1 explains.

Table 11-1   Differences between Shares and Bonds

Characteristic	Shares	Bonds
Lifespan	Once issued they carry on until the company ceases to exist, either because it goes to the wall or the shares are bought during a takeover or the firm itself buys back its own shares.	Fixed lifespan. The investor knows when the bond issuer will stop paying regular interest and give back the original investment.
Payment	Dividends are paid when things are going well with the company. The size and regularity of this dividend are entirely at the company's discretion.	A specific rate of return at regular intervals. This makes bonds a more certain investment than shares.

Characteristic	Shares	Bonds
Ownership	Shareholders own the company. They get invited to an annual general meeting (AGM) where they can vote on whether the board of directors should stay or not.	Bondholders don't get to sample the refreshments at the AGM and have no say in who runs the company.
Volatility	Day in day out share prices are far more volatile than bond prices.	Bonds can lose value on the open market, but the transition from star investment to absolute dud can be a lot more gradual than with shares.

Which are better, bonds or shares?

As far as long-term performance goes, money invested in shares comfortably outperforms cash ploughed into bonds. During the second half of the twentieth century bond prices grew at a far slower rate than shares.

Case closed then – ignore bonds and buy shares? Er, no. The performance of shares may have knocked that of bonds into a cocked hat over the long term but in recent years and for relatively long periods in the past bonds have returned more to investors than shares. Who is to say that during the five, ten, or fifteen years you have your money invested won't be a period when bonds once again beat shares. In fact, some money experts have suggested that since the bursting of the dotcom share price bubble we have entered a new era when bonds once again have the whip hand over shares and that this may last for decades.

If you want to take the balanced approach to retiring wealthy you shouldn't really think of choosing to buy *either* bonds or shares, instead you should look at buying *both* bonds and shares. Who knows what the future holds?

Hedging your share bets with bonds

Private investors are increasingly turning on to bonds. The bond market often moves in the opposite direction to equities. When shares are doing well bonds tend to do poorly and vice versa.

Bonds that don't act as a stock market hedge

Some types of bond don't work well as a hedge for investments in shares because they rely in part on the stock market to produce returns.

These bonds, known as hybrids, work by splitting investors' money into two – half goes into a savings account while the other half is invested in the stock market. If the money invested in the stock market does well the investor gets all or part of this growth. If, on the other hand, the stock market investment does poorly then the investor still has their original stake returned or in some cases 90 per cent of their original cash, as the interest earned on the half paid into the savings account is used to make good the losses on the stock market investment. These types of investment are often referred to as guaranteed bonds, because of the promise that even if things go wrong the investor will get most or all their original investment back.

Hybrid bonds are a pretty clever product, offering investors a taste of the stock market but backed up with the security of a standard savings account. And in recent years more and more banks and building societies have been offering this type of bond.

The reason for this is that pension funds and other major investors often sell shares when the stock market takes a tumble – this money has to go somewhere and apart from property the only other home for it is the bond market. What's more, bonds are generally safer than shares and this means that when there are economic problems investor money tends to flow where it's safest – bonds or cash on deposit. Therefore, as share prices fall demand for bonds tends to increase.

 You probably already own a fair number of bonds without even realising it. Bonds are bought in absolutely huge quantities by all pension funds. Therefore, buy a pension and you are in effect investing in bonds.

You can use this to your advantage. Many investors use bonds to balance their share investments. The hope is that if one type of investment is performing poorly the other will be doing well. In investment lingo this is called *hedging*.

However, hedging share investments with bonds isn't an exact science. At some points in the past both the bond market and the share market have taken a fall, particularly when there is a major world recession or currency crisis.

Bonds are usually safer than shares but not always. For example, a share in a multinational bank or oil company is probably a safer bet than buying a bond in a medium or small company. See later in this chapter for more details.

Using Bonds in Your Big Plan

Investing in bonds isn't a question of all or nothing. You shouldn't look to plough your entire fortune into them as they do come with risk but neither should you ignore them.

The key is to use bonds alongside as part of an overarching investment strategy. The watchword is diversity.

Use savings accounts and pensions as your base, providing you with short-term flexibility in the case of savings and long-term security with pensions. But neither your pension nor your savings account is likely to be a performance world-beater – you need to inject a little bit of growth to reach your retiring wealthy goal. This is usually the point at which property and shares come into the equation.

But hang on a minute – bonds can occupy their very own place in the risk middle ground between pensions and savings on one side and property and share investment on the other. Sometimes unloved, bonds are nevertheless unique as they offer a great degree of security and growth that can often be above that on offer through a savings account.

 The returns on bonds generally reflect the risk associated with them. The higher the risk of the bond the greater the return you can expect if the investment proves a sound one.

If you're looking to construct a truly balanced investment portfolio you should at least consider banking on bonds.

 Sometimes tying up your money in a long-term investment such as a bond can be a good move as it imposes a financial straightjacket which stops you from spending the cash on non-emergencies.

When it's unwise to use bonds

It's fair to say that the financial health warnings associated with bonds aren't as severe as is the case with shares. But this doesn't make them an absolutely rock solid investment in the same way as, say, National Savings.

Avoiding dodgy bonds

Financial product providers love the word bond. They know that in the minds of investors it suggests that their money is safe and the returns constant.

Bonds tend to appeal to people in late middle age, often close to retirement, who have plenty of cash to invest. As far as financial firms are concerned finding a product that appeals to these fifty and sixty somethings is equivalent to winning the lottery.

So guess what's been happening? The word bond has been used by financial firms to describe products that are a million miles away from the safety and security offered by, for example, UK government bonds.

The most recent scandal involved people being sold so called *High Income bonds* – the only part that was high, it turned out, was the high chance that the investor would lose their cash!

These products worked as follows: The investor was guaranteed a regular income but whether they got back their original stake depended on how the stock market performed. If it rose all was well they received an income – drawn from the growth in the stock market – and at maturity their original investment back.

But as it turned out the stock market fell and while investors still got their income their original investment shrank. This was because the money to provide the guaranteed income had to come straight from the original investment – as the stock market was not producing returns.

The original investment was caught in a nutcracker: It fell in line with the stock market and was further eroded by the guaranteed income. Result: Honest, hard working people had their life savings wiped out!

This whole sorry mess became known as the *precipice bond* scandal.

The regulator, the Financial Services Authority (FSA), has stamped down on the use of words like 'bond' and 'guaranteed' by product providers. But be on the lookout: Because a product uses the word bond or guaranteed doesn't mean that it's safe. Here are a few ways to protect yourself:

✔ Check on the FSA Web site that the firm is authorised to offer investments – if it isn't, the product's a scam!

✔ Take financial advice from a qualified professional before taking the plunge.

✔ Read the small print thoroughly. Ask yourself a simple question: Is my original investment 100 per cent guaranteed?

Sometimes an investor's financial circumstances are such that a medium-risk investment such as bonds is inappropriate. Bonds may not suit under the following scenarios:

✔ **The investor is new to saving:** Before taking the plunge into bonds it's important to have an easily accessible cash float which can help meet short-term emergencies. Rainy day savings are explored in Chapter 3.

✔ **The investor is going for growth:** An investor looking for growth may be better off buying shares or property.

If you feel that you fit into either of the above categories you should steer clear of bonds for the time being or at the very least seek financial advice from a qualified professional before investing. See Chapter 5 for more on how to find an independent financial adviser (IFA).

Getting to grips with bond credit ratings

The rate of interest paid by the bond issuer isn't the only factor to consider when buying a bond. Another major factor is whether the bond issuer will be able to pay the money promised on the due date.

After all, a bond promising to pay a whopping rate of interest is very nice, but if that proves to be just hot air the investor loses out – big time.

Bonds are issued by all sorts of organisations from the US Treasury to start-up cutting-edge technology firms. The US Treasury will pay up on the due date while the start-up firm may not be around to pay up. However, risk is reflected in the rate of interest on offer – the greater the risk the higher the rate of interest up for grabs.

Fortunately, money experts have drawn up a code so you can tell at a glance whether the bond issuer is as safe as houses or a risky gamble. The code isn't as difficult to decipher as the De Vinci code, you just need to know your alphabet.

The highest credit rating (the safest investments) is AAA, followed by AA, A, BAA, BA, BBB, BB, B all the way down to D. Plus and minus signs are also thrown in as well to add a few extra pointers. Essentially, the earlier the letter in the alphabet and the more letters used, the lower the risk. These bond ratings are not only used in the City – they are found in company analyst reports and sometimes the *Financial Times* newspaper.

A company or country doesn't just decide that it has an AAA or BB credit rating, it has to be awarded by a credit rating agency such as Standard & Poor's, Moody's, or Fitch. Credit rating agencies employ literally hundreds of analysts to pour over company accounts, and what they find dictates the credit rating awarded.

The highest credit rating – AAA – is reserved for bonds issued by governments from the world's largest economies including the US and UK. In addition, bonds issued by some major banks and other financial institutions also attract a triple A rating.

At the other end of the scale, the lowest credit rating, D, is normally reserved for firms that have fallen on hard times. These firms may have large debts and dwindling assets. Alternatively, they may be firms that are new to the bond market – they have no track record of paying bondholders. The message is simple with any bond issuer given a D rating: It stands for danger, so buyer beware!

The credit rating awarded to a particular company and even a country is regularly reviewed by the credit rating agency. You may find that the sure-fire AAA rated bond issuer over ten or twenty years falls to junk bond status.

Keep an eye out for the credit rating agencies downgrading a company, which is often reported in the *Financial Times*.

If it looks as if the bond issuer will not be able to pay – and this does happen – then the price of the bond will fall. If it looks as if the bond issuer will pay then it's likely the bond price will either rise or hold steady.

A bond is only as good as its issuer. Big companies and even some countries default from time to time. The most recent example of a country defaulting on its bond debt is Argentina in 2001. But in the distant past countries as important and powerful as Germany and Russia have also defaulted.

Junk bonds

There are bonds deemed too risky to be given a credit rating. The clue to the security of these types of bonds is in their name – junk bonds. Junk bonds are a very specialist investment that can pay off, as issuers promise to pay a high rate of interest to compensate for the risk, but they can also lead to investors losing their shirts.

If you fancy taking a punt on junk bonds there is a way you can reduce risk. Buy a diverse collection of junk bonds. That way, hopefully, the bonds that pay off will compensate you for any that prove a bad investment.

How to Buy a Bond

Three main ways to buy a bond exist:

- ✔ **Direct from the issuer:** When looking to sell a new bond issue the government makes it available to the public as well as major financial institutions.

- ✔ **Through a stockbroker:** New bond issues and bonds already issued can be bought and sold through a stockbroker. The stockbroker will charge a fee. See Chapter 5 for more on how to use a stockbroker.

- ✔ **By purchasing a bond fund:** There are literally hundreds of funds out there which pool investors' cash to buy bonds. These funds are explained in greater detail below.

Most small investors looking to invest in bonds do so through a *bond fund*. The idea of a bond fund is very simple: Funds pool investor cash to buy lots of different bonds.

Because funds invest in lots of different bonds, risk is reduced. Think about it: Even if one or two issuers default on a bond there will be plenty that will make their way to maturity without even so much as a hitch.

The vast majority of bond funds work as unit trusts. This means that when you come to invest or sell up you deal in units, and the price of these units mirrors the value of the bond held. If the bonds held by the trust rise in price so will the units and the return for investors. Unit trusts are explored in greater detail in Chapter 12.

The interest on most bond funds is greater than the dividends on funds that specialise in buying company shares.

Bond funds can be a very good way for small investors to get access to the bond market at minimum risk. They can be held in an individual savings account or ISA – see Chapter 10 for more on ISAs.

However, before plumping for a particular bond fund check to see what type of bonds it invests in. If the fund specialises in bonds issued by the UK government or big companies then it's likely that your money will be safe but growth no better than steady. But on the other hand if the fund invests in more exotic bonds such as those issued by governments in the developing world or small companies then there is a chance that you may lose your cash, but if all goes well the returns can be good. You pays your money, you takes your choice!

Bumpy ride for with-profit bond investors

With-profit bonds have been widely sold by insurance companies as the ideal vehicle for long-term savings. *With-profit bonds* are structured to smooth out the peaks and troughs of investment performance.

They achieve this smoothing by holding back some of the profits made from investments in good years with the aim of paying the cash out to policyholders in years when the investments aren't doing so well. With-profits pool investor cash to invest largely in shares, bonds, and property. This smoothing concept worked well for years and with-profit bonds were very popular.

But – and you just knew there had to be one of these – the stock market falls between 2000 and 2003 were so sharp and so sudden as to take a wrecking ball to the smoothing concept. Some managers of with-profit funds hadn't kept enough cash behind during the good years to continue to pay out annual bonuses to policyholders when stock markets fell. In fact, at one stage, it looked as if the whole with-profit edifice may come crashing down. As yet, it hasn't, and of late some funds have started to pay out hefty bonuses again, but investor confidence has been shaken in the smoothing mechanism of with-profits, perhaps even permanently.

Bond fund providers often levy an initial charge for investment. However, by using a fund supermarket you can get around having to pay all or some of this initial charge. Fund supermarkets buy in bulk from the supplier on the understanding that initial fees are waived. See Chapter 12 for more on fund supermarkets.

Chapter 12

Making Your Fortune through Shares

Say the word investing to most people and they'll probably think of the stock market. Fortunes can be made and lost on the movement of a company share price. A piece of stock market action can be just what you need to boost your retirement wealth.

In this chapter, I explain what shares offer investors and how to tell a potential money-making share from an absolute dud. I'll also take you through how to go about building your very own share portfolio. If that doesn't appeal you can let a professional fund management firm do all the hard work for you!

Figuring Out What Share Investment Has to Offer

Millions of Britons own shares and when you look at what's potentially on offer – provided you get your share selection right of course – you can see why they're such a popular investment.

You may own shares without even knowing it. Virtually all workplace and private pension scheme invest a large proportion of their cash in shares.

Shares offer the potential of both capital growth and a regular income. The capital growth is achieved when the price of the shares you bought rises. This happens when other investors see the company as doing well or as the likely subject of a takeover bid. Anyhow, the principle is that share price is dictated by investor demand.

Share price rises are usually relatively gradual but in some cases they can be sudden and sharp. Share investors have been known to double or treble their money in the same day.

You can get a regular income from the payment of share dividends. The company, provided it's doing well, will use some of its profits to pay its shareholders a dividend. More about this later in the chapter.

If the idea of investing for the sake of scooping share dividends appeals you may be best sticking to the UK stock market. Generally, companies listed on the UK stock market pay higher dividends then those in the US, Japan, and the continent.

Share dividends become particularly important if you're investing for the long term. In good years dividends can match or even beat rates of interest paid by National Savings or a building society savings account. Dividend payments can boost your wealth and help you get rich nice and slow.

Bear in mind though that the decision to pay a dividend is down to the company's board of directors. Of course, the board of directors can always be voted out if shareholders are unhappy with the decisions they take.

Sometimes companies can use their profits to buy back shares. What happens is that the company tells its shareholders that it is willing to buy a set number of shares at a particular price. Share buy-backs can be popular amongst investors because the price is invariably higher than can be had from selling the shares on the stock market.

Another big plus with shares is that there is a ready and sophisticated market for buying and selling. There are dozens of stockbrokers out there ready, willing, and able to allow you instantaneous access to the UK stock market and even, increasingly, those of other major world economies. You can buy or sell shares under the advice of the stockbroker or off your own bat. See Chapter 5 for the different levels of service offered by a stockbroker.

It's now easier than ever to trade shares. It can be done in seconds through a quick call to a stockbroker or a click of the mouse. Chapter 5 gives you the low-down on DIY Internet share trading.

Shares less ordinary

When reading the financial press you'll come across the phrase *ordinary share-holders*. This doesn't mean that the shareholder is actually ordinary or even simply average – lives in a semi-detached house in the suburbs, has 2.4 children, and works in the service industry.

There are two classes of shares to be had, preference and ordinary.

Holding preference shares means that you are first in line to get your money. If the company is short of cash then preference shareholders are more likely to get a dividend than investors holding ordinary shares. Likewise, if the company goes to the wall, preference shareholders have more rights to their cash than ordinary shareholders.

The bottom line is that preference shares are better than ordinary ones. Preference shares provide more security than ordinary shares but are often sold to large financial institutions rather then private investors.

Capital growth and a regular income can also be achieved through investing in buy-to-let property, examined in Chapter 15. But one advantage shares have over property is that they are far easier to trade.

Being alert to share price ups and downs

Having given the big up to shares, it's time for the downside! Shares come with a money health warning so big it should be visible from space. Remember Sir Isaac Newton's discovery that what goes up must come down? Well, it could have been designed for shares.

Shares can be a volatile investment. Firstly, investors are exposing themselves to the risk that the supposedly great company they have bought into turns out to be a dud. Secondly, investors are at risk from a general stock market collapse. Factors way outside the control of the individual investor such as war or a sharp rise in the price of oil can damage confidence and set stock markets tumbling.

And when a stock market tumbles then it's fairly inevitable that even good companies making nice fat profits also see their share price fall. Lots of times in the past – most notably 1929 and 1987 – stock markets have crashed without warning. When this happens it spells investor pain!

One way to sidestep the effects of a general stock market fall is to invest for the long term. The longer that you have money invested the better the chance of smoothing out the peaks and troughs of the market. For example, someone who bought shares in each of the largest 100 UK companies in early 1987 and then sold them a year later would have lost because the stock market crashed in October 1987. If they had held off selling until 1999 they would have made money because by then share prices had well and truly recovered.

It's never a good idea to have all your spare cash invested in the shares of just one company. Investment history is chock full of companies suddenly falling on hard times or even going bust, wiping out the fortunes of shareholders.

Working share investment into your big plan

Because shares are risky you have to be careful about the role they play in your retiring wealthy plan. Too much reliance on shares and you risk losing a fortune if the investment turns against you. But on the flip side, ignore shares completely or invest only a small fraction of your fortune in them and you may find that you can't quite reach your retiring wealthy goal. It's all a question of balance.

Free sandwiches alert for shareholders

Being a shareholder means that you'll get an invite to the Annual General Meeting (AGM). At the AGM you will be able to nibble on free sandwiches. More importantly, you'll also be able to quiz the board of directors on how good or bad a job they're doing. You will be asked to approve or, as has increasingly happened in recent times, throw out the directors' pay or remuneration package. If things are really going to the dogs you may be asked to vote on whether the board should be thrown out on its ear. It's your company after all.

Shareholder perks offered by UK companies include the Bloomsbury publishing house discounting the latest Harry Potter book by 25 per cent and Marks & Spencer sending out £20 gift vouchers. Both of these are useful when Christmas comes around!

Perks are often only available to *registered shareholders*. This means that the investor's name appears on the company's own register of shareholders. People who buy their shares through a stockbroker do not normally appear on the register, instead they are said to hold their shares in a *nominee account*, which means that they can't claim a perk – sorry!

While it's never a good idea to buy a share purely because of the perk on offer, it can be a nice little titbit, not to be sniffed at.

Here are the factors you should consider before spicing up your retiring wealthy plan with shares:

- ✔ **Your age:** The rule is the closer you are to retirement age then the less you should put into shares. Relatively volatile investments such as shares usually don't make good short-term investments. A stock market tumble can lead to you losing your fortune without having time to make any money back.

- ✔ **Your wealth position:** The golden rule with shares is don't go there unless you can afford to lose the money you're investing. Shares can rise and fall dramatically in value, quicker than almost any other investment.

- ✔ **Your other investments:** Throughout this book I've gone on about building something called a balanced portfolio. In short this means matching riskier investments such as shares with safe bets such as National Savings and building society savings accounts. Before ploughing your hard earned cash into shares make sure you have these safe investments in place.

- ✔ **Your know-how:** The future direction of individual company shares can be fiendishly difficult to call. The City of London is full of analysts who spend their careers examining the ins and outs of just a handful of companies – and guess what? They call a share price wrong, often. You need to do your research. See later in this chapter for more on reading up on a share.

Ultimately the advice is unless you know what you're doing steer clear of shares or seek financial advice.

Successful short-term share investment – from a few minutes to a few months – is very much about getting the timing right and spotting an opportunity. But usually the experts in the City of London are ahead of private investors on this score. See Chapter 17 for more on making a success of short-term share dealing, otherwise known as daytrading.

Zeroing in on Company Shares

Being a successful share investor has nothing to do with dressing in a bowler hat, donning red braces, and tucking a copy of the *Financial Times* under your arm. Instead, success comes from exercising a little common sense, harnessing the information out there about companies, and doing a bit of number crunching.

There are more than 800 companies listed on the UK stock exchange. And the choice of companies to invest in doesn't end there as you can buy shares in firms listed on the Alternative Investment Market

(AIM) or OFFEX stock exchanges. These exchanges are for small to medium-size firms.

In short the choice of shares is huge and bewildering and that's without factoring in shares in companies listed on the US, Japanese, or other major world stock markets.

No one individual, not even the supposed stock market experts you see interviewed on the telly, know everything about all these firms. So don't waste time swotting up on every company out there. By being clear about your own investment objectives you can narrow down your search.

And once you have narrowed down your search then you can use your research to work out the best investments for you and hopefully turn a profit.

Understanding that size does matter

One of the keys to share investing is to understand that the smaller a company is the more risky it is to invest in. This isn't always true of course but it is a general rule.

This 'small equals heightened risk' theory holds for two main reasons:

- ✓ **Competition:** The smaller a company is the less resources it has at its disposal to see off competition from larger firms.

- ✓ **Liquidity:** Shares in small companies tend to be less in demand than those in large companies. This can mean that when it comes to the time to sell there may be no buyers out there.

This shouldn't put you off investing in small companies. They can offer great growth potential. Remember today's multinationals started out as a small company and anyone buying shares in them in their early days made an absolute killing.

However, the heightened risk of investing in a small company should give you food for thought, particularly if you are near retirement and do not feel that you want to take on too much risk.

So one way of narrowing down your share choice is to decide whether you want to go large or small.

Whether a company is deemed to be small, medium or large is dictated by its market capitalisation. This bit of ugly jargon simply means the price of the share times the number of shares in circulation.

Judging whether a company is large, medium or small is made easy by the way the stock market is organised. The largest 100 firms by market capitalisation are in the FTSE100, then there is the FTSE 350 and finally the rest are to be found in the FTSE All Share index.

Taking the sector approach

Companies operate in sectors – markets if you like – and the stock market is subdivided to reflect this.

It's fairly easy to find out what the general view of experts is of a particular sector – the newspapers, magazines such as Shares and Investors Chronicle and Internet sites such as `www.motleyfool.co.uk` are full of articles of how particular sectors have performed and future expectations of them.

You may want to hone in on a sector that you know something about or think you can make a good judgement of. Retailing shares are popular amongst small investors because they can see during their weekly shop and through their daily conversations with friends and colleagues whether a particular retailer is doing well or not.

Share prices reflect not only how well a company is doing but also how investors view the sector that the company operates in. If investors feel that the sector is set to underperform the wider economy then the share price may suffer.

Narrowing down your choice

Having asked yourself what size company suits your taste for risk and what sector you fancy, you have probably successfully narrowed down the hundreds of shares out there to perhaps a dozen or so. That's a much more manageable number.

There are couple of other things to consider though before you start poring over the company numbers:

- ✔ Are you looking primarily for growth or income?
- ✔ Do you already own some shares?

If you do already own some shares then you should invest in the context of your wider portfolio. For instance, if you already have lots of shares in banks perhaps you ought to consider purchasing shares in a different sector. The idea is to hedge your bets. If banking shares nosedive perhaps your other shares will do OK, riding to the rescue. Having what is called a balanced portfolio of shares is a guiding principle of collective investment products and successful private investors alike.

Reading Up on a Company Share

Once you have drawn up your list of candidate shares for investment it's time to do a little research. So where do you look for information on a company?

The best place to look is the company report. All companies listed on the UK stock market are legally bound to send their registered shareholders a copy of their accounts once a year. And fortunately for would-be investors many firms make these company reports available online on their Web sites.

Losses in a company account are not represented by a minus sign – as you would think – instead the figures are enveloped in brackets. Keep an eye out for figures in brackets.

Some companies issue profit and loss accounts every six months, while a smaller band of firms do it every three months.

However – you've guessed it – these company reports are full to the brim with jargon. Here is your jargon busting guide to a reading a company report:

- ✔ **Turnover:** The amount customers spend with the company. It is usually the biggest figure you'll see in the report (yes, even bigger than the managing director's salary).

- ✔ **Cost of sales:** All the money the company has spent on raw materials. If this figure is bigger than the turnover then the company is in serious trouble.

- ✔ **Gross profit:** What's left after subtracting cost of sales from turnover. There is still a lot to take away from this figure.

- ✔ **Operating profit:** A bit of fantasy! This figure shows what the profit would be if there were no taxes – if only! – and no interest on business loans to pay.

- ✔ **Operating expenses:** The costs of running the business day-to-day, including staff salaries and rent on premises. This is where you'll find the dirt on directors' pay.

- ✔ **Exceptional items:** The clue is in the name: These are one-off expenses such as the cost of relocating the business or profits from the sale of a business asset.

- ✔ **Net interest payable:** Interest paid on any bank loans. Most firms have some sort of bank loan on the go. Occasionally, firms with a big cash pile – maybe following the sale of an asset – will be earning more interest than they are paying.

- **Profit before tax:** This is the biggie. Most media report the profit before tax figure.

- **Profit after tax:** We all have to pay tax, even companies. This is the amount of cash the company has either to reinvest or to dish out to investors in the form of a tasty dividend.

- **Profit attributable to ordinary shareholders:** Put simply this is the money that all shareholders have to share between them.

- **Retained profit for the year:** The money the board of directors has decided should be retained from profits for reinvestment. Hopefully a big retained profit figure will herald bumper profits down the line. All firms have to invest to grow.

- **Dividends:** The total cost of payments made to shareholders.

- **Earnings per share:** The profit attributable to ordinary shareholders divided by the number of shares. This is a key indicator favoured by many investors, described in more detail later in this chapter.

You shouldn't completely ignore any of the figures contained in a company report. If you see anything untoward try to find out a reason by looking at media reports on the company. The key with share investing is, if you're unhappy in any way with a company, don't buy its shares.

Being alert to profit forecasts and warnings

The City loves its forecasts. Analysts look at the ins and outs of the company, the sector in which it operates, and even the wider economy, and forecasts its profits.

Firms are expected to meet these forecasts. If they don't the City institutions often sell the shares – bringing the price down – and the board of directors had better start scanning the jobs pages.

Unsurprisingly, companies are very sensitive to forecasts – or market expectations as they are also referred to – and will give a heads up if they think that they risk missing them.

This is called a *profit warning* and it's a red alert for investors.

Whatever way you cut it a profit warnings is bad for investors as it can lead to a rapid sale of shares. However, some risk takers see them as an opportunity – a time to get in when many others are getting out in the big, and sometimes vain, hope that the company will pull its socks up and the share price soar again.

Earnings per share: the litmus test

Some investors swear by Earnings Per Share (EPS). It allows them to see at a glance if the company is doing better than it was in the past.

The pre-tax profit figure – reported by most media outlets – has the flaw that the firm may have boosted profits by buying up rivals. In order to buy up these rivals the company may have issued a lot more shares. The new larger company may be making higher profits but may not be making this money more efficiently.

The EPS figure cuts the crap: It gives you a benchmark you can use year in, year out to tell if the company is moving forward and working efficiently for its shareholders or not. After all, from an investor's point of view, that is the key.

A growing EPS is a hallmark of a company that is growing and working well for its shareholders, a falling EPS a sign that the firm may be struggling.

Taking into account other company indicators

EPS allows you to see whether the company is doing better or worse than it has done in the past but this gives you only a partial picture. For one thing the EPS may be growing because the company is in a sector that's enjoying stellar growth. It may well be that the company is actually a bit of a basket case but its luck is holding at present. Nevertheless, it may be a prime candidate for the knackers' yard just as soon as times get tougher in the sector it operates in.

So you need a figure that allows you to compare one company against another. This is where the *price/earnings ratio* (p/e) comes in.

You can get the p/e figure by dividing the company earnings into the share price. It tells you how many years of earnings you'd need to equal the share price. A p/e of 10 means that it should take ten years of earnings at their current level to match the share price.

Helpfully, the *Financial Times* share pages contain the p/e of each listed company.

Investors love p/e because it allows them to compare one firm in a sector with another. The rule of thumb with p/e is the lower the figure the better value the share ought to be. But on the flip side the p/e ratio may be low because earnings or company prospects are poor.

A high p/e can be an indication that the City sees the company's future prospects as rosy. Perhaps the firm has developed a new drug or has drilled a new oil field successfully. These events may not have fed through to the firm's earnings but have reached the share price. As a result, the p/e will be high. From a buyers point of view a high p/e indicates that the share price is inflated by market sentiment and you must ask yourself how much more upside is left in the share price?

Above all, you have to put the p/e ratio into context. Look at the company report, and check the firm's profitability and EPS. Also look at other firms in the sector to see how their p/e and prospects compare.

From time to time you will see a p/e quoted for the entire stock market. It's worth keeping an eye on this figure because if it climbs sharply it can be a sign that a bubble has developed and that a general fall in the market is due. For example, the long term average p/e for the US stock market is around 17 but just prior to the dotcom share crash of 2000 this had reached nearly 25.

Although EPS and p/e are important, there is no magic figure that will tell you all you need to know about a company – otherwise we'd all be using it to make a fortune!

Looking behind the dividend

Dividends are good, no doubt about it. They are how you participate in the company's profits. Once or twice a year, if all goes well, the company will send you a cheque of so many pence for each share you own. You can spend this money, save it in a deposit account, or even reinvest it in shares.

But dividends also give you a crucial clue as to a company's fortunes and can indicate whether it time to skedaddle or plough more money into its shares. You should also look at the dividends a firm pays before deciding to invest in the first place.

Here are some things to bear in mind when looking at dividends:

> ✔ **Size of dividend isn't everything:** If firm A pays a dividend of 50p a share and firm B 25p, which is best? That depends on how much it costs to buy the share in the first place. If firm A's share price is £5 while firm B's is just £1 then shares in the latter firm represent the best value. The figure you arrive at when dividing the share price by the dividend is called the *dividend yield*.

✔ **Sometimes it's good that there is no dividend:** From time to time companies choose to reinvest profits rather than pay shareholders a dividend. This can be a bit vexing but at the same time the investment may help boost long-term profits and hopefully the share price too. This scenario often holds true for small companies trying to become big. Remember shares are meant to be a long-term investment and if the directors' plans take off you may find that you win big in the long run.

✔ **Large dividends can spell trouble:** It's a fairly common tactic for companies that are down on their luck to pay a big dividend, even when they're making little money. The reason is that the board of directors is trying to keep its shareholders sweet. A firm's board of directors can be saying to shareholders: 'Please keep the faith, look at this lovely dividend.' Remember money paid out in dividends could have been reinvested to secure future profitability.

If you're a dividend hungry investor, you can use the dividend yield to compare one company with another. However, be aware that as share prices rise, the dividend yield is likely to fall.

Building Your Very Own Share Portfolio

I have already mentioned that really savvy investors buy lots of different shares rather than putting all their eggs in one basket. The beauty of having lots of shares is that if one performs badly another, hopefully, performs well.

This approach is called *building a portfolio of shares*. You can take a DIY approach or get a stockbroker to do it for you. See Chapter 5 for more on working with your stockbroker.

Constructing your portfolio

Think of building your own share portfolio as a microcosm of your overarching retiring wealthy plan.

Construct a portfolio with high-, medium-, and low-risk shares and balance these according to your personal circumstances such as how close you are to retirement, how much you have to invest, and your general attitude to risk.

The nearer you are to retirement, the less comfortable you are with the possibility that you may lose all the money invested, and so the greater the number of safer shares you should have in your portfolio.

Here are some fantasy portfolios to give you some guidance:

- **Safety first portfolio:** This will include predominantly large companies usually in the FTSE 100 index involved in traditional sectors such as oil, utilities, tobacco, mining, or banking.

- **Middle of the road portfolio:** Still plenty of cash invested in big blue chip companies but spread across more sectors perhaps taking in retailing, property development, pharmaceutical, support services, and new technology. The shares of some medium and small companies may be held also.

- **Adventurous portfolio:** Some cash in big blue chips, but much more money is invested in firms big and small in sectors that are predicted to grow sharply in the future such as the new technology, bio-technology, or healthcare sectors.

Buying shares for a quick killing

Throughout much of this book I bang on about how investments should be for the long term. But there are times when you see a bit of an opportunity to make a fast buck and as long as you're comfortable with the risk involved – which can mean losing all the money you invest – then there is nothing wrong with going for it.

Short term share investing is a bit of a gamble and gambling is supposed to be fun, particularly when you win!

Typical situations that may prompt a quick buy and sell include:

- **Takeover target:** Takeovers can cause a share feeding frenzy and invariably prices rise. Just be careful that the possibility of takeover isn't already factored into the price.

- **New product launch:** Perhaps the firm is about to announce a snazzy new product which you think will help it clean up, boost profits and therefore its share price.

- **Buying another company:** The company may have bought out a rival or is expanding into a new area. This can be a sign that profits are about to grow and with them the share price.

- **Management change:** If a firm's in trouble a management reshuffle often takes place. New management should bring new ideas after listening to what they have to say. It may be a smart play to buy, in the hope that many more investors will come to the same conclusions at a later date.

Blue chip companies can exist in sectors that may be considered a little risky. Retailing for example is seen as a little risky at present because of fears that shoppers, burdened by debts, have stopped spending, but shares in Tesco, the UK's biggest retailer, are considered one of the safest around. Being classed as a blue chip is more about the financial health and market position of an individual company rather than the sector in which it operates.

During economic downturns it's often traditional sectors such as oil, mining, and tobacco that do well. The theory is that firms in these sectors are a safe port from the storm producing consistent but unspectacular profits year in, year out. These firms also have a reputation for being consistent payers of dividends.

Some stockbrokers offer tailor-made share packages to investors. The packages often work in the same way as the three fantasy portfolios I have outlined above. A couple of things to bear in mind though: If the portfolio is defined as income it should be full of blue chip shares; if it's defined as growth it's likely to have shares from a larger number of small and medium-size firms.

All in all, though, no investor makes the right call all the time so it's unwise for you to risk a large part of your fortune on that supposed sure share winner.

Keeping track of your shares

Being on the ball and knowing what is going on with your shares is as important as deciding what shares to purchase and when to buy and sell them.

Ignore your shareholding at your peril. Share prices can quickly move against you and you must be prepared to sell at anytime.

Having said that, though, being too jumpy about every little move in the share price is not only a way to heart failure but can prompt you to sell a share when, in fact, you should be holding on.

As with everything else in the world of saving and investing it's about getting the balance right.

Every couple of weeks give your shares the quick once over.

The first place to start for share price information is national newspapers. In particular the *Financial Times* carries pages of up-to-date share prices. The BBC news Web site business section has a free-to-use price search which allows you to see same day share prices and even to plot their movements over several months. Check out www.bbc.co.uk/news/business for more. Other Web sites offering a similar service include Interactive Investor, www.iii.co.uk, Hemscott, www.hemscott.net, and Motley Fool www.motley fool.co.uk.

In addition, your stockbroker should be able to tell you the very latest price of your shares.

You may be best adopting a sell position with your shares. This is a point at which you automatically sell your shares. This can be when they have made a nice profit – say 50 per cent – or when you'd like to limit losses at say 20 per cent. Most successful investors adopt a sell position and – importantly – stick to it.

Knowing When to Sell Up

If I knew exactly when to buy and sell shares I wouldn't be writing this book: I'd probably be living on my own South Pacific island, worrying if today I'd go for the swordfish or the lobster. But that's not to say that there aren't events which happen to you or the company you are investing in when it becomes clear that it is time to get out, fast!

Here are some circumstances that should definitely prompt a rethink of whether you'd be better off selling up:

- ✔ **You get a takeover offer:** When one company wants to take over another company it will make its shareholders an offer it believes they cannot refuse. This is no Godfather style horse's head in the bed act of gentle persuasion – the offer will be cold hard cash or shares in the newly formed merged company.

- ✔ **You're nearing retirement:** Your share investment may have given you years of faithful service returning dividends and capital growth but now as you approach retirement your priorities may have changed. You may want an investment that provides an income with less risk. The best bet may be to sell your shares and use the money to buy a bond or an annuity.

- ✔ **The company is going under:** You won't get all your investment calls right – otherwise see you on that South Pacific island – and sometimes you'll find that your share falls sharply in value, perhaps to almost worthless. When a company is in real crisis the banks often end up owning it and in such circumstances the poor old shareholders may lose all their money. Perhaps it's best to sell at nearly any price. Hopefully with the use of a sensible sell position, as outlined above, you won't find yourself in this situation.

✓ **You think the market or share has reached its peak:** Lots of people who invested in dotcom companies wish they had sold up in 1999, because the following year nearly all these shares crashed and burned. If you think that there is a bubble in the market you ought to consider getting out. However, calling a market bubble isn't easy and you have to stick to your guns.

As you near retirement it doesn't mean you have to get out of shares altogether – instead consider the type of shares that you hold. If you own shares in riskier medium and small companies perhaps you should sell these and buy shares in big blue-chip firms.

Your employer may offer you access to a *share save scheme*. In this, you put aside a percentage of your earnings towards buying shares in your employer – often at a discount. These schemes can be an easy no hassle route into share investment but be warned if your company goes belly up you may well lose your job and the shares that you bought become worthless.

Letting Others Take the Strain: Collective Investments

Investing in individual shares is bit too seat-of-the-pants for many people's tastes. Not for them poring over company reports for hidden nasties or keeping a watchful eye on the share price pages of the *Financial Times* newspaper.

But at the same time these people don't want to miss out on the wealth boost that share investment potentially has to offer.

The finance industry has come up with a range of investments just for these slightly coy investors. They are called collective investments or funds. They come in all sizes and with risks to suit all investor tastes. Some funds only buy shares in the world's biggest companies while others will invest in companies from emerging economies such as China or India.

Essentially these investments pool investor cash to buy a basket of shares. The idea is that the value of the collective investment grows in line with the shares that it holds. If a few shares bought flop then never mind, there are hopefully other purchases that will do well. Collective investments are huge business all over the globe and some have been around for more than a century, making their investors a tidy pile of cash.

But be warned – collective investments are not immune to losing money. If you own shares in a really good company you may just be able to ride out or recover quickly from a general stock market crash. There is little chance of this for a fund which owns shares in lots of companies.

For example, following the bursting of the dotcom share bubble in 2000 some funds investing purely in new technologies lost up to three quarters of their value.

Two very distinct types of fund exist – investment trusts and unit trusts – with their very own advantages and disadvantages.

The US equivalent to unit trusts is called a mutual fund. The demand for collective investments is greater in the US than in the UK.

If you'd like to check out the performance of unit and investment trusts go to www.trustnet.co.uk. It's a free-to-use service which tells you all you need to know about most funds, even what shares they are invested in.

Unit trusts explained

Unit trusts are the most popular type of stock market fund. Investors buy units in the fund which own shares. The price of the units varies according to how well the shares do that the trust owns. If the shares held by the unit trust rise 10 per cent in value then the price of the units increases by the same percentage.

In recent years most unit trusts have morphed into something called OEICs, which stands for Open-Ended Investment Companies. The change is just a technical one and too boring for words. It doesn't matter a jot to investors whether they are investing in a unit trust or an OEIC, they are essentially the same.

Investment trusts exposed

Essentially investment trusts are companies listed on the stock exchange that own shares in other companies. By buying shares in an investment trust – in exactly the same way as you would a single company share – you are buying shares in lots of different companies.

Unlike unit trusts, investment trusts can borrow. This allows the fund manager to raise extra capital to buy shares when they see an opportunity – it also gives them carte blanche to get themselves into debt trouble. This all means that investment trusts have the potential to outperform unit trusts but they are more risky.

The share price of an investment trust rises and falls according to:

- ✔ The performance of the shares the investment trust has invested in.
- ✔ How the market sees the future performance of the investment trust.

The fact that the share price of an investment trust is affected by market sentiment means that at different times its shares can be valued higher or lower than the total value of the shares it holds.

When shares in an investment trust are valued at a lower level than the value of the shares it holds it is said to be at a *discount*. On the flip side, if its shares are valued at a higher level than the value of the shares it holds the investment trust is said to be trading at a premium.

Investment trusts are real companies – the biggest are worth over £1bn. Just like BP or BT they have boards of directors and shareholders who get to attend an AGM and vote on directors' pay and other matters.

Understanding different fund sectors

Both unit and investment trusts operate in specific sectors. Some invest only in the largest UK companies, others invest exclusively in the US, European, or Japanese stock markets. Some funds are very specialist, only investing in property, mining, or new technology companies.

Below is a guide to the sectors that both investment and unit trusts operate in:

- ✔ **UK all companies:** This is the biggest sector of the lot by number of funds involved and does exactly what it says – funds in this sector can invest in any company listed on the UK stock market.

- ✔ **UK smaller companies:** Again an easy one. Funds in this sector can invest in any company outside the FTSE 100 and even firms listed on AIM or OFFEX.

- ✔ **Global growth:** Funds in this sector invest in the largest firms, cherry picked from stock markets around the globe.

- ✔ **Emerging markets:** Unit and investment trusts in this sector invest in firms from countries that are considered to be on the up. Nations such as China, India, Russia, and Brazil are all considered to be 'emerging'.

✔ **Country and area specific:** These funds invest outside the UK, usually in the US, Japan, or Europe but also more exotic locales like Latin America and Australia. Country and area specific funds sometimes focus on either large or small companies.

✔ **Specialist:** Funds in this sector zero in on businesses operating in particular markets such as property, mining, pharmaceuticals, and new technology.

Funds are a cheap and easy way of investing in overseas stock markets. Only a limited number of UK stockbrokers offer clients the chance to buy shares listed in overseas markets.

Generally, funds own shares in anything from 70 to over 100 companies. But some unit trusts deliberately limit the number of companies they invest in to 30 or 40 at most. These *focus funds*, as they're called, have become a favourite amongst investors because the managers really earn their corn. If they get a share choice right it can make a big difference to the overall performance of the fund.

Buying a collective investment

There are hundreds of fund management firms out there. These management firms make money from the initial and annual fees they charge investors. As a rule of thumb if you buy direct from these firms expect to pay an initial charge of between 3–5 per cent and an ongoing annual charge of between 1–1.5 per cent on all money invested.

Tracker funds

As far as share investing goes trackers are as easy as it comes. You buy shares or units in a tracker fund and it buys shares in all the companies listed in a particular stock market index. The idea is to replicate the index by buying all the shares in their right weighting. For example a FTSE 100 tracker will buy all 100 shares but invest the most cash in the very largest of these companies.

Tracker funds have a manager but in reality the buying and selling is done by a computer. The idea is to closely replicate or track the index.

Many City insiders get very sniffy about tracker funds. These people bang on about how it's far better to invest in a fund with a manager who actively searches out shares to buy rather than just tracking an index. However, the evidence is that most highly paid fund managers fail to beat or even match the performance of tracker funds. What's more, the initial and ongoing charges levied by tracker funds tend to be much lower than is the case with actively managed funds.

But before going direct to the fund management firm, check to see if the fund is available through a fund supermarket. These supermarkets buy funds in bulk and in return the fund management firms waive part or all their initial charges.

Don't choose a fund because it has low fees, look at how the risks suit you.

You don't have to invest in a fund in one go. You can set up a direct debit or standing order to buy regular amounts of shares or units. This is called *regular saving*.

If you'd like to check out the performance of unit and investment trusts go to www.trustnet.co.uk. It's a free to use service which tells you all you need to know about most funds, even what shares they are invested in.

Part IV

Using Property to Boost Your Retirement Pot

– FORCED RETIREMENT –

In this part . . .

The saying goes that an Englishman's home is his castle; it can also be a passport to retirement wealth. In this part is everything you need to know as far as investing in bricks and mortar is concerned – from how you can increase the value of your own property to becoming a developer, through to buy-to-let investment and saving on your mortgage. For lots of people making money from property has a big appeal and this is the part to check out if you want to know how to do it with aplomb.

Chapter 13

Making the Most of Mortgages and Equity Release

In This Chapter

▶ Cashing in on your property

▶ Understanding equity release

▶ Bearing in mind the risks of equity release

▶ Paying off your mortgage early

▶ Getting used to moving your mortgage between providers

*I*n this chapter, I show you how you can turn your bricks and mortar into pounds in your retirement pot.

In addition, I outline how you can push down your mortgage debt, freeing you up to concentrate your financial firepower on bringing off your big retiring wealthy plan.

Cashing In Your Property

There are three main ways to use your own home to increase your retirement wealth pot:

✓ **Sell up and move somewhere cheaper**. The option of selling your home and buying somewhere cheaper can make a lot of sense, particularly if you own a family home and your children have now left and struck out on their own. Downsizing, as it's called, can help you free up cash and perhaps relocate somewhere that you really want to spend your autumn years.

✓ **Sell up and buy-to-let**. For many this is ideal scenarioville. You sell your main home, buy somewhere cheaper, and with a portion of your profit buy a place to let out. The income you receive from your buy-to-let helps see you through retirement and you have the option of selling the buy-to-let at any time. Buy-to-let in all its forms is covered in Chapter 15.

✔ **Equity release**. In effect you sign over a portion of your home to a bank or building society and in return receive either a lump sum or an income in return. Equity release is explored in much greater detail later in this chapter.

Exploding the 'property is better than pension' myth

You may have heard lots of people say that their property is their pension. What do they mean by this?

Well, they are trusting that the increased value of their property can be converted into a big enough income or lump sum to see them through their autumn years. Looking at what's happened in recent years – property prices booming while pension values have suffered due to stock market performance – you can see why choosing property over pension saving has become so de rigueur.

Case closed then, just go for property? Err, no! Pensions have an ace up their sleeve – you get tax relief on contributions.

If you're a basic rate taxpayer for every 78p you pay into a pension the government through tax relief will top it up to £1. Higher rate taxpayers get an even better deal – for every 60p they pay into a pension the government tops it up to £1. In effect the government – yes the government! – is giving you free money. And there's more: If you're a member of a workplace pension you may well find that your employer makes additional contributions into your pension – again, this is free money!

However, not all is rosy in the pension garden. You have to tie up your money for a long time and 75 per cent of the fund usually goes towards buying an annuity, an income for life. For more on pensions check out Chapters 6 through to 9.

On the down side for property, tax relief no longer applies to mortgage interest and over the long term a mortgage can cost you a lot of money in interest payments. For example, a £125,000 mortgage at a 4.7 per cent rate of interest will actually cost you £225,000 over 25 years and that all comes from after tax salary. Next time you hear someone boast about how much their property has increased in value, ask them if they've factored in mortgage interest payments – I bet you they haven't even thought of this huge expense!

Having said all that, I wouldn't be foolish enough to do down property as an investment. Some friends of mine have made an absolute killing in recent years and their retiring wealthy prospects have been given a stellar boost. The key is to have a balance of property, pensions, and other investments. Primarily, enjoy your property for what it is – a home – and if needs be use any increased value to boost your retirement pot.

In June 2007 home information packs – also called sellers' packs – are to be introduced. This means that when you put your home on the market you have to make available to would-be purchasers an information pack containing a survey of the property as well as local searches. This may add up to £1,000 to the cost of selling your home, but should cut the length of time it takes for property sales to complete.

Understanding Equity Release

Equity release gives older homeowners the opportunity to turn some of the value of their home into cold hard cash. For most people the path to equity release goes like this.

They buy a home with a mortgage, as they work they pay off this mortgage and the value of the property rises. The difference between the mortgage and the value of the home is called the property's equity. Many homeowners get to retirement or beyond cash poor but asset rich – they don't have a huge amount of cash tucked away but they do have the equity in their homes.

For some years now banks and building societies have been offering to free up this equity. Banks and building societies pay homeowners either a lump sum, a guaranteed regular income, or a combination of both; in return when the homeowner dies or sells up the bank or building society gets a slice of the property's value. Equity release is a lucrative business – for banks and building societies – and the number of older homeowners choosing this option has mushroomed in recent years (along with house prices throughout the UK).

The big idea behind equity release is that you bring in some extra retirement cash and get to stay put in the family home – this is what appeals to so many homeowners.

Different types of equity release explained

The idea behind equity release is pretty straightforward, but that doesn't stop banks and building societies complicating matters.

Over the years the straight equity release where you signed over a portion of your home in return for a cash pile has evolved into several different variants on a theme, each with their own advantages and disadvantages to be considered (see Table 13-1).

Table 13-1	Different types of equity release scheme	
Type of plan	*Advantages*	*Disadvantages*
Rolled-up interest loans		
You take out a loan against the value of your home but do not pay off any interest or capital until the property is sold.	The loan doesn't have to be repaid until you sell your home. If you choose you're able to stay in your home until you die, with the loan being repaid when the property is sold on your death. Under this type of equity release interest rates are usually fixed. This means that the amount you owe won't be affected by changes in rates throughout the wider economy.	If the loan runs for a long time you may end up owing more than your home is worth. This can be a real problem if subsequently you simply have no choice but to sell up – perhaps you become infirm and have to move into a residential nursing home or simply can no longer cope with stairs in the property."
Interest-only arrangements		
A bank or building society lends you money against the value of your home. You then make monthly interest payments but don't have to repay any of the capital.	The fact that you keep paying off the interest means that when you come to sell you only have to pay off the value of the loan. If in the interim the value of your house has risen you're able to pocket all or most of this profit. Likewise, if you leave your home to someone, they are able to pocket whatever's left after the loan has been repaid.	Interest rates may vary, which means that the monthly interest charge may go up or down. Interest charges can be quite hefty. In order to cope with meeting the interest payments, you have to have sufficient regular income in place.

Type of plan	Advantages	Disadvantages
Home income plans		
You take out a mortgage on your home and buy an annuity with the money raised. Mortgage interest payments are deducted from the annuity income. When you die the property is sold and the equity release provider gets back the money they lent you at the outset. Any cash left over goes into your estate.	The annuity provides you with a regular income for life and that is not to be sniffed at. If you live to a ripe old age you and your estate can end up winning on the deal. First up, live a long time and you can enjoy years' worth of income. Secondly, because you pay interest as you go along – from the annuity income – then on death the home income plan provider only gets the capital value of the mortgage. Hopefully in the interim property values have gone up sharply and the beneficiaries of your estate benefit from what's left over.	Home income plans have fallen out of fashion in recent years. They are very much the bell-bottomed flares of the equity release world. This is all due to a combination of falling annuity rates and super-boring complex tax relief changes. Put simply, the amount of income on offer through these plans has shrunk massively and subsequently so has their popularity.
Home reversion		
You sell your home in part or outright to a property investment company, but you remain living there as a tenant for the rest of your life, rent-free. If you and your partner sign up to the scheme, you both have the right to live in the property until death. On death the property is sold and the home reversion provider receives a share of the proceeds, in proportion to how much of the property you have signed over. Home reversion providers offer the options of a cash lump sum, an annuity, or a combination of the two.	You get to remain in the property and don't have to pay any interest, because you're not actually borrowing money, instead you're selling your property. Some schemes offer the option for you to choose to sell a proportion of your property when you need extra cash, for example start off selling 25 per cent at retirement, then a further 25 per cent every few years to give your finances a shot in the arm.	If you sign over your entire home then any future increase in value is scooped by the home reversion provider rather than by you or your relatives. You're in effect turning yourself from a property owner into a tenant. Some people consider this a step to far.

In the past few years equity release in most of its forms – the home income plan format excluded – has really taken off. Almost inevitability, there have been growing concerns that consumers can be mis-sold equity release. To head this potential problem off at the pass, where there is a mortgage involved equity release is now regulated by the City watchdog the Financial Services Authority (FSA). As for home reversion schemes, which have no mortgage element, the government has agreed that these too should be regulated by the FSA. The regulator will watch firms involved in equity release to ensure that they treat customers fairly and that their advertising isn't misleading.

If you fancy going for equity release, remember there are costs involved. You have to pay solicitors' fees and administration fees charged by the company arranging the scheme. Costs can vary markedly between providers. Some equity release providers charge hefty administration fees, so best avoid these.

Even if you sign over all your property through equity release you're still responsible for all repairs and building maintenance costs. You also have to pay council tax, electricity, gas, and insurance bills. Equity release is a big step – only do it if you're sure it's right for you.

Qualifying for equity release

All because you fancy the idea of equity release doesn't mean that providers will fall over themselves to dole out the cash to you. There are some hoops you have to jump through to get your hands on the money:

- ✔ **You need to own your home outright**. Most providers insist you've paid off your mortgage before they consider you for equity release. A few providers consider a property with a small mortgage on it just as long as the mortgage is paid off as part of the loan.

- ✔ **You have to be old enough**. Most providers insist that you're at least 60 or 65 years old before they consider you. This isn't because they're striking back against ageism – not a bit of it – the provider is making the cold, calculated analysis that the older you are the sooner you die and they get their hands on your property.

- ✔ **Your property has to be right for the provider**. Some companies don't consider certain types of property, such as flats, ex-local authority, or leasehold property. In addition, the property can't be a wreck. In short, it has to be in a reasonable state of repair.

Some providers are very strict about the type of property and person they consider for equity release. Other providers, though, are a little more free and easy in whom they consider, perhaps allowing people in their late fifties for equity release.

 You may well find that the valuation the equity release provider puts on your home is below what an estate agent may advise you to put it on the market at. This is because, generally, property does not fetch the full asking price. Property market experts reckon that sellers can expect to receive between 92 per cent and 96 per cent of the asking price.

Treading carefully with equity release

Just because you can release equity, doesn't mean you should!

Lots of good reasons exist for being ultra-cautious when it comes to equity release, either through a scheme or by selling up and buying somewhere less expensive.

I have heard some people say that they have no worries about their retirement because they will simply sell their home – but when it comes to biting the bullet it may not be so clear cut.

For most people the family home is a special place with memories, not just a pile of bricks and mortar. What's more, releasing equity from your home isn't straightforward – you can't sell up a brick at a time. The firms offering equity release are in it for the profit and want their pound of flesh.

They have done the sums and the offer they make factors in a healthy profit. You either have to fund their profit when you sell up or your estate does on your death.

As for selling up and moving somewhere cheaper, again it's easier said than done. Uprooting yourself in late life can invigorate you, but it can also lead to isolation and in some cases depression.

If you make plans early, save hard and invest wisely, then there is no reason for you to have to sell your own home just to provide life's basics or a few luxuries in retirement.

Many independent financial advisers I have spoken to view equity release – in all its forms – as an option of last rather than first resort.

Equity release is not to be taken likely. You should always take independent financial advice if you're considering equity release. A good adviser will assess the equity release provider's offer and see if it suits you. They can also suggest alternative strategies that you may not have even thought of, which can mean you don't have to start signing over your home to provide retirement income or a much needed injection of cash.

Pushing Down on Your Mortgage

Your mortgage is likely to be your biggest outgoing. Therefore, it stands to reason that if you work to reduce your mortgage debt you can divert more cash to savings and investments to bring off your big retiring wealthy plan.

Financial experts reckon that one of the smartest financial plays you can make is to pay off your mortgage early. Remember, the quicker you repay your mortgage the less interest you end up paying. For example, on a £70,000 mortgage just overpaying by £4.20 a day on your mortgage can wipe nearly ten years off the mortgage term. Just think about it, £4.20 a day – less than the price of a packet of cigarettes – and you can enjoy being shot of your mortgage 10 years sooner!

In the early years of a standard repayment mortgage a large portion of your monthly repayments goes to meet interest charges.

When you overpay on your mortgage your lender may ask if you'd like the money to go towards reducing monthly repayments or the mortgage term. The choice is really six of one or half a dozen of the other, but most people prefer the latter option, opting to slash time from their mortgage debt.

Getting the choice of mortgage right

Choosing a mortgage is one of the biggest financial decisions you ever make. However, in my experience many people spend little or no time at all choosing a mortgage, going for the lender which shouts the loudest through advertising or even simply rocking down to their bank and asking them for a loan without shopping around.

But believe me, failing to shop around for a mortgage can cost you thousands. The difference in interest rates between the best and worst buys may not sound much – 1.5 per cent or 2 per cent – but over 25 years it really mounts up. And it's not just headline interest rates that count. Some mortgages come with punishing early repayment penalties and set-up fees.

Only ever go for a mortgage which allows you to make overpayments. Most mortgages these days allow penalty-free overpayments but they usually put a cap on the percentage of the loan you can repay in anyone year. Expect only to be allowed to repay 10 per cent of your mortgage each year. You can still make larger overpayments but the lender may well hit you with an early redemption penalty.

You may be best seeking the advice of a specialist broker before choosing a mortgage. Just check that they don't charge you a whopping fee for the advice. Some firms charge 0.5 per cent of the money borrowed for giving advice, others don't charge their clients, instead collecting a fee from the lender they recommend. See Chapter 5 for more on financial advice.

There are several things you need to assess when choosing a mortgage including the following.

How is the loan to be repaid?

The choice is do you just pay off the interest – leaving the capital to be repaid at the end of the term – or do you pay off both the interest and the capital sum as you go along?

The former choice is called interest-only and the latter a repayment mortgage. Repayment is the safer option of the two.

Endowment mortgages are in effect an interest-only mortgage. You pay interest on the sum borrowed while investing in a separate investment vehicle – called an endowment policy – with the aim of building up a big enough cash pot to pay off the capital sum of your loan at the end of the term.

What is the interest rate?

In simple terms this means how much the money you're borrowing actually costs. This is expressed in the mortgage interest rate.

The lowest rates may not always be best. Some mortgage lenders have a really tasty headline rate but behind it lurk large redemption penalties, fees, and long tie-in periods (this is the length of time you have to wait to move your mortgage to another lender, without automatically triggering an early redemption penalty).

New rules introduced by the Financial Services Authority (FSA) mean that when you choose a mortgage the lender has to provide you with a Key Facts Information (KFI) document. These KFIs are very boring but, nevertheless, read them – they contain the low-down on the mortgage interest rate and fees as well as the full terms and conditions.

What happens to the interest rate in the future?

Many moons ago, as a borrower you had to take the interest rate
you were given by your bank or building society. Generally, you
were offered a mortgage pegged to the lender's Standard Variable
Rate (SVR); this would usually be around 1–2 per cent higher than
the Bank of England interest rate.

Boy have times changed! These days there is a huge choice of
lenders – literally hundreds to pick from – all offering different
interest rate packages.

In fact there is so much choice out there that it's all a little bewildering to say the least. Here is the low-down on the different mortgage
products you're likely to encounter:

- ✓ **Variable**. The interest rate on this type of mortgage varies
  according to moves in the lender's standard variable rate
  (SVR). In turn, the SVR is linked to the Bank of England base
  rate. As a rule of thumb, mortgages linked to the SVR tend to
  be the most expensive around. They are also, ironically, the
  type of mortgage most people have.

- ✓ **Fixed**. The interest rate is fixed for a specific term, usually 2, 3,
  or 5 years. Fixed rate mortgages are set a little higher than the
  Bank of England base rate but the borrower has the security
  that the amount of money they have to pay does not increase
  during the time the mortgage is fixed.

- ✓ **Tracker**. The rate is pegged to the Bank of England base rate.
  Usually, a little bit of profit is added by the lender, equivalent
  to say 0.5 per cent or 1 per cent. In effect this is a type of variable mortgage as the amount of money you pay goes up or
  down along with the base rate.

- ✓ **Discounted**. The rate is the lender's SVR with a discount
  thrown in, say 1 per cent or 2 per cent. For example, if the
  lender's SVR is 6.5 per cent a mortgage discount of 2 per cent
  will mean you're paying an interest rate of 4.5 per cent. Again,
  the amount you pay can vary – if the lender's SVR goes up you
  pay more and if it goes down you pay less.

- ✓ **Capped rate**. The rate you pay can go no higher than a
  pre-agreed level. The idea is to give you the best of both
  worlds – if rates fall so do your repayments, but if they rise
  then the damage they can do is limited because the capped
  rate kicks in.

- ✓ **Offset**. This type of mortgage came to the UK about 10 years
  after being pioneered in Australia. The idea is that you deposit

your savings with your mortgage provider and the interest on those savings goes to pay off the mortgage. Lots of people thought this was a great idea and piled into offset products. However, the rate of interest paid on the savings is below what can be had through the best High Street savings accounts, therefore offsets may not be that great a deal.

Instead of going for an offset simply shop around for the best savings account and use the interest you receive to overpay on your mortgage each month.

In life you rarely get something for nothing. Some great looking fixed rate, capped, or discounted deals come with long tie-in periods. Tie-ins mean you can't move to another mortgage provider without incurring a redemption penalty, which can be as high as 3 per cent or even 4 per cent of the amount of money you owe. Some lenders, once the discounted or capped period has expired, even move you onto a rate *higher* than the SVR. Be wary of this tactic, particularly on attractive-looking fixed and discounted deals.

Swapping lenders to save a packet

The lengths some people go to save money amazes me – cutting out coupons for two pence off a can of beans or driving miles out their way to fill up at the cheapest petrol station.

I suppose they are living their life by the maxim: 'Look after the pennies and the pounds will look after themselves.' However, they would do a lot, lot better by moving their mortgage between providers every few years. Most financial experts agree that banks' SVRs are a very bad deal. Far better offers exist, but these are only available if you switch providers. Remember, 1 per cent interest on a £100,000 mortgage is equivalent to £60 in monthly repayments. You can literally save thousands by steering clear of SVRs.

It's never been easier to switch and this is how you do it:

1. Apply over the phone to the lender.

2. Send proof of income (usually a P60 and your last three monthly payslips).

3. Fork out for the mortgage company's valuation of the property.

4. Get your solicitor to dot the Is and cross the Ts.

From start to finish the whole process shouldn't take any longer than four to six weeks. What's more, some lenders offer free valuation and legal fees to tempt you to switch your mortgage to them. Chapter 20 has more details on switching lenders.

Mortgage companies charge fees for switching – expect to pay anything from £200 to £500. But if you've chosen a good mortgage you may be able to make this back in reduced repayments within a year.

As soon as your present mortgage deal comes to an end look to move elsewhere, otherwise the lender shifts you on to an uncompetitive SVR or worse! If you really don't want the hassle, still tell your current lender that you're looking to move. They may well offer to reduce your interest rate to keep your custom – if you don't ask, you don't get!

Chapter 14

Maximising the Value of Your Property

. . . .

In This Chapter

▶ Realising how your home can help you retire wealthy

▶ Deciding on the right time to buy property

▶ Improving your own home for profit

▶ Developing a property for profit

. . . .

*F*or most of us our home has a double purpose. First, it's a roof over our heads, somewhere safe to bring the family up. Secondly, it's our main asset – when its value rises, most of us feel richer.

On the flip side, when it falls the reverse happens. Ask anyone who got on the property ladder ten, twenty, or thirty years ago and they can tell you just how important an asset a home can be.

In short, it's likely that your home plays a huge part in your retiring wealthy plan.

In this chapter I show you how to boost the value of your property investment by making home improvements, or by developing or building a brand new home from scratch. All in all, I outline the tactics you can use to ensure you're a winner when it comes to bricks and mortar.

Understanding the Importance of Property

There's no doubt about it; over the past decade property has been one of the best investments to be had. According to the Halifax bank UK house prices have more than doubled in the past ten years. During the same period, low interest rates have meant that even the highest paying cash deposit savings accounts have returned around 4–5 per cent a year.

During the same period share investments have done their own version of the hokey-cokey, in one minute, out the next. Overall, the index of shares in the UK's 100 leading companies has grown sharply since 1995, but between 2000 and early 2003 shares lost roughly half their value.

But being a property owner isn't just about capital growth. After all, you don't actually realise any growth in the value of your property until you sell it and many people are very happy staying put for years on end.

Investing in property can help your retiring wealthy plan in different ways:

✔ **You're not renting.** If you're not a property owner then you're likely to be a tenant. Friends of mine have often referred to rent payments as *dead money*, by which they mean that they are paying out but not seeing any return. At least if you have a mortgage (presuming it's on a repayment basis) part of your monthly payment goes to increasing the portion of the property that you own outright.

✔ **You can borrow more cash on better terms.** Lenders love homeowners. They have a major asset which can be used to secure a loan. Simply put, this means that if you as a homeowner don't keep up your repayments the lender has the option to come and take your home. This gives lenders the surety that come what may they get their money back. Loans *secured* against property are generally much cheaper than loans which are *unsecured* – under an unsecured arrangement the lender is relying on the individuals 'scout's honour' to pay the loan back.

The maximum amount you can borrow through a secured loan is closely related to the value of the asset – usually property – used to secure it. Secured loans tend to be of high value and are repaid over 25 years – the standard mortgage term. Unsecured loans, on the other hand, are usually capped to between £15,000 and £25,000. Unsecured loans have to be repaid within four or five years.

Just because property unlocks the door to cheaper and larger loan deals, doesn't mean you should necessarily take advantage. Sometimes it can be a good move to access a secured loan to invest in your future or to enhance the value of your property, but it's not a good idea if you only want to splash out on here today gone tomorrow possessions and holidays. See Chapter 2 for more on spotting the difference between good and bad debt.

Remembering Not to Overestimate the Role of Property

It's a fair guess that nearly every dinner party held in the UK in the past few years has probably not even reached the dessert stage without some discussion of house prices. Usually someone around the table announces that the value of their home has risen by 'X' per cent in no time at all.

But people who talk about how much they are making from their property sometimes forget three fundamental points:

- ✔ **You're incurring mortgage and other costs**. You need to subtract any money you pay in mortgage interest charges from the 'profit' that you make. In addition, there are lots of other costs such as solicitor and estate agency fees to factor in.

- ✔ **Property rarely fetches the asking price**. Just because a house is on the market for £200,000 doesn't mean it sells for that. Apart from when the housing market is in boom times, generally sellers work in a bit of wriggle room into the price. For guidance sake, sellers can expect to get between 92 per cent and 95 per cent of their asking price (provided, of course the asking price isn't unrealistically high).

- ✔ **Other house prices are on the rise**. If you sell your property what do you do next? For most people the answer is buy another one. If you buy a bigger place in the same area as you've just sold in, it's a racing certainty that you're actually upping your mortgage debt to do so. In truth, the only time you actually realise profit from property is when you sell and don't buy again, or purchase somewhere less expensive but probably smaller.

Putting all your resources into property may not be a smart ploy. There are big dangers in allowing your financial well-being to become wedded and chained to the value of your property. This is all fine if values rise, but several times in the recent past prices have fallen and many people's finances have sunk along with them. Try and aim for a balance of investments including cash deposit accounts, shares, and property.

Getting to grips with the house price cycle

House prices tend to move in cycles. Looking back over the past two decades, there was an inflationary cycle in the mid to late 1980s when annual house price inflation rose from 4–5 per cent to over 20 per cent a year. This period of price growth was followed by a market crash between 1990 and 1994 when prices fell by nearly a third (or more in some areas). The mid 1990s saw house price inflation rise at little more than inflation throughout the economy as people tried to recover from the shock of the crash. But from the late 1990s to 2004 prices at first picked up and then soared higher than ever as the wider economy enjoyed growth and interest rates fell.

In 2005–2006, house price inflation has ground to a bit of halt, this time due to the fact that prices have escalated so far away from wages that many younger people don't earn enough to enable them to borrow enough to afford to buy.

Generally, not all parts of the UK see house price rises or falls at the same time. In 2004, for example, the north of England, Wales, Scotland, and Northern Ireland all saw house price rise by 10 per cent, while London and the south of England saw prices stand still and even fall in some parts.

But most property market experts reckon that a fresh cycle of house price rises or falls starts in London and the south east and then a wave effect washes over the country. This is because London and the south east are by far and away the wealthiest parts of the country and what happens there today affects the rest of the country tomorrow. This has proved right again recently; in 2005 house price inflation has slowed dramatically in the north of England, Wales, and Scotland, mirroring the previous year's slowdown in London and south of England.

Taking the Property Plunge

In order for your property purchase to be a sound investment you have to be able to resell it with ease.

Get your property purchase wrong and it can be an albatross around your neck – it can mean you have to stay put and can't move up the property ladder.

Here are some key factors which influence the marketability and therefore the price of property:

- ✔ **Location, location, location**. Any estate agent will tell you that where a property is located is selling point *numero uno*! Be near good schools, transport links (although not too near a road or train station), a nice row of shops and restaurants, and a property is far easier to sell.

✔ **Freehold basis**. Can you do what you want with the property or is there a separate freeholder charging a fortune in service charges and ground rent? Having the freehold or a share of the freehold can add up to 15 per cent to the value of a property.

✔ **Good decorative order**. Are the outside and inside of the property smart? Are there wow factors, like real fireplaces or a beautiful garden?

If you're looking at buying a leasehold property, check out how much it will cost to buy the freehold. You may well find that buying the freehold is a sound investment as it boosts the value of the property.

Some ex-local authority property – particularly in high-rise blocks – and property on a short lease can be very hard to get a mortgage on. If you want to buy this sort of property then you probably need to be a cash buyer and accept that when it comes to resale time your market may be limited to other cash buyers.

Deciding when to buy property

Like any investment buying property is about timing. Some may think the only timing involves trying to successfully second guess the property market, the big idea being to catch a wave of house price inflation just as it forms and riding it to wealth. However, timing markets is notoriously tricky and dangerous.

The type of timing I am referring too is gauging whether it's the right time in your life to make such a huge financial commitment. Whether you're a would-be first time buyer, buy-to-let investor, or are considering trading up your property for a larger one, ask yourself the following questions before setting your sights on property purchase:

✔ **Are your finances in place?** Figure out what your finances will look like after you have bought the property. Remember to factor in all costs, including moving in and redecoration as well as stamp duty, legal fees, mortgage arrangement charges, and funding a deposit. If after all this your finances are wiped out, perhaps you need to save a little more before taking the plunge.

✔ **Is your job secure?** Be honest with yourself: Is there a chance you can lose your job anytime soon? Perhaps the project you're working on is coming to an end. I have come across some horror stories of people taking on a whopping mortgage debt only to lose their job soon after or even on the day of completion. If you don't have a degree of job security, the next best thing is being secure that if you lose your job you have transferable skills which allow you to work freelance or get a new job quick. In the modern world few of us have 100 per cent job security. All in all whether you're confident in your employment prospects is your call.

✔ **Can you afford the mortgage?** After you have made your mortgage repayments, are you still able to afford to pay the bills, socialise, and meet emergency household expenses – without borrowing more money?

✔ **What can you do if interest rates rise?** In recent years interest rates have been historically very low but they may not remain that way in future. In the early 1990s hundreds of thousands of homes were repossessed when interest rates spiralled. Look at your projected mortgage repayments, double them, and calculate if you can afford them or not.

Just because you fall down on one of the above questions, it doesn't necessarily follow that you should not buy property. You may have an ultra secure job, which means you can safely say you're able to build your savings back up after purchase. If, however, you fall down on more than one factor, think seriously about postponing your property owning ambitions for the time being.

Always try to put down as big a deposit as possible on your property purchase. For starters, the bigger the deposit the less you have to borrow and the smaller your mortgage repayments. What's more, having a large deposit provides you with a financial cushion, just in case property prices fall.

Trading up: Playing the home ownership game

Climbing the property ladder not only means you get to live in bigger and smarter homes with enough room to spread yourself around and bring up a family, it can also mean – as long as you're savvy about when you buy and sell – that you boost your chances of retiring wealthy.

You've probably seen friends and family alike climb the property ladder, moving from one-bedroom, to two-bedroom, to larger three-and four-bedroom homes with nice gardens. Hopefully along the way they have sold their homes at a profit, using the equity to fund more ambitious property purchases. What's more, most people tend to get wealthier and find better paid work as they progress through their twenties, thirties, and forties. This combined with money made on the sale of previous property means that lenders are happy to lend them more money.

Ultimately, the big idea for most is to find a place that they are happy to settle in for the long term and work to pay off the mortgage. When they come to retirement, all being well, they own a great big asset – all that originating from their first tentative steps on the property ladder.

Improving and Extending Your Home

One of the main ways to increase the value of your home is to make improvements to it.

Sometimes it can be much more cost-effective to extend your property rather than move to a larger home. By choosing to extend rather than move you save on estate agency, stamp duty, and legal fees.

Currently, you have to pay stamp duty at 1 per cent on property purchases over £120,000. The stamp duty charge rises as you buy more expensive property. Stamp duty rises to 3 per cent on property over £250,000 and 4 per cent over £500,000.

If you want to retain or boost the marketability of your property best avoid making too much of a 'statement' in any renovation or redecoration you undertake. Avoid bright colour schemes and renovations which have a limited appeal – that's a thumbs-up to en suite bathrooms and new kitchens, but a thumbs-down to pigeon lofts and even swimming pools.

Home improvements may involve a trade-off between satisfying your own tastes and making the property appealing to buyers.

Always try and improve with one eye on the future saleability of the property. Ask yourself the following questions:

- ✔ Does the renovation or redecoration add value to the property?

- ✔ How much value does the renovation or redecoration add and is it more than the cost of the work?

- ✔ Does the renovation require you to move out while the work is complete? If so how much does alternative accommodation cost?

Improvements that can add value to your property include the
following:

- ✔ **Loft conversion**. Creating an extra bedroom through a loft
  conversion can add value. However, properly done conversions are not cheap, in fact they can cost well over £10,000
  (depending on what you want done).

- ✔ **Extra bathroom**. Having more than one bathroom is a big
  boon. En suite bathrooms are all the rage, adding that little bit
  of luxury and privacy.

- ✔ **New kitchen**. A modern, tastefully designed (and properly
  installed) kitchen can be a huge selling point, particularly for
  buyers with families.

- ✔ **Garage**. Having safe off-street parking means lower car insurance premiums and provides welcome extra security for
  buyers.

Some improvements that may not be worth it:

- ✔ **Swimming pool**. Generally, a pool costs a lot of money to
  maintain and often needs to be rebuilt every twenty or so
  years.

- ✔ **Reducing the number of bedrooms**. Usually, the number of
  bedrooms a property has is key to its value. Therefore, don't
  be tempted to create large master bedrooms by losing a spare
  bedroom. Reduce the number of bedrooms at your peril, no
  matter how 'boxy' they are!

Improvements done on the cheap or to a low standard can actually
reduce the value of your property rather than increasing it.

If you know any friendly local estate agents, ask their opinion on
whether the improvement you plan adds value or not.

Some renovations require planning permission and have to comply
with building regulations. Loft conversions are a good example of a
renovation which needs planning permission. Don't be tempted to
renovate without proper permission – you risk having the council
ordering you to tear the work down. What's more, when it comes
time to sell up, your buyer's solicitor is likely to discover what
you've done and either halt the sale or demand money off.

If the work you are undertaking has to comply with building regulations the local authority sends a planning officer out to you at the
start of the job. The planning officer makes clear what you have to
do to comply with building regulations. The officer returns once

the job is complete and checks that you have followed what she/he has said. You are then issued with a document stating that the work complies with regulations.

Developing Property for Profit

No matter how hard you work at it or how tasteful and carefully thought through your home improvements, they're unlikely to make you a fortune big enough to allow you to retire wealthy.

But two other ways can turn property into big profit. So big are the potential profits on offer that it can give your retiring wealthy plan a real push in the right direction:

- ✔ Become a developer by buying a property wreck and doing it up.
- ✔ Build a new property from scratch.

A house, bungalow, or flat bought with development in mind is often referred to as an *investment property*.

For more information on the management, building, and technical issues involved, take a look at Nicholas Walliman's *Self Build and Renovation For Dummies* (Wiley).

Becoming a property developer

It seems every other TV programme is about property development. In recent years, as the property market has boomed, literally thousands of people have given up the day job and turned their hands to development.

The big idea behind development is that you buy a property, do it up, and sell it on for profit. It's quite often the case that the more work you need to do on a property, the greater the potential to turn a profit.

The following costs have to be taken into consideration:

- ✔ Expenditure on labour and materials.
- ✔ Mortgage repayments during the time it takes to renovate and then sell the property.
- ✔ Legal and estate agency fees.

✔ Any fees charged by architects or project managers you
employ.

✔ Compensation for the time you spend seeing the project
through.

With property development time is very much money. The longer
you take to complete your project the more you have to pay in
mortgage interest.

If you take out a mortgage to fund a property development with
the aim of selling it on at a profit, then you're probably best going
for an interest-only mortgage. As the name suggests, under this
type of mortgage you pay only the interest on the loan rather than
the capital sum. Interest-only mortgages generally mean lower
monthly payments, helping keep your overheads to a minimum
during the project.

Whether you just develop a property which you go on to live in or
take it on as a career choice, you're best following these simple
steps.

Have a full survey done

With development property it's vital to have as extensive a survey
as possible done before purchase. The survey should give you an
idea how much work you need to do to the property to bring it up
to A1 condition. Expect to pay around £700 or £800 for a full structural survey.

Draw up a realistic budget

Talk through your development plans with the builder. Submit
clear written instructions before any work starts and always obtain
a written quote. On top of this add the mortgage costs, legal, estate
agency, stamp duty, and any other fees.

Once you've got a budget, it's crucial to stick to it. Every penny
you go over your budget eats into your potential profit.

Property developers I have spoken to recommend that once you
have a plan for your development in place you stick to it. Chopping
and changing designs and plans mid-way through a development is
a recipe for delay, error, and extra cost.

One of the biggest mistake novice property developers make is to
get carried away with creating a dream home, without keeping a
tight rein on expenditure.

Have a resale price in mind

If you're developing for profit, get to know the local market. The aim is to gauge, as precisely as possible, how much your property may fetch on the open market once all the work you plan is complete.

Some properties are listed, which means that they are considered of particular historical significance. The rules governing renovation of listed properties tend to be very strict and the penalties for breaking them severe. For further information on listed properties check out English heritage at www.english-heritage. org, Cadw in Wales www.cadw.co.uk, Scottish Heritage www. historic-scotland.gov.uk, or the Environment and Heritage Service in Northern Ireland www.ehsni.gov.uk. Ultimately, though, the best advice may be not to buy a listed property to develop in the first place.

For more on property development, check out Melanie Bien's *Buying a Home on a Budget For Dummies* (Wiley).

Buying on the cheap: Property auctions

A property auction is often a great place to find homes to do up. Generally property sold at auction fetches far less than it would through an estate agent. However, be aware that you only have 28 days once you successfully bid for a property to complete the purchase. (You have to pay a 10 per cent deposit on the day.)

Best get your skates on. Have a full structural survey done, so that you can gauge how much the whole project is going to cost and whether it's worthwhile.

During an economic recession you often find the number of properties being sold at auction rises sharply. This is usually because mortgage companies have repossessed the property and are trying to offload it to recover the debt. If you have the spare cash, this can be a good time to pick up a property bargain.

Building a property from scratch

Building your own home seems like a huge hassle – and guess what, it is just that. However, it can be a cheap way of getting on the property ladder. What's more, going down the self-build route means you can get just what you want from the property (just as long as you can afford the land and the work to be done).

Self-build properties are generally anywhere from 25 per cent to 35 per cent cheaper than buying a ready-built home. All it costs is the price of the land, the labour, and materials. Crucially, you're not boosting the profits of a multinational developer.

Self-builds can be a huge, expensive undertaking. The average self-build costs £150,000 plus. A number of Web sites offer advice on how to undertake a self-build – check out `www.selfbuild.abc.co.uk` or `www.buildstore.co.uk`.

Very few self-builders actually throw up a home themselves. Instead the vast majority trust to professional builders and architects to see their dreams into reality.

Funding a self-build project

The financial side of self-builds works differently than a standard mortgage on a pre-built home.

The bank or building society assess how much it is willing to lend you in the normal way – taking your income and financial commitments into account. However, your lender isn't just going to give you a big pile of cash and let you get on with it. They want to keep their hand on the rudder, to a certain extent, just to ensure that you are doing things in a timely and efficient manner. There are two types of self-build mortgages available:

- **After work is completed**. The mortgage company only pays you the money once the work is complete. Generally, they break down the work into four parts and then release funds only after a particular stage has been completed.

- **Prior to the work starting**. The lender lets you have the cash before the work is done. Again they do this in stages – once one stage is completed they then release the money to start the next stage of the project. This type of mortgage was once rare but has come more to the fore of late.

Expect to be able to borrow a maximum of between 3 to 4 times your income if you're undertaking a self-build project.

Getting the basics of self build right

You're going to need to call in the professionals if you want to make a success of your self-build project.

It is a case of all hands on deck and you're likely to need the following people:

✔ **A surveyor to value the plot of land you're buying**. It can be hard to gauge off your own bat if you're paying the right price for land.

✔ **An architect to draw up your plans**. At the early stages of a self-build project the architect is key. They listen to what you want and draw up precise plans for the builder to follow. Architects are skilled people and do not come cheap. Try to find one who has experience of self-build; they have a good idea of what is possible and what isn't.

✔ **A builder to carry through your plans**. Word of mouth is often the best way of finding a quality builder but if you don't have someone specific in mind, make sure you go with one that is a member of the industry organisation the Federation of Master Builders. This gives you an avenue for complaint if they don't do what you ask. Builders often get a bad press, but in reality people don't help themselves by purely hiring whoever's cheapest, rather than going for experience, even if it costs a little more.

✔ **A project manager**. This is someone who oversees your plans to fruition. You can do this yourself or you can hire a professional. An experienced and capable project manager can be a godsend – they see that materials are delivered and the work is done on time and to the right specification.

✔ **A good solicitor**. You need to pick a solicitor with experience of buying and selling land rather than just houses. They do searches in the same way as for a standard home.

You need planning permission to develop the land and whatever you do must comply with building regulations.

Chapter 15

Buy-to-Letting Your Way to Riches

*I*n recent years buy-to-let property has become the must-have investment.

Nowadays, when people talk about having their very own portfolio they are just as likely to be talking bricks and mortar as shares. It seems everybody fancies life as a landlord.

In this chapter I explain the role buy-to-let can play in your big retiring wealthy plan as well as the benefits and pitfalls of the landlord life.

 If you want more information on the mechanics of buy-to-let, pick up a copy of Melanie Bien and Robert S. Griswold's *Renting Out Your Property For Dummies* (Wiley).

Choosing Buy-to-Let

Get a buy-to-let property investment right and it offers the El Dorado of regular income and capital growth. The hope is that the rental income from the property will cover the costs of maintaining the property and any outstanding mortgages. Anything over and above this gives the investor a return on their investment – otherwise known as the buy-to-let investment yield. More on this later in the chapter.

Seeing the buy-to-let advantages

It's not hard to see why buy-to-let has caught the imagination of the investment community, particularly when you consider the following factors:

- ✔ **Other investments doing badly.** Shares took a hit after the dotcom bubble burst in 2000. Many small investors lost a fortune and are now reluctant to return to shares.

- ✔ **Pension problems.** Following mis-selling scandals and the collapse of some workplace pension schemes, people's confidence in pensions has been shaken.

- ✔ **Property confidence boost.** People have seen the value of their own homes rise and this helps give them the confidence to buy more property in the hope that they can strike lucky again.

- ✔ **Being their own boss.** Buy-to-let gives people the chance to strike out on their own and run a business, perhaps in their spare time from their day job.

- ✔ **Mortgage market changes.** Lenders have been falling over themselves to offer buy-to-let mortgages. The range of buy-to-let mortgage products has expanded and the cost fallen. See more on this later in this chapter.

- ✔ **Interest rates are low.** Interest rates have more than halved since their height in the early- to mid-1990s. This fall in rates makes borrowing cheaper and savings less rewarding, tempting people to borrow cash to invest in property.

- ✔ **Greater mobility.** People move around more than ever for their work. This can tempt some to buy homes in different parts of the country.

Few people are rich enough to buy property with hard cash. Instead they have to borrow the funds through a buy-to-let mortgage.

Understanding the drawbacks of buy-to-let

Buy-to-let isn't a one-way street to profit. There are some downsides, such as the following:

- ✔ **You can't get your money out in a hurry.** Even under a best-case scenario it takes at least a couple of months to offload a buy-to-let property. If the housing market is in the doldrums it can take a year or so to sell a property.

✔ **They are difficult investments to manage**. Even if you employ a letting agent to do the hard work for you there is still stacks for you to do as a buy-to-let investor. From repairs to ensuring the mortgage is paid, the lot of the buy-to-let investor is much more taxing than having the money tucked away in a savings account.

✔ **It can unbalance your investment plans**. Buy-to-let property is a huge investment – it's not only the costs of purchasing the property, it's also the ongoing repairs, furnishing and, if it's bought with a mortgage, there are interest payments too. The danger is that buy-to-let investors have all their eggs in one basket.

✔ **It can be an uncertain business**. Think of it this way: If you buy a bond or savings account you receive interest as regular as clockwork, but have a time when your buy-to-let property sits empty and you will have nothing coming in – not a sausage! All the time, though, you still have to fork out for the upkeep of the property, council tax, and mortgage repayments.

Knowing Your Target Group

It's vital to the success of buy-to-let to have a good understanding of your target group. Usually, landlords aim to attract tenants from one or more of the following groups:

✔ **Students**. Gone are the days of Rick and Vivian from TV's *The Young Ones*. Students today have ready cash (usually borrowed) and want a few of life's luxuries; and they often houseshare, which means you have more than one point of contact to chase should the rent be late.

✔ **Young professionals**. For many landlords this is the dream group. They are less destructive than students to a property, and have good jobs earning enough to pay rent. What's more, property that caters for young professionals tends to be easy to sell on.

✔ **Families with children**. This can be a very broad-ranging group from lone parents on benefits to working families looking for short lets before moving into their own home. They tend to be respectable tenants, although children can create problems for neighbours and damage the odd bit of décor.

✔ **Professional high earners**. These people want the best and are willing to pay for it, generally being older higher earners, successful in their careers perhaps needing to rent following a divorce or having to take on a project or new job far away from the home they share with their family.

If you draw anything from the seemingly hundreds of property makeover programmes on TV it should be to decorate your buy-to-let property with your tenants in mind. If you're going for the young professional market they're likely to like modern and stylish décor rather than lots of chintz and Formica!

You may want to designate your property non-smoking. This should help you save on your buildings insurance and minimise the damage to your property from burns and smoke staining your décor. However, by barring smokers you are automatically excluding one in four of the population and therefore reducing your target market.

Getting the Property Location Right

It may be a bit hackneyed but the desirability of a property and therefore its saleability and value depends in great part on its location. Think about it. Where would you rather live – near decent transport links, shops, and a good school in a nice neighbourhood, or in the shadow of a flyover . . . next door to a glue factory?

People who rent probably have very specific needs other than a roof over their head. The more you offer your tenants in terms of location and facilities the more likely they are to stay put and keep boosting your bank balance.

You need to pick your location with your target tenant in mind. Therefore, if you're looking to attract university students best buy a place as close as possible to the university – although not so close that you are swamped by student houses which can put off potential buyers for your property later down the line.

Buying a buy-to-let property *off plan* – meaning not yet built – seems a painless route into the world of being a landlord. What's more lots of off plan properties come with sweeteners such as cash-back to cover stamp duty fees. But there are hidden dangers with buying off plan. Firstly, you'll be paying top price because the property is brand new and secondly, if lots of other properties in the development are bought by other buy-to-let investors, a glut in the local market may be created forcing down rents across the board.

Here are some things you should bear in mind when choosing a location:

- ✔ **Closeness to shops**. One of the first things people look for is how far they have to go if they need the standard pint of milk. The rule is close to shops but not too close; that is, not actually living above a retail premises.

- ✔ **Transport links**. Same rule again – close is good but not so close that the tenant will be woken by all-night freight traffic.

- ✔ **Local schools**. If your target tenants are families with children being in the catchment area of a good school can be a real boon. There are even cases of families renting property just so they can send their little treasure to the right school.

- ✔ **Neighbourhood**. Yes to leafy environs and nice families, no to boarded-up shops and graffiti. Ask yourself: Is the property located somewhere that if push came to shove you'd be OK living in yourself? If the answer's no, then walk away.

Making the most of property shortages

In parts of the UK there aren't enough houses to go around. An increasing population, strict planning regulations, the curtailment of council house building, and the fact that there are more households due to divorce and lone parenthood, all result in demand for housing outstripping supply.

The government is always saying it will 'do something' about the housing shortage – that is, build homes – but so far nothing concrete (geddit?) has happened. Everyone knows more houses are needed but no one can agree exactly where they should be built, of what type they should be, or even how many are needed.

What does this shortage of housing mean for the would-be buy-to-let investor? In one word: opportunity. If you own any asset in short supply then it's bound to fetch a good price both in terms of rental and when it comes time to sell on.

However, the housing shortage isn't universal across the country – in fact in the north of England it can be said that there is over supply. Shortages are mainly concentrated in the south of the country. Some buy-to-let investors haven't cottoned onto this north–south divide and have continued to merrily snap up property where there is actually plenty of stock – over the long term they may find it tricky to turn a profit! So before taking the plunge check to see what the local housing supply situation is. If there is for example a major governmental or housing association housebuilding project underway it is an indication of a need but can equally be a sign that it's being addressed.

You may have to make some concessions to your budget when picking a location. Avoid unnecessary expense by plumping for highly desirable areas that are inappropriate for your target group. What's the point, for example, of shelling out extra for property in the catchment area of a good school when you're looking to attract university students?

 It may be tempting to pick up a cheap property in an awful location, on the premise that it's a bargain way to get rental income. However, this purchase can be a mug's game because it can prove both difficult to rent out and ultimately to sell on.

 One good way of assessing the health of the local buy-to-let market is to call a letting agent posing as someone looking to rent. Ask them what the choice of property is and whether you can negotiate on rent. If it appears that there is lots of property choice and that the rental asking price can be negotiated downwards, perhaps you ought to consider buying elsewhere.

Getting Your Buy-to-Let Finances Right

Treat your buy-to-let investment like any other. Be calculating and rational about it – sit down and do the sums.

 Before investing in a buy-to-let do some thorough research on what the property is likely to fetch in rental. Check out local newspapers for similar properties advertised and talk to letting agents.

Your buy-to-let property really must cover the following expenditure:

- ✔ The mortgage.
- ✔ The letting agent's fees.
- ✔ Council tax, water rates, and other charges.
- ✔ The cost of insuring the property.
- ✔ The cost of advertising the property if you're renting it out yourself.
- ✔ Maintenance of the property and its furnishings.

Add up all these costs and anything above this figure you make in rent is profit.

In a perfect world your profit should beat what you would get if you had the money you have spent on the property invested in a bank or building society savings account.

At present the very best savings accounts available are paying between 4 and 5 per cent interest a year before tax.

Taking tax into account

Sadly, no free tax ride exists when it comes to buy-to-let. The Revenue has a few little tax nasties tucked up its sleeve.

Fortunately, as a landlord, tax breaks are available to you to cut your bill, including:

- ✔ **Income tax:** Your rental income is subject to income tax but with an important caveat. Income tax is only due on profit – defined as the difference between rental income received and mortgage interest costs and the other *allowable expenses* (including insurance costs and letting agent's commission).

- ✔ **Capitals gains tax (CGT):** If you sell property which isn't your main residence (where you live) any profit you make is subject to CGT. Use your CGT allowance to the max – you have a tax free CGT allowance of £8,500 (in the 2005–2006 tax year), so use this when selling up your buy-to let property.

 If you decide to take the plunge and purchase a buy-to-let property why not get an accountant to fill in your tax return? A good accountant should be able to take advantage of whatever tax breaks are available.

 You may be able to claim an allowance of 10 per cent of the rental income you receive from the property to cover wear and tear on the property.

Understanding and using property yield

A quick sum can work out whether your buy-to-let investment is worth it.

It's very simple: Divide the value of the property by the monthly rental and, hey presto, you get the property yield. For example a £200,000 property let out for £1,000 a month has a yield of 6 per cent.

Deciding the level of rent

Setting and then ultimately increasing the level of rent that you ask for your buy-to-let property is a crucial decision. Get the level of rent wrong, and you can either be giving a bit of a free ride to your tenants or be left with an empty property.

If you employ a letting agent he or she should give you a good idea of what the going market rate is. If you're managing the property yourself then do your research; check out the competition – what is being asked for similar properties? You can even be a little cheeky and go and see rival properties, posing as a prospective tenant. This makes it easier for you to judge what rent you should charge.

At some point you also need to increase the rent. Best review the rent you charge once a year. This can be a tricky business – you don't want to get the tenant's back up to such an extent that they move out. After all, a vacant property is a drain on your finances. The art of gentle persuasion is the key: Remember, good tenants are worth keeping sweet. Regularly review the local rental market – if other landlords have been raising their rents perhaps you should follow suit. Don't forget that your tenant is likely to have a pay rise once a year. They should understand that from time to time you need a little extra.

But this quick calculation doesn't give you the whole picture. You need to take into account all the expenses outlined above and any period in which the property will be vacant – and therefore not earning rent.

The Association of Retail Letting Agents (ARLA) estimates that the average buy-to-let property is vacant for on average around two months a year. Apply a two month void period to the above example, and the annual rent falls to $10,000 and the yield to 5 per cent.

Factor in your expenses and the property yield falls. But don't despair: Capital growth may ride to the rescue.

No one knows for certain where the property market is headed, although lots of people claim to have insider knowledge. If the past is anything to go by then over the long term property should do as well as shares or any other type of investment.

Stellar growth in property prices – more than doubling over the past six years across the UK – is the exception rather than the rule. If you bank on this repeating itself you may come a cropper. Factor in steady growth, perhaps 5–7 per cent a year, and be prepared that if you hold property for a long time then it may go through periods when its value stagnates or even falls.

Renovating a property for profit

The idea of taking a wreck of a property and turning it into a rental goldmine appeals to many investors. Properties sold in poor condition to people looking to renovate them for rental or to sell them on are called *investment properties*.

However, for every successful investment property venture there are plenty where investors find the going too tough, give up, and go home to lick their financial wounds.

There are lots of things to bear in mind with investment property, not the least of which include:

✔ **The property may not be in a good area**. Remember the house I mentioned under the flyover and next to the glue factory. Well, think of it again but this time requiring renovation as well.

✔ **Difficult to raise finance**. Mortgage companies rightfully get very twitchy about investment property and may not lend until the repairs have been carried out. This can put you in a catch-22 situation. You are likely to have to borrow against your own home or other buy-to-let property, if you have any, to get a mortgage.

✔ **You may not have the skills and money**. Even if you're going to employ trades-people to do the hard graft, do you have the contacts and the skills not to be ripped off? Are you au fait with local planning and building regulations? Anyone who has ever taken on a renovation project will tell you it's much harder and more expensive than you first realise.

Having put the frighteners on you a couple of plus points apply to investment property. Firstly, get it right and it can be a lower cost way to become a buy-to-let landlord. Secondly, there are grants and relief from stamp duty available for people looking to renovate property in inner city areas. Check with your local authority and the Office of the Deputy Prime Minister (ODPM) Web site for more on housing, www.odpm.gov.uk.

Arranging a buy-to-let mortgage

With the price of housing so high few people can afford to purchase buy-to-let property outright: They need a mortgage.

Buy-to-let mortgages used to be a very specialist financial product with few providers – most of them charging the earth.

However, the recent boom in buy-to-let has led mainstream mortgage lenders to rush into the marketplace. Nowadays, plenty of competition exists and there are some good deals to be had. Nevertheless, you still have to jump through a few hoops to get your hands on the cash.

Interest rates on buy-to-let mortgage rates are generally 1 or 1.5 per cent higher than the rates that someone using a mortgage to purchase a home to live in has to pay.

Understanding lenders' calculations

Lenders will assess you and the property before making a decision on whether to lend you the cash to buy the property.

They make their decision based on the following factors.

Loan to value limit

Banks and building societies calculate a figure called the Loan to Value (LTV) which is the largest proportion of the property price that they'll lend you – the rest you fund as a deposit. If you're purchasing a home for yourself to live in you can get an LTV of 90, 95, or even 100 per cent of the purchase price. Buy-to-let mortgage lenders tend to be a little more cautious and will lend you between 70 and 80 per cent of purchase price. This means you need a hefty deposit.

The likely rental income

The lender will look at the property you plan to buy and assess what rental income you can reasonably expect it to bring in. As a rule, lenders insist that the likely rental income should more than cover the mortgage. Typically the rent will have to be anything from 1.3 times to 1.6 times the monthly cost of mortgage repayments, a nifty number called the *cover*. The lender will adjust the amount it is willing to lend you so that it tallies with the cover. Ultimately, this may mean that you have to find a bigger deposit than would be the case if you were only trying to meet the lender's loan to value benchmark.

In general, the higher deposit you're prepared to pay, the lower the rate of interest on your mortgage.

Before signing up to a buy-to-let mortgage you may want to take financial advice from a professional who specialises in mortgages. Many mortgage brokers offer advice, including Charcol www.charcol.co.uk, London and County www.lcplc.co.uk, and Towry Law www.towrylaw.com. A good independent financial adviser who specialises in mortgages can also help; check out www.unbiased.co.uk for a list of local IFAs.

Looking at different buy-to-let mortgages

First you have to choose between a repayment or interest-only mortgage. Under a repayment mortgage each month you pay enough to cover interest charges and to repay a small part of the original loan. With an interest-only mortgage your monthly payments cover the interest but you are still left with the capital sum to pay off at the end of the loan. In short, the choice is do you want to pay now or later? Many people may instinctively say later but you may not be in a position to pay the capital sum 25 years down the line – the standard mortgage term. See Chapter 14 for more on mortgages.

Next you have to choose between a fixed, variable, or discounted rate of interest. The differences are as follows:

- ✔ **Fixed rate**. Repayments are fixed at a particular level for a set period of time, usually, 2, 3, or 5 years. Once the fix comes to an end you move to a variable rate, and if you want to move to another mortgage provider you may find that you're asked to pay an *early redemption penalty* – nasty!

- ✔ **Variable rate**. The rate will move up and down with interest costs in the economy as a large. They can be a good bet if you think that rates are heading downwards.

- ✔ **Discounted rates**. This tends to be a bit of hybrid between fixed and variable. The rate you pay is linked to the variable rate with a pre-agreed percentage lopped off (discounted), so you pay less interest. However, discounted rates, like fixed rates, often come with early redemption penalties.

Early redemption penalties are worked out as a percentage of your loan. For example if an early redemption penalty is set at 2 per cent and your loan is £100,000 then the penalty to move your mortgage is £2,000. The good news is that early redemption penalty periods come to an end – eventually!

Check out all mortgage fees. Some mortgages have an attractive rate of interest but come with larger than normal arrangement and survey fees.

Fixed rate mortgages tend to have higher fees than variable rate ones.

Making a Success of Your Buy-to-Let

Having identified your target tenants, found a location, and sorted out the finances, the next thing to get right is to manage your investment properly. After all, your buy-to-let property may well be your biggest investment of the lot and your passport to retiring wealthy.

Don't forget to tell your home insurer that the property is being rented out. Buildings insurers usually charge landlords more than owner-occupiers. If something happens to your property such as a fire and you haven't been 100 per cent honest then the insurer is well within their rights to turn down your claim.

You've got to decide whether you are going to take on managing the property yourself or put your faith in a letting agent.

You may see adverts for firms offering managed investment properties. The idea is that you give these firms money, they go out and buy you a property, do it up and rent it out, giving you back a regular yield. However, some firms offering managed investment property are simply scamsters, disappearing with your cash and leaving you with no property or ramshackle rubbish. Avoid these like the plague!

Often it's best to invest in property close to where you live. For one thing you know the area – the good parts from the bad – and it is easier for you to keep an eye on it, even if you do use a letting agent.

Using a letting agent

Letting agents offer two levels of service:

- **Part management**. They find the tenant, organise the documentation and the handover of keys, and collect the rent. They act as a go-between you and the tenant.

- **Full management**. They do all the above but also have a plethora of local tradespeople on hand to make repairs and have the property cleaned when the tenants leave. This is the service to go for if you're inexperienced or live a long way from the property.

Of course, the more you ask the letting agent to do the more they charge. Each letting agent has his or her own scale of charges but as a guide expect to hand over between 10–12 per cent of the rental income in the case of part management and 15–18 per cent in the case of full management.

Only use agents that are a member of a reputable industry body such as the Association of Residential Letting Agents (ARLA). Members are listed on their Web site at `www.arla.co.uk`. This way you can complain to the trade body if you feel you have been badly treated. Also check to see that they are a member of the Client Money Protection Scheme – this protects your rent should the letting agent go bust.

If you sign up to a letting agency you may find that you automatically grant the agent to undertake emergency repairs – such as fixing a faulty boiler – without your advance approval. Read the small print!

Choosing DIY property management

This is the riskier but potentially more financially rewarding route. You take on the whole kit and caboodle of managing the property.

Be honest with yourself: A letting agent may be more up to the job of managing your property than you. An agent will know the local market, have an army of local tradespeople to carry out repairs and, crucially, employing an agent will free up your time.

If you manage the property yourself you will have to be prepared to do all the following:

- ✔ Advertise for tenants.
- ✔ Check to see that prospective tenants are bona fide.
- ✔ Arrange for the tenancy agreement to be drawn up.
- ✔ Monitor that rent arrives on time and is the right amount.
- ✔ Repair and maintain the property.
- ✔ When the tenant leaves arrange for the cleaning of the property.

Quite a lot of work, I hear you say – but if you feel up to the job you can save a packet on letting agents' fees.

Dealing with problem tenants

If you're a landlord for a long time it's a racing certainty that you come up against a problem tenant at some point. You can expect to encounter at least one of the following bad tenant nasties:

- Late payment of rent.
- Unauthorised additional occupants.
- Noisy tenants.

When you have a problem with a tenant your first port of call shouldn't be eviction. Talk to the tenant, establish what has happened and why they are acting in the way they are. Make clear in a letter to your tenant what you expect them to do to rectify the situation – pay the back rent, move out the additional occupant, or keep quiet in future. Try to be fair but don't get walked over.

If there is no improvement then move to evict the tenant. You may be able to negotiate a voluntary move out, but if not you have to go to court. Evicting a tenant can be a long drawn out process involving serving legal notices and seeking count court judgments. If you find yourself with a bad tenant then consult your letting agent, if you have one, a solicitor, or make an appointment at your local Citizens Advice Bureau. You can also check out *Renting Out Your Property For Dummies* by Melanie Bien and Robert S. Griswold (Wiley) for more on tactics on how to deal with problem tenants.

Instead of going to a solicitor each time you need a tenancy agreement you can purchase standard one-size-fits-all agreements off the shelf at stationery shops such as WH Smith.

Whether you employ an agent or DIY ultimately you're relying on your tenant to behave fairly. There are countless horror stories of tenants not paying up and actually damaging property. Make sure you or your agent take proper work and personal references before renting your property out to a new tenant.

Building a Property Portfolio

You may have heard stories of twenty or thirty somethings becoming buy-to-let millionaires. How do they do it?

To get to this fortunate position you have to borrow smart. A common tactic is that, after a few years of owning a buy-to-let and hopefully seeing its value on the open market rise, you borrow against this increased value to fund a further property purchase. This can work fine, just as long as the property continues to attract tenants in order to service the debt. The danger comes though when you need your money back quickly and have to sell the property. If the property market is doing badly it can be tricky to get the right price.

Someone may be called a buy-to-let millionaire because the total amount his or her property is worth is vast. But it's likely that in order to acquire this property in the first place they have had to borrow huge sums.

The key advantage of owning lots of properties is that when one is empty hopefully the other properties will be full. Having lots of properties should mean a regular income stream.

Selling Your Buy-to-Let Property

Selling a buy-to-let property can be just like any normal house sale. It's advertised with an estate agent and Mr and Mrs Bloggs put in an offer, arrange a mortgage, and move merrily to completion. At other times though buy-to-let investors look to sell to other investors as it helps secure a quick sale.

The buyer gets his or her hands on an established rental property. They can see accounts detailing the rental yield that has been gained from the property in the past. However, they can expect to pay top dollar for the property because in effect they are buying an established business.

Timing the property market can be very risky. No one can be certain what's going to happen to property prices next week, never mind in twelve months' time.

Serious buy-to-let investors sometimes try to play the housing market, selling some of their properties when they see property prices at a peak. They then sit on their cash and wait for prices to fall and when they do, they buy back into property.

If you sell your buy-to-let property, any profit you have made may be subject to Capital Gains Tax (CGT), see the earlier section 'Taking tax into account' for more on tax and buy-to-let.

Investing in property abroad: Fly-to-let

Increasing numbers of people are choosing to invest in property abroad. The take-off in no frills airlines means it's cheaper than ever to reach even far-off destinations where property bargains can be snapped up.

The phenomenon of investing in homes abroad has been dubbed *fly-to-let or jet-to-let*. The return on the investment is likely to come from short-term holiday lets rather than long-term tenancy.

If you fancy buying a place in the sun then you have to tread very carefully. Here are some of the things you have to be aware of:

- ✔ **Surveying the property**. It's always a good idea to get a full structural survey done before buying any property. This is especially true when buying abroad. Some European countries have building regulations that simply don't pass muster. Horror stories abound of Britons buying abroad without a survey and finding that their property is unsound or even unsafe.

- ✔ **Local laws**. Laws governing property ownership and planning regulations vary wildly from country to country. Use a local solicitor to manage your purchase. The last thing you want is to be embroiled in a land dispute or to be hit by a surprise local property tax.

- ✔ **Property management**. Face facts, you're not going to be able to do everything yourself. Hopefully, your holiday let will be successful which means the property will have to be cleaned and made ready for new tenants in double quick time. You're going to need someone on the ground to do the donkey-work and this will cost money.

- ✔ **Mortgage**. You may find it tough to get a mortgage on property overseas. You may have to raise the money through remortgaging the property you hold in the UK.

It's easy to be persuaded to overpay for property abroad, so make yourself familiar with the local market. And remember that most European countries aren't as obsessed with property ownership as the UK, which can mean that it's hard to sell up if you need to.

Buying into Commercial Property

Buy-to-let isn't the only way to make money from property. You can invest in commercial property too – offices, warehouses, retail outlets, and factories.

Watch out, REITS are about!

The government has said that it will allow the setting up of American-style Real Estate Investment Trusts (REITS) in the UK from January 2007. REITs are companies that directly own property but with the twist that they are free of Corporation Tax.

In the US, the tasty tax-free carrot has tempted many firms to spin off the buildings they own into REITs and invite people to buy shares in the property. As a result, in the US it is possible to own shares in hospital buildings and prisons. The buildings are leased to local authorities and firms in return for rent which is paid back to the investor.

Over US $170 billion (£100 billion) of investor cash has been ploughed into REITS across the pond since 1993, and when they come to the UK they may prove equally popular.

Investors like commercial property for the following reasons:

- ✔ The rental to be had from top-class commercial property in a good location can be very high.

- ✔ Businesses often sign long leases. This can mean a steady flow of income.

- ✔ Commercial property, like residential, can grow in value.

However, downsides exist to commercial property investment, namely:

- ✔ Commercial property can be in an area that goes out of fashion fast or it can become subject to new, and expensive, environmental regulations.

- ✔ If there is a recession the commercial property sector is often badly affected.

- ✔ Unless you have a spare few million quid – in which case you don't really need to worry about retiring wealthy – you can't buy commercial property in expensive well-heeled areas outright. This is not to say that small commercial properties, such as retail units, are out of the question.

If you're not rich enough to own an office block or shopping centre, don't despair – you can invest in commercial property in many ways. These include:

- ✔ **Buy shares in a property company**. Lots of firms build or own commercial property. By buying shares in a property company you are in effect gaining exposure to that market.

Should there be a boom in the property market your share investment should grow in value.

✔ **Invest in property unit trusts**. These are funds which pool investor cash to buy shares, in this case in companies investing in property. Funds are generally lower risk than buying shares in a single company. Again, if the property market booms so should the fund.

See Chapter 12 for more on unit trusts and how to distinguish between good and bad company shares.

Part V

Alternative Investment Strategies: The Wealth Is Out There

"Well....sho much for inveshting in wine!"

In this part . . .

Strap yourself in and prepare for a journey on the investment wild side. In this part I examine exotic stock market investments as well as popular collectables, all with the aim of showing you how you can make some money without falling into an investment trap. If you're a big profit hunter this may well be the part for you, but be warned – dangers lurk in the undergrowth.

Chapter 16

Making a Mint from Collectables

In This Chapter

▶ Understanding what collectables have to offer

▶ Investing in wine and racehorses

▶ Making money from classic cars, art, antiques, and stamps

*I*nvesting for a wealthy retirement doesn't have to be all boring savings accounts and pensions – it can also be a lot of fun.

In this chapter, I examine the world of collectables – from movie posters to antiques – showing you how it is possible to mix pleasure with top-notch investment returns.

Understanding What Collectables Have to Offer

Investment in collectables such as classic cars, art, and antiques can hopefully help you get rich while bringing with it the simple pleasures of ownership. Think about it: You can't take a savings account for a Sunday drive and you can't drink a company share – unless you put the certificate in a blender, but I don't recommend it.

Here are some golden rules to follow when looking to make a fortune from collectables:

✔ **Knowledge is power**. The world of collectables is every bit as complex as the market in shares or bonds. Don't invest if you don't know what's what. And if you want to spot a bargain and avoid getting ripped off, do your research.

✔ **Invest in something you like**. Collectables should be about having fun as much as making a profit. What's more if you're interested in your investments you're more likely to be a successful investor.

✔ **Invest properly**. This is as much about approach as doing your research. Some collectable markets – such as classic cars and stamps – are notoriously prone to ups and downs. In order to smooth out these peaks and troughs you should look to invest for the long term – at least five years.

If you're serious about retiring wealthy you should first have a base of money in savings accounts to meet emergency expenses, cash invested in shares and bonds for long term growth, and of course your own home. Only after all these bases are covered should you even consider putting large sums into collectables. See collectables as nothing more than the icing on your investment cake.

Table 16-1 compares the different types of collectables dealt with in this chapter.

eBay or auction room?

In the past, you bought or sold a collectable either at auction or privately. Basically this is still the case but with a twist. Nowadays you can buy or sell your collectable on online auction houses such as eBay, and gain access to literally millions of potential buyers and sellers.

eBay is mega business, some bright sparks estimating that the total value of goods changing hands is larger than the economies of some African countries.

eBay is cheaper than an auction house as the sales commission is rock bottom. What's more, if you're a purchaser there is plenty of choice and sellers often benefit from lots of competition between buyers. Some collectables can go for stunning amounts of money.

But buying and selling online does have a downside.

If you're purchasing through eBay you have no real guarantee as to the quality of the collectable, while at auction you can see it. With many collectables even the slightest imperfection can seriously harm its value.

Find out more about eBay in Marsha Collier and Jane Hoskyn's *eBay.co.uk For Dummies* (Wiley).

Table 16-1		Summarising the risk			
Collectable	**Risk level**	**Minimum investment**	**Usual Term**	**Easy to invest?**	**Watch out for**
Wine	Medium	£200	Medium to long	Yes	Storing your wine, changes in quality
Racehorses	High	£20,000	Short	No	Injured or poor-performing horses
Memorabilia	Medium	£50	Short to long	Yes	Authenticity
Classic cars	Medium	£1000	Medium	Yes	Stolen cars, maintaining condition
Art & antiques	High	£100	Medium	Yes	Rogue traders
Stamps	Medium	£5000	Medium	Yes	Rogue traders
Gold	Medium	£200	Long	Yes	Falling prices

If you keep a high value collectable at home you must inform your home contents insurer. Being honest with your insurer may lead to a higher premium but if you're burgled and you haven't told your insurer about the collectable your insurer may refuse to meet any claim.

Soaking up Some Profit: Investing in Wine

Britons have developed quite a taste for wine. From a generation ago where a bottle of plonk was something quite exotic, we now down nearly as much wine as the French.

Likewise, over the past couple of decades wine has become an increasingly popular investment and it's not hard to see why:

✔ It's easy to buy and sell wine and the commission charges for sales are relatively low.

✔ Lots of sources of information exist for investors on what types and vintages of wine to buy.

✔ Wine is a tangible and fun investment. If your wine doesn't make any money you can always choose to drown your sorrows.

Some wine connoisseurs invest to subsidise their pastime. They buy say a dozen cases of wine which if all goes well increases in value – they sell some to cover their initial outlay and drink the rest.

To retain the value of your wine it has to be stored correctly. The best way to do this is in a temperature-controlled warehouse. It costs anything from £8 to £15 a year to store a case of wine this way.

Telling vintage from vinegar

You have to carefully source your sauce. Investing in wine isn't just a matter of popping down your local Threshers and buying whatever case of plonk is on special offer – it's very unlikely that this will be of high enough quality to be classed an *investment wine*.

Wine dealers offer investment packages. You pay your money and they go and buy the wine for you. This is a very unemotional way to buy wine but may be best if your knowledge isn't good.

Generally, it's French red wines where the money's really at. A sophisticated market in French reds has been about for many years. Literally thousands of French reds exist, but the wine dealers concentrate on about 30 famous brands. Look for wine hailing from Burgundy, Bordeaux, or Rhone.

It's not only reds that sell – a smaller market exists in white wine, where again French *vin* dominates.

The market is growing in wines from Spain and the so-called New World wines, hailing from South America, Australia, and South Africa. However, you need to exercise caution when you invest in wine from these countries. On occasions in the past a new wine has burst on the scene in a blaze of glory only for the growers to cash in by upping production, usually at the cost of quality.

Take the example of Liebfraumilch. This was considered a good quality wine in the 1960s but by the 1980s massively increased production had led to a sharp fall in quality – this affected the reputation of the wine and killed it as an investment.

Expect to pay around 10 per cent commission when buying and selling investment wine at auction.

If you want the low-down on wine then check out *Decanter* magazine or the Web sites of wine dealers such as Berry Brothers and Rudd at www.bbr.com or Farr Vintners at www.farrvintners.com.

Buying early or playing the waiting game?

Making money out of wine – like any investment – is a matter of timing. Get the wine and vintage right and you can make a real killing. However, the longer you leave it after the wine has been bottled the less likely you are to make a bumper profit. You have to decide whether to buy your wine bottled and cased on the open market – when you have a good idea of the quality and potential investment return – or before it has been bottled, which is called buying *en primeur*.

Buying en primeur is a bit of a risk. It may turn out that your investment – of between £200 and £1,000 a case – is declared a classic or condemned as just plain old plonk – but if you're lucky you can make a fortune.

When a bottled wine is first traded on the market it achieves an *opening price*. This should give a good idea of how the wine is regarded by the market. Occasionally, the market misses a trick and the opening price underestimates a wine's true value. For example a case of French Le Pin 1982 achieved £185 a case at opening – a case is now worth around £30,000.

Don't leave it too long to sell your wine, otherwise it can go off. Generally wine is considered mature and at its most drinkable after around 15–25 years. However, some wines mature much later.

From Nags to Riches: Pinning It All on a Racehorse

Being a racehorse owner can be the stuff dreams are made of – but can you really turn your love of the turf into a profit?

Fortunes are to be made on the track if you own a champion horse – stud fees alone can run into the millions for a proven winner.

However for every Nijinsky, Shergar, or Rock of Gibraltar there are thousands of also-rans. Prize money in British racing is notoriously poor: You need to be winning a race or two a year to break even.

Buying at auction

At auction you can pick up a horse for as little as a couple of grand. The more you pay though the better the lineage of the horse. Racing ability is said to pass down through the genes. A horse's ancestry is very important: If a foal was sired by champions expect to pay mega-bucks.

 Some horses bought at auction prove to be poor performers or injury prone. In fact, it's quite possible that the horse you buy may never actually race. Owning a racehorse is an expensive pastime rather than a serious retirement investment.

Horse auctions take place all over the country – the most famous one are held at Newmarket run by Tattersalls. For a schedule of auctions look at Tattersall's Web site www.tattersalls.com.

 Navigating the world of horse auctions is notoriously tricky. You'd be well advised to employ a bloodstock agent to source and buy a horse for you, if you're serious about your investment. Expect to pay up to 5 per cent commission for their services. Check out the British Horse Racing Board Web site at www.britishhorseracing.com for a list of reputable agents.

 Experts estimate that it costs anything from £15,000 to £20,000 a year to own a racehorse. You need to pay the trainer, jockey, transport, race entry fees, insurance, and veterinary costs. You can't own a racehorse on the cheap, even if it's a three-legged old nag.

Clubbing together to back a winner

One way of spreading the cost of owning a racehorse is to join a racing syndicate. Members pool their money to buy, train, and race a horse or even a selection of horses.

Shares in a syndicate can vary from a few hundred to tens of thousands of pounds. If you fancy keeping costs to an absolute minimum then join a syndicate with lots of members.

However, as with everything in life, you get what you pay for with a racing syndicate. As a rule of thumb the more you pay the more extensive the ownership experience. Some trainers bar members of large syndicates from entering their yards or watching horses on the gallops. Also members of large syndicates may not be granted entry into the owners' enclosure on race day.

If you want the full racehorse owning experience – visiting the yard, watching the horse on the gallops, or hobnobbing in the owners' enclosure – you'll have to either own a horse outright or be a member of an expensive syndicate.

The South African golfer Gary Player once said 'the harder I prac- tise the luckier I get'. In the case of horse racing the more you shell out the luckier you may be. If you want to turn your passion into profit then don't cut corners – employ bloodstock agents, buy a good horse, and stable it with a winning trainer.

Moving in on Silver Screen Bargains

Movies mean glamour, and that can often translate into profit. You can make a tidy packet from silver screen memorabilia, but the key is to identify a sure-fire classic movie or one likely to catch the public mood of the time. For example, memorabilia from the early *Star Wars* movies – made in the Seventies and Eighties – can be worth a fortune.

A ready market exists for the movie related memorabilia such as:

- ✔ Posters
- ✔ Props
- ✔ Toys

The most recent films from which memorabilia have become col- lectable include the *Lord of the Rings* trilogy and Harry Potter films.

Posters have been a popular collectable for years, with buying and selling more akin to the art market with specialist galleries and dealers.

Some simple rules on memorabilia to bear in mind:

- ✔ You may be best buying memorabilia related to films that have wide appeal – this should make it easier to sell on.
- ✔ Web sites such as eBay should give you a good guide to the current price of memorabilia. This can also be a great place to auction your collectable. See below for more on eBay.

Scoring a money making hit

The British are sports mad – well some are anyway – and the market in memorabilia has exploded in recent years. Football shirts once worn by famous players can go for tens of thousands of pounds and even cricket bats – particularly after England's ashes victory – fetch a fortune if they were once wielded by one of the sport's master batsmen.

Golf is the sport where the real money is, because there is huge interest stateside. Ancient clubs can go for hundreds of thousands of pounds and anything associated with one of the game's great players can be worth a fortune.

✔ If you're buying a prop from a film – some studios auction off props after a film has been shot – then ask for a certificate of authenticity from the studio.

✔ If you can mix one field of collectables with another you can be quids in! For example, the Lego version of the Harry Potter films' Hogwarts Express was originally sold for £80 but now fetches £500.

 If you're serious about making money from collectables then it's a smart play to keep all original packaging. Collectors simply love to buy items which come in original shop condition – some comic collectors for example never open the original packaging, leaving their pride and joy unread. A bit strange you may think but if you want to turn a profit you've got to play the game – actually, on second thoughts don't, just leave the game in the box!

 If you'd like to know more about buying movie props check out the Movie Props Association at www.moviepropsassociation.org. For movie posters try www.atthemovies.co.uk.

Banking on an Old Banger

Classic cars are hugely popular. They can be practical runarounds or ornate vintage vehicles sweeping their owners back to an earlier age of motoring. Classic cars are also an important investment which can increase in value over time.

But be warned: The market in classic cars is far from a one-way money-making street. Several times in the past – most notably in the late eighties – a bubble has developed where vehicles were changing hands for fortunes only for prices to crash, usually when the wider economy had gone into recession.

On the other hand, classic cars – like any other collectable – can offer the double whammy of profit growth and fun. And of late classic car prices have been rising again.

Classics are advertised in magazines such as *Auto Express* and *Dalton's Weekly*. You should also check out the specialist press. Magazines such as *Practical Classics* and *Classic Car* give the low-down on what's hot and what's not in the world of classic motors. And don't forget to browse those classified adverts.

Once you've identified which type of car you want to buy, check out the owners' club Web site. Club members – who often look after their cars well – advertise them for sale on these sites.

Avoiding buying a wreck

Here are some tips for buying a classic:

- ✔ **Join a member's club**. Just about every make of car has an owners' club. These clubs will have information on what you should be looking for when buying.

- ✔ **Get the car inspected**. Members' clubs and motoring organisations such as the RAC or AA offer to inspect the car you're looking to purchase – for a fee of course. They check to see that it's mechanically sound and bona fide. Motoring organisations charge around £140 for this service, some members' clubs may do it for less.

- ✔ **Check the car's history**. The AA does this for you for around £40.00: It searches vehicle registration databases and the records of lenders to check that what you're being told about the car's history is correct.

If you buy a car that is either stolen or is the subject of an existing credit agreement, you're not the legal owner and may well be forced to hand over the car and be left having to pursue the person who sold it to you for compensation. A lot of rogues are out there!

The cost of insuring a classic car is often lower than a modern high-tech motor. The reason for this is that insurance companies reckon that classic car owners drive their pride and joy less frequently and more carefully than they would if it was a modern car. Another plus point: All motor vehicles registered before 1973 are exempt from UK road tax.

Keeping your car in classic condition

It's pointless buying a classic car and then leaving it to fall into rack and ruin. In order to retain, and hopefully increase their value, classic cars need to be kept in A1 condition. Here's how to do it:

✔ **Keep the car garaged**. Older cars tend to be prone to rust, therefore it figures that you should keep them away from the elements.

✔ **Rust proof and wax**. Even if you garage the car it will still be open to the elements when it's driven. Get a garage to rust proof your car or do it yourself, also clean the car regularly and keep the bodywork waxed.

✔ **Keep documentation**. Cars with a service history are worth more than ones without. When you get anything done to your classic, keep the bills so to show any prospective buyer that everything's above board.

✔ **Fit original parts**. Classic car buyers are very choosy and they are looking for a motor that is as close as possible mechanically to the day it rolled off the production line. Remember, retaining your car's authenticity is vital to boosting its value.

 If you get sucked into the world of classic car ownership you may hear motors described as being in concourse condition. This means that the car is in such tip-top nick that it's considered fit to be displayed at owners' club meets. Clubs run regular competitions where owners compete – often very fiercely – for who has the most original and best turned out motor. Concourse condition is the blue ribbon of classic cars; expect cars in this condition to attract the highest prices.

 For some people the challenge of classic car ownership is finding a car that is only fit for scrap and transforming it into a prize-winner. It can cost thousands and take years to do up a classic and often when they finish these enthusiasts will sell the car on – to fund their next project. Such cars can be a bit of a bargain because they have had lots of TLC lavished on them and the price asked is often far lower than the amount that the enthusiast has spent doing them up!

Introducing a Little Culture: Investing in Art

Art lifts the soul but can it lift the bank balance? The world of art is not an easy one for amateurs to get their heads around. The problem is that investment choice is absolutely huge. Try buying a contemporary piece of art and you find hundreds of artists out there, with art dealers and galleries located in most major cities. Even if you decide to buy older artwork you have an incalculable number of artists to choose from.

Face facts, the cases of people spotting a long lost masterpiece at a flea market and then buying it for peanuts are very few and far between.

Some things you should bear in mind when investing in art:

- ✔ **Concentrate on one art movement**. If you know about watercolours then stick to watercolours, if conceptual art is your bag – or your lobster – then stick to that.

- ✔ **Buy art that you like**. You may have to hold on to your art investment for a long time – you don't want something you hate hanging up in your house. Art investment should be enjoyable.

- ✔ **Consider using a dealer**. You can ask a dealer to do the legwork for you. You give them some cash and they go out and buy a portfolio of art for you; they can even keep it under lock and key. However, dealers don't pass exams – you're relying on their experience and know how.

Top art auction houses charge hefty sales commission. At Sotheby's for example, there is a buyer's premium of 20 per cent on hammer price – pay £10,000 for an artwork and you also have to find £2,000 in commission. Sellers also face similar sales commission charges.

If you want to keep your commission charges down when buying or selling artwork you may be best selling or buying through a small auction house or an art dealer. However, if you're selling remember the wealthier buyers naturally gravitate to the large auction houses.

Putting a Price on the Past: Buying and Selling Antiques

Buying and selling antiques has become a popular pastime. If the plethora of TV programmes on the subject is anything to go by, it seems the nation's obsession with owning a bit of the past is only rivalled by its desire to make money through the housing market.

Antiques, like artwork, are amongst the most tangible of assets and are collected as much for their aesthetic appeal as their value.

In general, you pay the most for an antique in a shop and the least in an auction room. Think of an auction room as a wholesale outlet and an antiques shop – and this includes antiques fairs and car boot events – as retail.

Action at the auction

Buying and selling at auction can be fun, but you should follow some rules:

- ✔ Get there early and look at the items due to go on sale – check carefully for damage if you find something of interest.

- ✔ Pay close attention to the description of the item in the auction house catalogue and the guide price given.

- ✔ Don't get carried away. Go along and just watch a few times. Familiarise yourself with the auctioneer's style and what type of items come up for sale before sticking your hand heavenwards and bidding.

For a list of auction rooms check out www.auctioneers.com.

Buying and selling antiques at auction can be real seat-of-the-pants stuff. The auctioneer may well give an item a guide price – the sum of money he or she thinks it will achieve – but no guarantee exists that this will be reached. In fact, anyone who goes to auctions can tell you that there are days when you get lots of serious buyers and on other days there are only a few.

If you're selling, to protect yourself from the misfortune of catching a duff day at the auction make sure you put a reserve price on your prize antique. This way if it fetches too little you have the option of taking it away and trying to flog it elsewhere.

Get to know the auction rooms which specialise in buying and selling the type of antique you're interested in. Some auction houses have a reputation as being a good place for picking up furniture, others for china, and so on.

Fun at the fair

In recent years car boot sales and antiques fairs have become incredibly popular.

Like auction rooms they can be lots of fun. Don't just pay the price asked as the seller expects you to haggle!

However, stories abound of crooks selling stolen or fake antiques at these fairs and then doing a disappearing act.

You're very much on your own at one of these fairs so best exercise caution – if you smell anything fishy simply walk away.

Posting a Profit: Investing in Stamps

Stamps may be tiny but they can be worth a lot of money. Some rare stamps hailing from exotic locations or linked to a particular event in history can be worth thousands and in some exceptional cases hundreds of thousands of pounds.

The reputation of stamp investing has soared in recent years. Stamps as an investment are being taken more seriously because they have proved a real winner.

Since 1998 the price of the world's 100 most frequently traded stamps – called the Stanley Gibbons 100 index – has increased in value by around two thirds. This is far better rate of return than the stock market or a savings account.

To find out more about stamp collecting – prices, what to look for, and how to care for your stamps – check out the annual edition of the *Stanley Gibbons Catalogue* or check their online stamp catalogue at www.stanleygibbons.com/priceguide.

Just because stamp investing has produced good returns for investors doesn't mean it's a safe investment. Back in the 1980s the market in stamps crashed. Only invest what you can afford to lose. If you can't afford to buy a portfolio you shouldn't be risking your money investing in stamps.

The China syndrome

Like everything else in the world economy the Chinese have the potential to have a major impact on stamp investing. Until recently stamp collecting in China was illegal!

Nevertheless, an estimated 18 million Chinese are now philatelists – the name for stamp collectors – and once they get involved in the international market it may boost prices significantly.

If you fancy having a go at investing in stamps then be aware of the following:

✔ Rare and exotic stamps are the most collectable and therefore the most saleable. Not much of a market exists for modern stamps apart from first day covers.

✔ Don't just blow a fortune on a single stamp – try to buy a portfolio and therefore spread your risk. Stamps are a bit like company shares – some can rise in price while at the same time others fall in value.

✔ You can go it alone, buying stamps without advice at auction, but you may be best taking advice from a dealer. A dealer can help you build a good portfolio of stamps.

✔ Stamps are very portable way of holding wealth and the worldwide market is huge.

✔ If you want to buy a portfolio of stamps then it is going to cost you quite a bit of money. Stamp dealers offer ready-made investment portfolios starting at around £5,000.

There are some rogues in the stamp investing world. Contact the Philatelic Traders' Society for a list of bona fide dealers. Its Web site address is `www.philatelic-traders-society.co.uk`.

Going for Investment Gold: Buying into Bling

Gold is a classic hedge investment. When other investments are going awry or the world economy is up the creek without a paddle you often find that the price of gold rises. It is traditionally an investment of last resort.

Of late, due in part to escalating oil prices and worries over the world economy, gold has been increasing in price again and investors' profit antennae have been twitching.

Gold may be on the up at present but this is after 20 years or so of prices falling. In fact, since 1980 gold has been one of the worst investments you can have had. For more on gold investing check out the World Gold Council Web site at `www.gold.org`.

It's relatively easy to buy gold. For starters you can buy jewellery, but bear in mind this isn't the cheapest way to invest in gold as you're paying extra for the styling.

Keeping an eye out for scams

Getting the buying and selling of collectables right often depends on know-how. From art to wine you need to gen up as best you can – remember that knowledge means power and maybe some profit. However, let's be honest, few of us have the time to become collectable experts. This opens the way for scamsters.

Lots of people operate collectables scams looking to part the unwary with their cash. Scams are particularly prevalent in wine and art, the two most sophisticated collectables markets.

Scamsters rarely take the money and run – that would be simple theft and relatively easy for the authorities to spot. Instead they cannily prey on the ignorance of investors and get them to pay way over the odds.

One scam I've come across is an absolute classic. Investors were offered paintings produced by a supposedly famous Spanish watercolour artist. They were told that the value of the painting would rise over time and that a host of businesses were falling over themselves to pay rent for the privilege of hanging the artwork in their offices. Anyone falling for this sales patter – and believe me it suckered lots of people – found that the supposedly famous artist was in fact a nobody and that the army of firms didn't actually exist. Angry investors looking to complain then faced the usual problem of tracking down the scamster who had been operating from a P.O. Box number.

How to avoid falling victim? The key is to exercise caution: Don't rush into anything without checking out what's on offer very carefully. Also, remember that just because the company offering the collectable investment has a flashy brochure it doesn't necessarily follow that it's bona fide.

Ultimately, if an offer looks too good to be true it's probably a scam.

If you want to own gold and be able to touch it, generally the cheapest route is to buy it in bar or coin form.

Buying coins

The two main types of gold coins available are South African Krugerrands and UK Sovereigns.

Generally, Krugerrands are available in greater quantities, and they can be bought at lower prices than any other gold coin. Their production quality is consistently high, and it is also easy to compare prices, as they contain exactly one ounce of fine gold. Sovereigns, on the other hand, offer a more attractive and more historic coin than Krugerrands.

Buying gold bars

Buying a gold bar can be cheaper than buying the same weight of gold coin, but it has disadvantages:

- ✔ **It's a substantial investment**. Even the smallest bars set you back around £6,000, while you can buy a single ounce Krugerrand for about £200.

- ✔ **Gold bars can be hard to sell**. Only a specialist gold dealer will give you a good purchase price for a bar.

You don't have to buy gold bars or coins to benefit from the rising price of gold. Instead you can buy shares in gold mining companies. In theory as the price of gold rises so should the price of mining company shares. See Chapter 12 for more on share investment.

If you buy gold you have to store it. You are best keeping it in a bank deposit box or in a safe at home.

Chapter 17

Taking a Walk on the Wild Side: Alternative Investments

. . . .

In This Chapter

▶ Risking it with hedge funds

▶ Looking at derivatives

▶ Daytrading your way to riches

▶ Beating the odds through spread betting

▶ Balancing alternative and standard investment

. . . .

*R*oll up, roll up, for the ride of your investment life! Alternative investments – hedge funds, derivatives, spread betting et al – all offer you the chance to take home the retiring wealthy prize in double quick time. But guess what, they're also wrought with danger.

Many of these investments are akin to gambling – except that in some cases you can lose more than your original stake. Yikes!

In this chapter, I lay bare the world of alternative investments, showing you how they work while making the risks abundantly clear.

Hedging Your Bets

Ever since the turn of the century hedge funds have been the 'must have' investment. Whereas most collective investment schemes – such as unit trusts, investment trusts, and pension funds – were battered by falling stock markets between 2000 and 2003, some hedge funds produced eye-popping returns for investors.

So what's been the secret of hedge fund success? The answer lies in the unique way that hedge funds work which allows them to make money even when the general market they are investing in is doing poorly. The trend-bucking potential of hedge funds is due to the following:

- ✔ **Flexibility**. Most hedge fund managers are given carte blanche to invest in companies, currencies, or commodities which they feel will return a profit. They're also free to invest for as long or as short a time as they see fit. Basically, the manager can do whatever it takes to turn a quick buck!

- ✔ **Manager incentives**. The manager usually has a substantial stake in the hedge fund. In short if their investment performance is poor then they lose out too. From a fund manager's perspective, hedge funds are where the money is at. This means that some of the brightest stars in the fund management world gravitate to hedge funds.

- ✔ **Use of derivatives**. Hedge fund managers employ derivatives such as futures and options to make the most of market situations. Derivatives allow them to make money even when the price of their underlying investment is falling – see later in this chapter for more information on derivatives.

- ✔ **Borrowing**. If a hedge fund is free to borrow money and if the manager sees an opportunity to make a killing then they can really go for it! Borrowing is called *gearing* in the UK and *leverage* in the US and can also magnify losses if the investment turns out to be a poor one.

Hedge funds are a US invention and the 'land of the free' is still the centre of the hedge fund universe, so much so that no matter where a fund originates they work in US dollars.

Hedge fund managers are free to plough money into investments they think will sink, making money as the underlying investment falls in value. This technique is called *short selling*. In contrast, it is illegal for a pension fund manager to adopt short selling tactics.

Understanding the downside of hedge funds

The very things that enable hedge funds to make money even when the general market is falling – flexibility, use of derivatives, and the ability to borrow – can also amplify loss making.

Huge power is vested in the hands of the fund manager and there are few checks and balances in place. Get a good manager who knows what they're doing and you can be quids in but, on the other hand, back one who makes the wrong moves and it can all go horribly wrong.

Hedge funds are high-risk investments and are not for beginners. The golden rule is never invest what you can't afford to lose – because believe me, with hedge funds you're running the risk of losing your entire stake.

Noting the hedging principle

First let's get one thing straight: Hedging is good. It can protect companies and banks against unexpected price movements. Hedging has been around for over a century. Initially, it was commodities like coffee or wheat that were the subject of hedging. A company that needed a regular supply of a commodity would pay a little extra to secure the right to buy their chosen commodity at an affordable price in the future. This provided a hedge against a sudden rise in the price of the commodity.

Nowadays just about everything can be hedged – shares, bonds, currencies, even the creditworthiness of investors.

Hedging is carried out through using derivatives such as options and futures, which are explained later in this chapter.

Hedge funds are so called because they deploy many of the tactics used in hedging, such as the use of derivatives. But whereas hedging is all about minimising risk, hedge *funds* use derivatives and borrowing to actually take greater risk in a bid to maximise returns.

Spotting hedge fund tactics

Hedge funds try to make money through following one or all the following tactics:

- ✔ **Relative value**. Through this tactic the hedge fund tries to profit from price differentials between the same or similar investments in different markets. Margins tend to be low as does the risk.

- ✔ **Company events**. The fund buys into a company which is or is likely to be the subject of a takeover or merger. The hope is that they will be able to demand top whack for their holding as the bidding for the company hots up.

- ✔ **Opportunism**. The fund bets on the directions of the share, bonds, commodity, and even currency markets. Funds deploy derivatives such as options and futures and short selling as ways to make money from market moves.

For more in-depth coverage on hedge fund tactics check out *Investing For Dummies* by Tony Levene (Wiley).

Hedge funds use derivatives and borrowing to move billions of dollars around the globe overnight to take positions. These positions are in essence bets on future market moves. The most famous instance of this – from a British perspective – was when George Soros, through his Quantum Fund, bet millions that UK would be forced to devalue in 1992. He won his bet and became known as 'the man who broke the pound'.

Scaling hedge fund barriers

Hedge funds are not an everyday investment. Many are based in tax havens and what managers do comes under very little scrutiny. In the hedge fund universe managers rule and they don't want much truck with small investors – they cost too much to administer and they do annoying things like ask questions!

The fund manager wants the right sort of investor. This doesn't mean that you have to be one of the old school tie brigade – they are only interested in how much money you have to invest.

The clientele of most standard hedge funds are rich individuals and financial institutions such as banks. You have to have a large stake to play at the hedge fund table. Some hedge funds set a minimum investment level of a quarter of a million or even half a million US dollars. If you have this much cash then, in the world of hedge funds, you qualify as a 'serious' investor.

But such high stakes are too much for 99 per cent of people – even if they remortgaged their home, which would be far too risky. But don't despair, you can have a piece of the hedge fund action by investing in a *fund of funds*.

As the name suggests funds of funds invest in a basket of hedge funds, usually anything from 5 to 40. Increasingly major UK fund management groups such as Schroders, Close Brothers, and even HSBC offer funds of funds.

These fund management groups are less sniffy about dealing with ordinary people with a few grand to invest. Minimum investment levels start at £1,000.

The more hedge funds a fund of funds has a stake in, the lower the investment risk. In theory, if one hedge fund underperforms another should ride to the rescue by performing well. This doesn't always work though.

You should have no more than 10 per cent of your investment portfolio in hedge funds and other alternative investments. See later in this chapter for getting the balance right between alternatives and other types of investment.

Looking at Derivatives

Mention derivatives and most people either don't have a clue what you're going on about or they think of risky investments.

But derivatives have a long tradition, having been in use for over a century – they haven't always been the preserve of the City wide-boys!

In simple terms derivatives derive their value from the price of an underlying investment.

Derivatives allow traders to hedge their bets. Usually, the subject of derivatives are commodities, shares, bonds, or currencies.

Sorting through derivatives

There are three main types of derivatives, outlined in this section.

Futures

A futures contract is an agreement to buy or sell something at a later date for a set price. These agreements provide security and they don't come free. A fee has to be paid to secure the futures contract. The size of this fee depends on the risks the issuer is bearing – therefore if there's a good chance the contract may benefit the buyer then the fee will be higher.

For about a century futures were used to protect companies and banks from sudden moves in the price of a commodity. In the 1980s traders increasingly bought and sold these future contracts. This is now a huge global business.

Options

Options are an agreement which gives someone the option to buy or sell something at a set price at a later date. Options were invented because people liked knowing they could buy or sell at a certain price but wanted the chance to profit if the market price suited them better when the option expired.

Like futures a fee is levied. An option is in essence a type of future. Options are also now bought and sold in mind-boggling quantities and are available on just about anything.

Swaps

As the name suggests, swaps are an exchange of something. For example, a company may want to swap a variable interest rate for a fixed one to minimise uncertainty. Swaps are very much the little brother of the derivatives world and the preserve of big financial investors rather than small investors – so we won't pay them any more attention.

Although the majority of hedge funds are focused on large investors the derivatives used by these funds are now open to anyone. Increasingly, small investors are buying options and futures as a way to hedge their share bets or as stand alone investments.

Understanding the appeal of derivatives

Investment houses, banks, and companies can't get enough of derivatives because of the following benefits:

- ✔ **Flexibility**. Derivatives allow someone to bet on price movements without actually owning the item. For example, an investor can take a punt on the price of coffee without having to actually buy any coffee.

- ✔ **Gearing**. The derivative can be geared up to be worth many times the price moves of the underlying asset. For example, the price of the asset may only move £10 but the value of the derivative can change by £100. This is where the big bucks can be won and lost.

- ✔ **Insurance**. An investor can buy a derivative which bets that the market will move against their original investment. The idea is that they either win through their original investment or their derivative.

Derivatives can be high-octane, dangerous investments. 'Rogue trader' Nick Leeson famously broke the UK's oldest investment bank Barings by gearing up on derivatives traded in the Far East.

If you use derivatives to provide insurance against your share investments going awry, then bear in mind that even if you don't need it the cost of the option or futures contract will eat into your total return.

Getting In on the Derivatives Act

Derivatives have long been the preserve of the super-rich and the big financial institution and companies. But times are changing.

More then ever derivatives are finding their way onto the radar of private investors. Some investors love the idea of being able to invest in the underlying price of an asset rather than the asset per se. They can be gung-ho types, looking to gear up their investment bet in a bid to turn a little money into a lot. Alternatively, they can be cautious souls wanting to use derivatives to hedge against their investment turning out to be a poor one.

Stockbrokers now offer small investors a route into the high-pressure world of derivatives. As well as offering standard share purchases stockbrokers offer access to future and options contracts. Usually, these are futures and options based on individual shares or whole stock markets, such as the FTSE.

Considering contracts for difference

Recently, a new type of low-cost investment has emerged that is open to small investors, which is in essence a derivative. It's called contracts for difference (CFDs) and it allows investors to make a little money stretch a long way, all in a bid to increase investment return.

Under a CFD a deal is struck between two parties – an investor and a CFD broker – agreeing to pay the difference between the opening price and the closing price of the contract. The difference is then multiplied by the number of shares specified in the contract.

Here's how a CFD can work in practice.

In January you agree to a CFD for the purchase of 5,000 HSBC shares at £5 a pop, total value £25,000. But instead of parting with a cool £25,000 to buy the shares outright you lodge a 10 per cent deposit with the broker – just £2,500. You stand to benefit from any growth on £25,000 worth of shares, but you're also tied in to foot the full bill if the share price falls.

By June you're in luck, the price of HSBC shares moves to £7 each, and you agree to sell at this level, thereby calling time on the CFD.

You're quids in – the difference between the start and end of the contract is a whopping £10,000 and what's more your 10 per cent deposit is returned.

Needless to say, CFDs are ultra high-risk investments. If you turn the above example on its head you can see if the HSBC share price had fallen to £3 at the end of the contract then you would have been liable for every penny of the difference in the opening and closing price of the contract, a rather eye-watering £10,000.

Because you can lose a lot of money on CFDs brokers often insist that you hold at least £10,000 on account before being allowed to trade.

You can trade CFDs on most large UK companies and stock market indices. The advantages of CFDs are as follows:

- ✔ They allow gearing – for a relatively small outlay you can gain big exposure.

- ✔ No stamp duty is due – on a standard share trade you'd have to pay 0.5 per cent.

- ✔ There is no Capital Gains Tax to pay on any profits. This is because in essence a CFD is a gamble!

Commission charges on CFDs can really mount up. You pay around 0.5 per cent commission on each buy or sell. That may not sound like much but when you consider that CFDs are designed for frequent trading these charges can mount up. Keep a beady eye on CFD commission charges – some brokers lower charges to 0.25 per cent if you trade frequently.

If you're brave enough – or should it be foolhardy enough? – to invest in CFDs then you're well advised to put a stop-loss in position. A stop-loss does exactly what it says on the tin – if you start to lose lots of cash the stop-loss kicks in and automatically closes your position, stopping the haemorrhage of cash. Ask your broker about stop-loss arrangements.

Lifting the lid on covered warrants

In return for a premium, covered warrants allow investors the option of buying or selling a share at a fixed price at a specified later date. Warrants are cheaper than shares and ultimately all you stand to lose is the price of the warrant.

You can use covered warrants as a hedge in case other share investments go awry.

For example, you buy 10,000 shares in a company priced at £5. At the same time you buy a covered warrant giving you the option to buy a further 10,000 shares at £4.80 at a later date. If the share price falls to £4.90 you would have lost £1,000 on your original investment.

This is when the covered warrant works its magic. You're now allowed to buy a further 10,000 shares at £4.80 which is below market price. You can now either sell the option to buy at £4.80 for a profit or exercise the option to buy the shares and then sell your entire holding to cover any loss on the original share purchase of 10,000.

However, remember that warrants are far from an investment panacea – you have to pay a premium. And in general warrants are far more volatile than shares, exaggerating the price movements of the underlying stock.

Covered warrants are – you guessed it – high risk. If the warrant calls the future price wrong, the value of the covered warrant can shrink to nothing. For example, if a covered warrant allows the investor to buy a share at £2 but the price of the share then drops to £1, no one is going to pay for the right to buy a share at double the going rate!

Daytrading Your Way to Riches

At the height of the dotcom boom in the late 1990s it seemed that the world and his wife were getting into share investments. Some optimistic souls even gave up their job and became daytraders – private investors who approach share dealing as if it is their full-time job. They hired expensive market-enabled computer terminals for their homes or desk space at daytrading firms and started to buy and sell shares in a bid to make their fortune.

There was talk of a 'new investment paradigm' as stock markets rode the crest of the new technology wave (although some day-traders still managed to lose cash even back then).

But this new investment paradigm was never going to last. When dotcom and technology stocks crashed in early 2000 it put paid to the hopes of thousands of daytraders across the globe, bankrupting many.

However, a few daytraders managed to keep their heads above water and learned how to make money in falling markets, using derivatives such as options.

If you fancy a crack at daytrading you need the following:

- ✔ **A trading vehicle**. At the very least you need a telephone or Internet share trading account with a stockbroking service. Check out Chapter 5 for more on the different levels of service stockbrokers offer. You also probably want to arm your home PC with an up-to-date stock analysis software package; see more later in this chapter.

- ✔ **Lots of time**. As a daytrader you're trying to beat thousands of City professionals whose job it is to know everything to do with shares. You have to really do your homework otherwise you're relying on hunches and guesses and that way an empty bank account lies!

- ✔ **Plenty of cash**. To make daytrading worthwhile you need to be turning a decent profit. You need capital to invest and you need money to live on. In short, think about how much your everyday job pays you and that should be the minimum amount you look to make from daytrading.

If you're serious about daytrading you may be best buying some real whizz-bang software to help you analyse your stock selections. The best software provides thorough stock analysis and portfolio management. Expect to pay between £70 and £100 for the right software. Magazines such as *Investors Chronicle* regularly review investment software.

You can approach daytrading in a low-tech or high-tech fashion. You can go the whole hog and buy a very expensive computer, load it up with whiz bang software, and trade online through a stockbroking account. Alternatively, you can go low-tech, simply making do with a telephone or Internet share trading account, and quarter hourly share price updates on page 220 of Ceefax.

The simple truth is that unless you're a real expert and have lots of time to do your research as well as plenty of cash to burn you really shouldn't consider daytrading for a living.

Some firms offer courses in daytrading and promise to show you sure-fire ways of making money on the stock market. Take such promises with a huge pinch of salt. The stock market and sure-fire winners don't mix. All too often, these courses are hugely over-priced and badly run. Keep your money in your pocket.

Making Money from the Grim Reaper: Death Futures

Yes, it seems in the heady world of alternative investment everything, even death, has its price.

Through something called *life settlement* terminally ill people are offered the option of selling their life insurance policy. The person selling the policy gets a payday – they receive anywhere between 60 per cent and 80 per cent of the policy's value. The buyer then collects on the policy when the seller dies.

Traders study the prognosis of the policyholder to see how long they have to live. If the prognosis is wrong and the person lives on then inflation starts to erode the investment. If, on the other hand the person dies quickly then a big profit can be made. All pretty brutal in-your-face stuff, so no wonder some call life settlement *death futures*.

Death futures have been big business Stateside for decades. However, they have only recently started to creep into the UK. Check out the Web sites of the Association of Policy Market Makers www.apmm.org.uk or the Association of British Insurers www.abi.org.uk for details on which firms deal in death futures.

You can invest direct in a single policy or buy into a fund which invests in a basket of policies. The fund route should be the safest as investment risk is spread.

At first – not to say second or third – glance death futures may seem both morbid and distasteful, but they do provide a service for the seller who wants quick cash.

Beating the Odds: Spread Betting

Spread betting is booming. From virtually nowhere a few years ago, the industry is now worth hundreds of millions of pounds. Spread betting firms such as www.cantorindex.co.uk, www.igindex.co.uk, and www.cityindex.co.uk have sprung up offering punters the chance to bet on just about anything, from whether a company share goes up or down to how many times the Chancellor utters the word 'prudent' in his Budget speech.

Spread betting is simple: The spread betting firm makes a prediction on a particular aspect of a sporting event, share price, or stock market index. You simply decide whether their prediction is too high or too low.

If you think the prediction spot on, you don't bet. But if you think they're too low or too high with their prediction you can make a killing through *beating the spread*.

Steering clear of get rich quick

Lots of people are looking to diddle you out of your cash pile. The golden rule is if something seems too good to be true it's probably a scam! Here are some of the classic scams out there – you may recognise some or all them.

Nigerian advance fee fraud

A letter, email, or fax arrives offering to share a huge sum of money in return for using your bank account. Usually the fraudster claims to be a relative of an African official who has pilfered a huge sum of money from his country and now needs to get it abroad.

If you hand over your details the fraudster simply empties your bank account of its funds. Alternatively, they tell you that money is needed upfront to bribe officials. Whatever story is spun the upshot is the same – get involved and you pay the cost.

Pyramid schemes

These offer a return on a financial investment based on the number of new recruits to the scheme.

Investors are promised that they will double their money at worst. However, the scheme relies on each new member's subscription paying the person who recruited them. Ultimately, pyramid schemes are doomed to failure because they run out of people to recruit and the scheme collapses.

Prize draws

Unsolicited telephone calls, letters, and emails tell people they have been entered into a prize draw. Later, they receive notification that they have won but in order to collect their prize they have to pay an administration, legal, or tax charge. Of course, there is no prize and the scamsters simply pocket the cash.

If you even reply to a scam mailshot you're probably added to a *sucker list*. These lists are traded between scam networks. Suckers find that they are targeted by ever increasing number of scamsters. If you get an unsolicited email, letter, or fax promising you untold riches, just bin it!

Cast your mind back to the Bruce Forsyth TV show *Play Your Cards Right*. The basic concept behind spread betting is similar. Brucie asked the contestants if they wanted to go 'Higher' or 'Lower' – if they got their guess right they won, if not they lost! With spread betting, though, the amount you win or lose depends on how right or wrong you are.

Spread betting is gambling but with the twist that the potential for winning and losing is virtually open-ended. It's possible to lose far more than your original stake and needless to say this makes it very high risk.

If you fancy having a go, approach it as a bit of fun. Remember, beating the spread is far from easy and the average punter loses more often than they win.

Taking a Punt: Investing in Venture Capital Trusts

Venture Capital Trusts (VCTs) are collective investment schemes which specialise in taking a stake in newly formed firms. The big idea is that by buying a stake in a small firm they will be able to sell it later on for a fat profit. Any profit is then reinvested in other small firms.

As you can imagine, VCTs are high-risk investments because for every firm that turns into a goldmine there are usually plenty more which go down the swanny.

In fact, VCTs are far more risky than other collective investments such as unit or investment trusts which buy shares in often long-established companies.

However, as with everything in the investment universe, the higher the risk the greater the potential reward. If the VCT manager gets their picks right then investors can see their cash pile turn into a towering money mountain.

The government simply loves VCTs. This is because VCTs provide a much needed investment in small and medium size businesses. In order to boost the VCT market the government has started to give 40 per cent tax relief on investment. So if you buy £10,000 worth of VCT shares the government gives you £4,000.

Understandably, the idea of free money from the taxman has excited investors and up to £400 million was invested in the

2004–05 tax year. There are lots of VCTs out there – check out the Web sites of the British Venture Capital Association www. bvca.co.uk and the Tax Efficient Review online at www. taxefficientreview.com.

The 40 per cent tax relief only applies to initial investments in VCT shares. If you sell your VCT shares within three years of purchase you have to pay back the initial tax relief.

The tax relief on VCTs is very tasty, but don't invest just to get your hands on it.

Getting the Balance Right Between Alternative and Standard Investments

A smattering of alternative investments can add a much needed boost to your retiring wealthy plan. But unless you really know your way around the complex worlds of hedge funds, derivatives et al, you shouldn't stake your retiring wealthy dreams on what is in effect gambling.

A sensible private investor only considers alternative investments after they have plenty of money safely tucked away in savings accounts, shares, and property. In fact, many people make it to a wealthy retirement without putting so much as a penny into alternative investments.

All in all, the best approach to alternative investments may be simply to consider it a bit of fun – if your gambles pay off then great, if not then no sweat. Don't bet your future on alternatives.

Part VI
The Part of Tens

"Here we are, Gladys – a telegram from the
Queen & an insolvency notice from your bank."

In this part . . .

This part contains four vital chapters that show you how to boost your income, reduce your tax bill, avoid money pitfalls, and sort out your personal finances.

If you choose just a handful of tips from this book you're best off drawing them from the chapters in this part, because they explain in an easily digestible form how to save and make money – the key ingredients of retiring wealthy.

Chapter 18

Ten Ways to Cut Your Tax Bill

In This Chapter

▶ Being clever with your savings

▶ Reducing your tax through work

▶ Paying into a pension

▶ Beating the Capital Gains Tax rap

*L*ots of people choose to bury their heads in the sand when it comes to tax. They are confused by it and perhaps a little intimidated by the thought of dealing with the UK's gargantuan tax authorities. But here's the bottom line: Every penny that you save in tax is extra cash that can go towards reaching your retiring wealthy dream. Get with the tax-saving programme and I guarantee it's much easier to retire wealthy.

In this chapter, I outline some simple, yet perfectly legal, steps you can take to ensure your tax bill is as low as it possibly can be.

Minimising Tax on Savings and Investments

If you have savings and investments it's best to put them into an Individual Savings Account (ISA). An ISA is a wrapper which protects your savings and investments from tax. You're allowed to pay up to £7,000 a year into a maxi ISA, which can only be invested in stocks and shares. When you come to sell these investments you do not have to pay Capital Gains Tax, because they are in an ISA.

Alternatively, you're allowed to put £3,000 into a mini cash ISA and £4,000 into a mini stocks and shares ISA. Any money interest earned on the mini cash ISA is free from tax; likewise any growth in the value of investments held in a mini stocks and shares ISA is free from CGT. ISAs – and in particular cash ISAs – are a bit of a no-brainer.

Just about everyone would benefit from sheltering their savings from tax in a cash ISA. However, a stocks and shares ISA is a different kettle of fish – this type of investment can be high risk and may not be right for those who can't afford to risk losing money.

You can't open a maxi ISA and a mini ISA in the same tax year. See Chapter 10 for more on ISAs.

Claiming Your Tax Back on Savings

Your bank or building society acts as a tax collector for the government. Any interest you earn automatically has tax deducted from it at a rate of 20 per cent (unless of course the money is held in a mini cash ISA, see earlier in this chapter). But you may not have earned enough during the year to qualify to pay tax.

During the 2005–06 tax year anyone earning less than £4,895 should not be paying tax on their savings and this figure is even higher for people over the age of 65. If you're a non-earner, simply ask your bank or building society to give you form R85, fill it in, and send it off to the address stated on the form – allowing you to receive interest free of tax.

On the other hand, if you earn enough to qualify as a higher-rate taxpayer you're in line to pay even more tax. It's up to you to contact the tax authorities and tell them you should be paying top-rate tax on your savings.

Normally interest earned on savings is taxed at 20 per cent if you're a basic-rate taxpayer or at 40 per cent if you're a higher-rate taxpayer.

Making the Most of Tax-Free Perks

During your daily working life you can be missing out on tons of opportunities to grab a tax freebie.

Your employer may be able to claim tax relief on computer equipment they provide you with to work from home. Likewise, if you persuade your employer to buy a bike for you to get to and from work, which they lease to you, then your repayments are allowed to come from gross rather than net salary. Play your cards right and you can get the taxman to spring for up to 40 per cent of the cost for the bike, presuming you're a higher-rate taxpayer.

Check out *Paying Less Tax for Dummies 2005/2006* by Tony Levene (Wiley) for the full list of tax-free workplace perks you can enjoy.

Working from Home and Saving Tax

If you're self-employed and work from home then you can be in line to claim some tax breaks.

You may be eligible to claim a proportion of the household expenses, such as heating, lighting, and telephone calls.

The amount which can be claimed for heat and light, for example, is the proportion of the bill calculated on the basis of the number of rooms used for the business against the total number of rooms in the house.

 Business expenses can be claimed through your self assessment tax return. See later in this chapter for more on self assessment and working with an accountant.

Making the Most of VAT Registration

Becoming VAT registered means that every time you do something for a customer you have to levy VAT. In effect, you become a tax collector. You have to account for every penny paid to you in VAT and ensure it finds its way to the tax authorities.

Doesn't sound very appealing so far, does it? Ah! But a big plus point to becoming VAT registered is that you can claim VAT back on any item you buy for your business. So buy a computer or stationery for your business and you can claim your VAT back from the tax authorities. In fact, if you're really clever about it you can claim VAT back on any number of goods and services, just as long as it is a business-related expense.

 The VAT threshold is determined by total sales and not profit. Once you're a business owner and your company turnover is greater than £60,000 (2005–06 tax year), you have to register for VAT. Currently VAT is charged at 17.5 per cent.

Remembering to Contribute to a Pension

One of the most lucrative tax breaks is the one that allows you to make pension contributions from gross rather than net income. If you're a basic rate taxpayer this means in effect that for every £78 in pension contributions you make the government will top up your pension fund to the tune of £22. And from April 2006 the amount of money you can contribute to a pension, tax-free, will rise to 100 per cent of your earnings up to a maximum of £215,000 a year.

The tax break available on pension contributions if properly exploited can give a massive leg-up for your retiring wealthy plans. Pensions are such a big deal that Part II is devoted to them.

 Pension saving isn't everyone's cup of tea. In return for tax relief the government insists that money paid into a pension stays locked away until you reach age 50 (55 from 2010). What's more, you may end up using most of your fund to buy an annuity – income for life – before age 75. Such lack of flexibility has turned some people off pensions.

 With a pension not only do you get tax relief on contributions but you may be able to take 25 per cent of your total pension fund tax-free on retirement. In addition, your employer may pay into your pension scheme.

Working to Reduce Your Inheritance Tax Bill

If on your death your *estate* – everything you own – is worth more than £275,000 (2005–06 tax year) then every penny over this threshold is subject to Inheritance Tax (IHT) at a whopping 40 per cent. You may think this doesn't matter much because you're no longer about – but when the taxman cometh it can create merry hell for your beneficiaries. I have come across cases where the family home has had to be sold to pay an IHT bill.

However, there are gifts you can make during life, and on death, which are free from IHT. All gifts made between spouses and same-sex couples who have gone through a civil partnership ceremony are IHT exempt, and all gifts to charity and political parties are IHT exempt.

While alive you're allowed to make what are called *exempt gifts* to whomever you please. You can give away up to £3,000 a year in a single exempt gift as well as one-off gifts to your children or grand-children when they get married. The beauty of an exempt gift is that it won't count as part of your estate when you die.

If you have a spouse (or same-sex civil partner) and children, one of the smartest IHT saving ploys you can make is to leave just enough to support your partner while giving the rest to your children, up to a maximum of £275,000 (the IHT threshold for the 2005–2006 tax year). So long as the amount you leave your children is no more than the IHT threshold, it goes to them tax-free.

If you think your estate is likely to be subject to IHT then you can take out an insurance policy that pays out on your death enough cash to cover any IHT due. For more on how to reduce IHT check out *Wills, Probate and Inheritance Tax For Dummies* by Julian Knight (Wiley).

The threshold for IHT rises to £285,000 in 2006–2007 and then to £300,000 in 2006–2007.

Sometimes you see the IHT threshold described as the *nil rate band*. This is because every penny under the threshold is subject to nil IHT.

Getting to Know Your Tax Code

You definitely know your name – even after a night on the barley wine, that's still probably the case – and you may even have your National Insurance number off pat, but do you know your personal tax code? The answer may well be no. Yet your personal tax code is vital. It dictates exactly how much or how little tax you pay and disturbingly, HM Revenue and Customs frequently get people's tax codes wrong, meaning that many are paying too much in tax without even realising it.

Your tax code represents your *taxable allowance* – the amount of income you're allowed to earn before you become liable to income tax.

Your tax code is displayed on your pay slip and consists of three numbers followed by a letter. The following are the most common letters for a tax code:

✔ L – You're entitled to the basic personal allowance of £4,895 (2005–06 tax year).

✔ P – You're between the ages of 65 and 74 and entitled to a higher personal allowance of £7,090 (2005–06 tax year).

✔ Y – You're over 75 years of age and entitled to an even higher personal allowance of £7,220 (2005–06 tax year).

The numbers preceding the letter are the amount of allowance you're allowed minus the final digit. Therefore, if you are entitled to the standard personal allowance for people under the age of 65 your allowance will be 489L. But this is adjusted if the Revenue wants to collect on a taxable benefit such as a company car.

If you find there is something awry with your tax code, contact your local HM Revenue and Customs office ASAP. Ask them to investigate if a mistake has occurred and if so, ask them to give you back your overpaid tax.

Using Your Capital Gains Tax Exemption to the Max

When you sell a share investment or a major asset such as property (other than your main residence) for profit then it will be subject to Capital Gains Tax (CGT). CGT is a really tax nasty, weighing in at an unpalatable 40 per cent. But each year you're given a CGT allowance; this is an amount of money you're allowed to make in profit before the tax authorities want a slice.

In the 2005–06 tax year the annual CGT allowance is £8,500 (in 2005–2006). But this may not be a large enough allowance for you during a bumper year. Here are some ways you can work the system to minimise your CGT exposure:

✔ **Gift assets to your spouse or same-sex civil partner**. They will have their own personal CGT allowance against which they can offset the profit from the sale of the asset, if owned jointly.

✔ **Offset gains with losses**. If you make losses on an investment in one tax year you can carry this forward into another to offset a taxable charge. For example, lose £30,000 on an investment in one tax year but make £35,000 on another the following year and you can offset the £30,000 loss against your tax bill – which means you won't be hit with CGT on your £35,000 profit.

✔ **Sell your assets gradually**. If you don't need to sell up all at once try the gradual approach. Spreading the sale of assets that can be subject to CGT over a number of years means that you can offset each tasty morsel of profit with a fresh annual CGT allowance.

Letting an Accountant Take the Strain

If you have complex tax affairs or are self employed you may be best advised to let an accountant take the strain. Getting a good accountant on your side can be invaluable, as they should know the fiendishly complex UK tax system like the back of their hand. In my experience a good accountant usually more than pays for their fee with the useful tax-saving moves they can make on your behalf. What's more, an accountant can ensure that you don't miss crucial tax deadlines. You'll find tips on getting yourself a really good accountant in Chapter 5.

If you're asked to fill in a self assessment tax form, you'd better not be late. HM Revenue and Customs levies an automatic £100 fine for late filing. If you have an accountant they can ensure your self assessment tax form is filed on time.

You have until the end of January to file your self assessment tax form relating to the previous tax year.

Chapter 19

Ten Things That Can Stop You Retiring Wealthy

In This Chapter

▶ Getting into debt

▶ Choosing risky investment strategies

▶ Mixing mortgages and investment

▶ Getting caught up in legal and tax issues

*T*his chapter is this book's equivalent of Madame Tussaud's Chamber of Horrors: chock full of financial nasties that can throw your retiring wealthy plan off course.

In some instances you can take evasive action, but in others you have to face the fact that sometimes life can just go plain wrong – no matter how canny a saver or investor you are. Under such circumstances the key is to have enough of a financial cushion in place and – where applicable – the right insurance policy to protect your grand retiring wealthy design.

Coping With Stay-at-Home Children

A recent survey found that clothing, schooling, and feeding a child up until the age of 21 costs parents on average £166,000. That's a lot of money, roughly equivalent to the price of an average home in the UK, according to the Halifax. But what are you supposed to do? They're your children and you undoubtedly want to provide for them. Where parental duty spells danger for your finances is when a child continues to depend on you for support well into their twenties and even thirties.

This phenomenon has been given its very own acronym, *Kippers*, which stands for Kids In Parents' Pockets Eroding Retirement Savings. And adult children don't have to remain at home to play the role of Kipper. They can come calling for 'loans' that never get repaid – some parents give their kids a leg-up onto the property ladder by funding a mortgage deposit.

A growing trend is for parents to stand as a mortgage guarantor for their kids. Being a guarantor can ease the concerns of mortgage lenders and help your kid buy their first home. However, think carefully before agreeing to act as guarantor. It's a serious undertaking – if your child can't meet his or her loan repayments you'll be left to pick up the tab.

Getting Deep into the Red

Beware of building up so much debt that you have little chance of retiring wealthy. Temptation is all around – from credit card offers to no-questions-asked personal loans – but if you're serious about retiring wealthy then avoid getting into debt, even if it means forgoing a few of the finer things in life.

Some elements of the media push the view that getting into the red is a sign of consumer greed. Examples of feckless twentysomethings maxing out on their credit cards so that they can get a flash car, high-definition TV, or that killer pair of heels are frequently quoted. In some cases these stereotypes are spot on, but in my experience of interviewing hundreds of people in debt, excessive borrowing is often closely related to depression following a sad event such as the breakdown of a long-term relationship.

If you find yourself in debt, think about the deeper underlying cause. Whatever the scenario, you need help to get out of debt and there are places that advise you what to do for free. Go see your local Citizens Advice Bureau or call the following charities: National Debtline on 0808 808 4000 or the Consumer Credit Counselling Service on 0800 138 1111.

Having warned on the dangers of debt, I can add a caveat. Not all debt is bad. Some, such as a mortgage, helps you invest for your future through buying property (and we all know what a good investment that can be!) or starting your own business.

You can also borrow to pay for courses to improve your skill base, which can in turn unlock the door to a better job and higher earnings. See Chapter 2 for more on spotting the difference between good and bad debt.

Taking on debt to invest for your future is a far better idea than doing it to buy here-today-gone-tomorrow possessions.

At all costs avoid taking out a consolidation loan. You have probably seen the daytime TV adverts promising to convert your debts into 'one manageable monthly repayment'. This is simply a tarted-up second mortgage, with exorbitant fees and uncompetitive interest rates. It's a very bad deal and the firms that flog such loans are nothing more than vultures!

Failing at Business

It's fair to say that Britain is second only to the US when it comes to entrepreneurial spirit. Nearly two million of us are business owners. We seem to love the idea of making it in business on our own. And being a successful small business owner can be a great passport to a wealthy retirement.

However, if your goal is to retire wealthy, just a small word of caution. The majority of businesses fold within their first year and if your enterprise is among this number, it can really set back your retiring wealthy plan. If your business fails you get no reward for the time and capital you put into it, and if you borrowed big you can be declared bankrupt.

In 2004 the bankruptcy laws changed and it's now possible to be discharged from your debts within a year. However, this doesn't make bankruptcy a soft option. Your creditors can still take your home and you're unlikely to be able to get further credit for at least six years.

Putting Your Eggs in One Investment Basket

If you plough the majority of your resources into one investment you become ultra dependent on its performance for your future financial wellbeing. All can go well if the investment performs as you want, but it can spell the death knell for your retiring wealthy plan if it goes wrong.

Aim to build up a range of investments such as property, cash deposits, bonds, and shares. The idea behind this strategy is if one investment performs poorly another may well ride to the rescue of your big plan by doing really well.

Getting Your Investment Risk Wrong

If you're nearing the age at which you want to retire or don't have much cash then you should avoid high-risk investments like company shares. The golden rule with high-risk investing is you should only ever invest what you can afford to lose – if you can't afford to lose it don't even go there.

At the other end of the scale, be too cautious in your investment and you can end up missing out on the retiring wealthy prize. For example, a thirtysomething who has all their cash tied up in low interest paying government bonds or building society savings accounts is unlikely to enjoy the sort of investment growth necessary to build up a big retirement pot.

Your investment choice depends on your age, income, and long-term financial goals.

An independent financial adviser (IFA) should be able to help you make the right investment choices. However, IFAs don't dole out advice for free. See Chapter 5 for more on how to find a good IFA and what you can expect to pay to access their wisdom.

Mixing Mortgages with Investment

Remember endowment mortgages? Well, I'm afraid millions of endowment mortgage holders are still counting the cost of having chosen them.

The idea behind an endowment mortgage is beautifully simple. You take out a mortgage on an interest-only basis while at the same time paying a certain amount of cash each month into a separate investment called an endowment (the performance of which is partly linked to the stock market). All things going well, at the end of the mortgage – when it's time to pay back the capital sum borrowed – the endowment has grown in value to not only meet this expense but provide a healthy profit. All sounds good? Back in the 1970s and 1980s endowment mortgages were about the only game in town, with insurers shifting them by the truckload.

But – and you knew there had to be one of those – a combination of low interest rates and the stock market crash of 2000–03 has meant millions of endowments have performed badly. As a result homeowners have been left at the end of their mortgage term with the grim reality that their endowment won't even cover what they owe the mortgage lender.

Fortunately, relatively few endowment mortgages are sold these days, but their failure points to an investment no-go. Borrowing to buy property is a risk – you may, for example, lose your job – and pegging the ultimate repayment of mortgage debt to an investment is doubling the risk. Mixing mortgages and investment can go badly wrong!

Taking Account of Personal Disasters

Life has a habit of bowling you a googly from time to time. In the perfect scenario you work for a certain number of years, enjoying perfect health, and build up a tidy cash pile to be able to really enjoy your retirement. But many people have to stop work early due to ill health or redundancy. In fact, the average man in the UK stops work (notice I don't write retires!) at between the ages of 61 and 63. This is short of the present state pension age of 65.

The upshot of all this is that you should be prepared for the possibility that at some point you may not be able to work even if you really want to.

 You can insure yourself against accident, illness, or even being made redundant. These types of insurance can be expensive, but they can really help dig you out of a hole if you find that you have to stop work early.

Ignoring the Taxman

No one really likes to pay tax and many of us feel intimidated by the thought of having any dealings with HM Revenue and Customs. However, don't be tempted to leave your head in the sand when it comes to tax. Ensure if you have any taxable earnings that don't go through the Pay As You Earn (PAYE) system that you tell your local tax office. If you don't, believe me they will catch up with you eventually and when they do you can at the best face fines and, in serious cases of tax fraud, imprisonment.

About ten million people in the UK have to fill in annual self assessment tax forms. The deadline to get the completed form and payment of tax due to HM Customs and Revenue is the end of January each year. Fail to meet this deadline and you will be hit with an automatic £100 fine. Each year, as regular as clockwork, about 900,000 people miss this deadline and have to pay a fine.

Chopping and Changing Your Investments

Moving your money from one investment to another is sometimes necessary – perhaps you want to collect some profit or you have had enough of losing cash through a dud investment. Yet by being too willing to chop and change you can harm your long-term wealth creation prospects.

Often when you switch investments you attract exit or entry fees, dealing charges, tax, and sometimes penalties. The idea of being a fleet-of-foot investor, willing to follow an investment hunch, in order to grab the chance to make a killing may appeal. But always ask yourself how much you lose in commission and penalties for switching.

In financial circles, chopping and changing is called *churn* and banks, stockbrokers, and building societies want you to do as much churning as possible (as long as you're churning in their direction) as they earn fat fees and commissions.

Being Sued

The problem of being sued following an accident in which you're involved is a growing one. Egged on by no-win-no-fee law firms, people in the UK are becoming a litigious lot. If you cause injury or libel another person and they sue you successfully, you may well find that your retiring wealthy plan goes up in smoke.

Ensure that your home and motor insurance policies come with hefty legal expenses cover – and by hefty I'm talking in the million pound-plus bracket. Furthermore, do ensure that you keep up-to-date with your insurance premiums and don't do anything that can invalidate a claim. When it comes to insurance, honesty is always the best policy.

Chapter 20

Ten Savvy Financial Moves

*I*n this chapter, I outline some simple steps you can take right now to turn around your finances and give yourself a real fighting chance of retiring wealthy.

Moving Your Mortgage

The potential for money saving through remortgaging is huge. If you have been with your mortgage provider for quite some time, it's a racing certainty that you can find a better deal by moving your mortgage to another lender.

Remortgaging has never been easier. This is how you do it.

1. Apply over the phone or at the branch of the lender you're looking to switch to.

2. Give them proof of income – your most recent P60 tax summary and three payslips should suffice.

3. Produce proof of identity – a utility bill and a passport are normally acceptable.

4. Pay for the mortgage company valuation – this should cost no more than £200.

5. Get your solicitor to talk to the mortgage company and draw up the paperwork – again, this should cost no more than £200.

6. Pay any mortgage set-up charges, anywhere from £200 to £500.

Remortgaging can be your passport to big financial savings. If you have a £100,000 mortgage cutting your mortgage interest rate payments by 1 per cent can save you £60 a month.

Some lenders offer unbelievably good rates at the start of the mortgage term, but then after a while they move you on to a much higher rate of interest. Just to turn the screw a little more, some lenders insist that you sign up to a tie-in period. During a tie-in period the lender has the right to impose an early redemption penalty if you move your mortgage elsewhere. Read the small print!

At least once a year check to see if your current mortgage is competitive. If it isn't then move to another lender.

Starting Paying Off Your Mortgage Now

Your mortgage is likely to be your biggest financial commitment. It stands to reason, therefore, that the faster you throw off this financial commitment the more resources you can dedicate to saving for retirement. What's more, by overpaying on your mortgage you reduce your debt and the amount of interest you have to pay. See Chapter 14 for more on how paying off your mortgage can benefit your finances.

Some lenders allow you to overpay on your mortgage, but others don't. Aim to find a lender that lets you overpay without imposing any charges or penalties.

Striving for a Big Mortgage Deposit

When buying a property try your hardest to put a big deposit down.

Having a big deposit offers the following advantages:

- ✔ You pay less interest as you're borrowing less cash.
- ✔ It allows you to access the best mortgage deals – lenders often reserve their best rates for buyers who put down a deposit of around 20 per cent.

✔ You protect yourself against negative equity – even if the property's value falls it should still be worth more than your mortgage debt.

Changing Your Current Account Provider

It used to be the case that people were more likely to get divorced than change banks. Skating over what this says about the institution of marriage, the reason often given for such reluctance to switch providers was that people didn't want to go to the hassle of moving their direct debits.

However, like remortgaging, switching is now easier than ever. Banks and building societies have whole departments which will do the legwork for you. In most cases, all you need do is contact the provider you'd like to switch to, provide proof of identity, and sign a form giving them the go-ahead to switch. The provider then organises the transfer of funds, direct debits, and standing orders. If you're in paid work, let your employer know your new account details so you get your salary!

But why switch? Answer: To get a higher rate of interest. Some providers are willing to pay you up to 5 per cent on money you have in your current account, whereas the big banks including HSBC and NatWest pay a pittance, just 0.1 per cent. They are banking – geddit! – on customer inertia. They figure that they already have more than enough customers and can get away with paying microscopic interest.

You can find which current account pays the highest rate of interest by logging onto www.moneyfacts.co.uk or www.moneysupermarket.co.uk.

Taking Advantage of Zero Per Cent Deals

If you must use credit cards then go for one offering a 0 per cent introductory interest rate. Generally, credit card interest rates range between 10–20 per cent. But in order to attract new custom some providers say they won't charge interest for the first six or twelve months that you're with them. The trick then is to shift to another provider offering a 0 per cent initial deal as soon as the introductory period comes to an end. Lenders are betting that you forget or can't be bothered to move your money once the introductory period comes to an end.

 More often than not 0 per cent interest only applies to debt transferred from another provider, while new purchases incur the standard interest rate.

 Some providers are getting wise to people moving cards between providers to take advantage of a 0 per cent offer, only to shift again as soon as the offer ends. To deter so called *rate tarts* some providers have started imposing balance transfer fees. Avoid these providers like the plague!

Joining Your Workplace Pension

If your employer offers a pension scheme you should seriously consider joining. Many employers make contributions into their workers' pensions. In effect this is free money and all you have to do is join the scheme and make your own contribution into it.

Pensions may not be everyone's cup of tea, but they do come with great tax breaks and can – provided you pay in enough and investment performance is good – help boost your income in retirement. See Chapter 6 for more on workplace pensions.

 Most financial experts reckon that you should have at least some of your retirement cash fund invested in a pension.

Putting Money Aside Each Month

If you're serious about retiring wealthy you're going to have to show commitment and be disciplined with yourself.

One of the best ways of kick-starting your retiring wealthy plan is to draw up a list of your outgoings and income and arrange for part or all of what's left over to go into a savings account each month. It need only take a few minutes to sort out. Look for the savings account paying the highest interest but also offering easy access to your money without penalty. Set up a direct debit or standing order from your current account into the savings account and watch your money pot grow.

You need only use your savings account as a starting point. Once you have a tidy sum in your account, you can start taking some money out and putting it into investments which offer a potentially better return such as bonds or shares.

 It's always a good idea to have a cash float equivalent to say three or six months' salary. This money gives you the security that should you lose your job you will be able to keep the wolf from the door for a while.

Making Sure You Start Early

The younger you start saving and investing towards your retirement the better the chances you have of building up a money pile of skyscraper proportions.

Starting young can mean the following:

- ✔ Your investments have plenty of time to grow.
- ✔ You have a long time left in work to earn income.
- ✔ You can take a few risks, as your finances have time to recover if an investment goes pear-shaped.

If you're not in the first flush of youth, don't despair – you still have lots going for you in the retiring wealthy stakes. Most of us don't reach the top of our careers until we get into our forties or fifties; this is the time when potentially you can put some really big sums aside to ensure your autumn years are a little bit special.

Playing the Stock Market

The evidence of the past century is that share investing offers the potential for top drawer performance. In fact the performance of shares knocks that of bonds and savings accounts into a cocked hat. As for property, well until recently, shares won hands down in performance charts.

However, you can lose your shirt with shares – unlike most bonds and savings accounts – so it's not for everyone. But if you have time on your side – say more than five years until retirement age – seriously consider putting a bit of cash into the stock market.

And you don't have to be a City whizz-kid to make a mint. You can invest in collective investments such as unit and investment trusts which pool investor cash to buy a basket of company shares.

If you're not prepared to do your homework and take risks, avoid buying shares in individual companies, since their performance tends to be volatile. Check out Chapter 12 for tips on how to tell a poor company share from a good one.

 You can benefit in two ways when buying a company share. First, if you're lucky, you make a profit when you sell at a higher price than you bought. Second, many firms pay their shareholders annual dividend income. Over time, dividends can really mount up and some shares are worth owning mainly for the likelihood that they yield a dividend.

Arming Yourself with the Right Advice

The range of scope of savings accounts and investments is absolutely huge. No matter how organised you are, you simply can't know it all. There will be times when you feel you have reached the limit of your knowledge; perhaps you receive a fiendishly complex tax form, want to purchase shares, or are looking for insurance against getting ill and being unable to work.

In short, there are lots of scenarios where a bit of sensible advice would not go amiss. This book offers lots of tips on what you should be doing to boost and protect your finances – as do other For Dummies books, forgive the plug! – but sometimes a bit of face-to-face advice may be the best option. See Chapter 5 for more on finding a good adviser, accountant, or stockbroker.

 There are two main types of money adviser – financial adviser and independent financial adviser (IFA). They both have to pass exams to dole out money advice, but financial advisers work for banks, insurers, and building societies, while IFAs work for themselves or in a network and are independent of product providers. Generally, IFAs are better than financial advisers, but they can cost more money.

Chapter 21

Ten Ways to Boost Your Income

*Y*ou may know where the best places are to save and invest, but if you're not earning enough in the first place to be able to afford to follow your hunches then it's all a bit pointless.

In reality the bulk of your income is going to come from your job or, if you're an entrepreneur, your business. But there are some simple, easy to follow ways that you can maximise your income stream, allowing you to save and invest even more for a wealthy retirement.

In this chapter, I outline 10 easy-to-follow income-boosting tactics.

Taking in a Lodger

Say the word lodger and you may think of fierce Blackpool land-ladies or even, heaven forbid, the character Rigsby from TV's *Rising Damp*. But landlords, landladies, and lodgings in general have come a long way in recent times. Lots of people take in a lodger to help cover the mortgage, pay the bills. or just for a bit of company.

Renting out a spare room to a lodger can be a great way to boost your income stream. Under the government's *Rent a Room* scheme the first £4,250 of rental income you receive from letting out a room in your house is tax-free. This is an annual limit – exceed it and you must pay tax. In addition, the scheme is strictly limited to renting out a room in the house you occupy. You can't use the scheme's tax-free allowance to shelter rental income from a buy-to-let property.

A large number of people are often looking for lodgings, particularly if you live in a big city. You may be best off aiming for professional types who want a nice room in a quiet house, perhaps only on a Monday-to-Friday basis, leaving you free to enjoy the property at weekends.

If there are any major employers near you, why not contact them and ask if they have any contractors or workers from other parts of the UK who will need a room?

If you choose to advertise your room through a letting agent, they demand a chunk of the rent. Expect to have to hand over up to 10 per cent of the rental income if you go through an agent. What's more, some agents ask for an up-front fee before agreeing to advertise your room.

Renting Out a Parking Space

Parking! It's a real bugbear. From the explosion in numbers of traffic wardens (in one London borough they have started to give wardens mountain bikes so they can get around more quickly and issue more tickets!) to the rapid introduction of residents' parking zones, finding a safe, legal place to park is a bit of a modern-day nightmare.

No surprise, therefore, that motorists pay good money for places they can park while they go about their daily business. If you have a garage or driveway space you don't use, this can present you with a lovely money-making opportunity. Why not advertise your garage or driveway for hire? You may find a queue of motorists looking for somewhere out of the clutches of the dreaded traffic wardens and light-fingered dishonest types.

Before starting to rent check out local car parks – how much do they charge motorists to park their cars? Most car parks do special monthly rates. Check these out as it gives you a good idea how much you should be charging.

If you earn any income from renting out your garage or driveway it is taxable (unless you earn too little to pay tax). You're legally bound to tell the tax authorities about your new income source.

Working from Home

If you spend a lot of your time at home – perhaps because you have to care for a child or elderly relative – you don't have to call time on your money-making ability. You can work from home. You're not going to make a fortune, but you may be able to stop your retiring wealthy ambition from going off the rails. There are any number of things you can do at home to earn extra cash, from childminding to proofreading or tutoring. Inevitably, you stand a better chance of earning decent money if you have marketable skills such as journalism or caring.

Some firms advertise home-working projects, making items like Christmas crackers or envelopes. These firms don't pay well – in fact many pay an absolute pittance – and some even have the brass neck to charge new workers a fee for instruction on how to make the product in question. Avoid these home-working firms like the plague.

If you're in receipt of benefits you may have these stopped if you earn extra cash at home. Talk to your local benefits office before taking on any extra work to check what the situation is. Above all, don't be tempted to cheat the system – the penalties for working while claiming benefit can be severe.

Hiring Out Your Home as a Film Set

If you're a homeowner you can consider hiring your home out as a film or TV set to earn extra cash. Film and TV companies are always on the lookout for homes to use for filming. It's cheaper to hire a property than to build a whole new set from scratch. Also the film company can be pretty sure you'll go along with what they need to do.

Your property doesn't have to be a stately home or even a period terrace to attract film-makers. A normal everyday semi can be fine – it all depends on what the production company is looking for. But if a TV or film production company does want to hire out your home then be prepared for lots of disruption. They may want you to move out while the filming takes place.

Like to hire your home out but don't know where to start? Contact the BBC location department on 0208 576 8863, or the Location Partnership on www.locationpartnership.com or www.locationworks.com. You can make anything from £300–500 a day for a small place or £1,000–2,000 if you're lucky enough to own a really grand pile.

The film company may want to make some cosmetic changes to your home – no knocking through walls – but the contract for hiring your property should specify that they put everything back as it was before they started.

Buying and Selling on eBay

Becoming an eBay trader is so simple millions of people around the world are doing it. At the simplest level, you can use eBay to sell stuff you no longer want. You may be surprised how much you can get – remember, one person's junk is another's invaluable collectable.

If you fancy taking eBay a little more seriously, you can try to buy in order to resell at a profit. Thousands of items are up for sale at any one time and plenty of bargains are to be had. Numerous guides exist on how to buy and sell on eBay – check out *eBay.co.uk For Dummies* by Jane Hoskyn and Marsha Collier (Wiley) or *Starting a Business on eBay.co.uk For Dummies* by Dan Matthews and Marsha Collier (Wiley) for starters.

Like any other marketplace, eBay has its crooks. One criminal gang was caught offering what turned out to be non-existent items for sale. Bidders were told that they had been outbid, but an identical item was available if they transferred payment by money transfer. It turned out the identical item didn't exist and the crooks pocketed the payment.

If you buy or sell on eBay, remember to always use Paypal. Paypal is a safe, guaranteed means of transferring funds between bank accounts. Never wire funds or use cash as you then have no protection against con artists.

Driving Up Your Income

Most people see owning a car as a necessary expense, but being a motorist doesn't have to drain your resources. You can put your car and driving skills to money-making use.

Here are some ways you can employ four wheels to give your income a much-needed boost:

- **Becoming a mini-cab driver**. The demand among cab firms for good reliable people (with their own cars) is huge. You can make good money and you can work the hours to suit. Mini-cabbing doesn't have the greatest reputation. However the image of dodgy drivers picking up drunks outside the kebab house on a Saturday is changing and some cab firms are now quite slick operations. Bear in mind cab firms will ask you to pay a rental fee for the hire of a radio connecting you with the office, which distributes the jobs, as well as handing over part of the fares you collect.

- **Hiring out your services as a chauffeur**. Again, if you're reliable, smart, and know how to drive then you can be in line to make some extra cash. You don't even need your own car – most chauffeuring companies have a supply of suitably upmarket motors. Chauffeuring needn't be that hard work – you would probably spend most of your time doing airport runs, ferrying rich types to posh shops, or simply twiddling your thumbs. Expect to make £8 an hour minimum.

- **Becoming a driving instructor**. If you're really good at driving why not pass on your knowledge by becoming an instructor? You need to qualify as an approved Department of Transport driving instructor. To do this you need to pass three exams and mustn't have any recent criminal convictions. You also need to hire or buy a car with dual-driving controls. The going rate for a driving instructor is around £15 to £25 per hour.

If you use your car to boost your income, just make sure that you're earning enough to cover your petrol, insurance, and repair costs. Also, in theory, each mile extra you put on your milometer reduces your car's market value.

Getting Physical to Up Your Fiscals

If you're physically fit – and I mean really physically fit – why not become a gym instructor or personal trainer? You can pick hours to suit and you spend most of your time telling other people what to do while watching them suffer – one for the sadist in us all!

One of the good things about being a fitness instructor is that you're in the highest demand in the evening and at weekends. This means that it may be possible to juggle a full-time job and a bit of gym instruction to bring in some extra reddies!

If you take a class you should aim to charge each student £3–5 a time. One-to-one personal trainers regularly charge anything from £20–35 for a single half-hour session.

Banging Away to Earn Extra Cash

No, this isn't something X-rated. By banging away I'm referring to putting your DIY and odd-job skills to good use to turbo-charge your income stream. I'm a complete dunce when it comes to something seemingly as simply as putting up flat-pack furniture (nuts and bolts are always left over when I've finished) and millions of people like me are either too cack-handed or don't have the time to do those household jobs or repairs. Why not make money out of people like me?

One of the best – and cheapest – forms of advertising is word of mouth. Tell your friends that you're available to do odd jobs and repairs, and ask them to put cards up in their workplaces so you can attract custom. Remember to stick to jobs you can do – a reputation is hard won but easily lost!

Exercising Mutts to Make a Mint

People love dogs but in our time-poor society they may not have time to take them on their daily constitutional. As a result, professional dog walkers have come into vogue. For a fee – of course – these people take dogs for a walk for an hour or so a day. Dog walkers often take several pooches at once, as it's a great way to earn cash. If you love animals and have spare time, why not exercise a pooch – or several – and provide extra cash for your retiring wealthy plan?

Aim to charge owners between £6 and £10 an hour to take their beloved pooch for walkies. Take four or five at one time and you have a lucrative sideline. It can also be lots of fun if you love dogs.

Just because you don't need professional qualifications to be a dog walker, it doesn't mean that you shouldn't take it seriously. People love their dogs and they won't trust you to look after them unless they see you as someone who can be trusted, has common sense, and genuinely cares for our four-legged friends.

Being a Computer Whizz-Kid Spells Wealth

If you're au fait with computers and cyberspace you have a real skill, which you can use to boost your cash pile. Most people are generally intimidated by all things techy, which means you can charge to do any of the following:

- ✔ **Wordprocessing CVs**. Top agencies charge anything up to £250 to draw up a bang-on CV. If you have technical know-how and a background in personnel, you can advertise your services as a CV writer and make a packet.

- ✔ **Desktop publishing**. Maybe some local clubs and businesses can do with someone to knock up a nifty bit of promotional material or a newsletter? Of course, you have to be skilled and have the right software and computer, but you can charge a minimum £20 an hour for your work.

- ✔ **Web design**. If you're a keen surfer, why not turn your hobby into a money-making enterprise you can do in your spare time? Lots of clubs and businesses still have no online presence of any sort and they are missing out on lots of custom as a result. Again if you have the software, computer kit, and skills you should aim to charge £150–200 for designing a basic home page. If they want extra, they have to pay more.

Index

Notes

Notes

FOR DUMMIES

UK editions

HOME

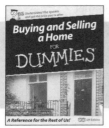

Buying and Selling a Home FOR DUMMIES

A Reference for the Rest of Us!

0-7645-7027-7

Renting Out Your Property FOR DUMMIES

A Reference for the Rest of Us!

0-7645-7016-1

DIY & Home Maintenance ALL-IN-ONE FOR DUMMIES

0-7645-7054-4

PERSONAL FINANCE

Investing FOR DUMMIES

A Reference for the Rest of Us!

0-7645-7023-4

Paying Less Tax 2006/2007 FOR DUMMIES

A Reference for the Rest of Us!

0-470-02860-2

Sorting Out Your Finances FOR DUMMIES

A Reference for the Rest of Us!

0-7645-7039-0

BUSINESS

Starting a Business FOR DUMMIES

A Reference for the Rest of Us!

0-7645-7018-8

Understanding Business Accounting FOR DUMMIES

A Reference for the Rest of Us!

0-7645-7025-0

Business Plans FOR DUMMIES

A Reference for the Rest of Us!

0-7645-7026-9

Other UK editions now available:

Arthritis For Dummies
(0-470-02582-4)

British History For Dummies
(0-7645-7021-8)

Buying a Home on a Budget For Dummies
(0-7645-7035-8)

Cognitive Behavioural Therapy For Dummies
(0-470-01838-0)

Diabetes For Dummies
(0-7645-7019-6)

Divorce For Dummies
(0-7645-7030-7)

eBay.co.uk For Dummies
(0-7645-7059-5)

Gardening For Dummies
(0-470-01843-7)

Genealogy Online For Dummies
(0-7645-7061-7)

Golf For Dummies
(0-470-01811-9)

Irish History For Dummies
(0-7645-7040-4)

Marketing For Dummies
(0-7645-7056-0)

Neuro-Linguistic Programming For Dummies
(0-7645-7028-5)

Nutrition For Dummies
(0-7645-7058-7)

Small Business Employment Law For Dummies
(0-7645-7052-8)

Starting a Business on eBay.co.uk For Dummies
(0-470-02666-9)

Wills, Probate & Inheritance Tax For Dummies
(0-7645-7055-2)

8386_p1

FOR DUMMIES

Do Anything. Just Add Dummies

LANGUAGES

Spanish
0-7645-5194-9

French
0-7645-5193-0

Italian
0-7645-5196-5

MUSIC AND FILM

Guitar
0-7645-9904-6

Filmmaking
0-7645-2476-3

Piano
0-7645-5105-1

HEALTH, SPORTS & FITNESS

Fitness
0-7645-7851-0

Exercise Balls
0-7645-5623-4

Asthma
0-7645-4233-8

8386_p3